"This book is on one level what one should expect from someone as intelligent and articulate as Al Herzog. That is not what makes it valuable. Al's understanding of the real issues surrounding sociology, disability, and Christian ministry, combined with his almost relentless quest to synthesize a more healthy understanding of how we can better understand and engage one another positively around these issues is, in a word, priceless. Al takes us beyond understanding, toward enrichment. Here you will find a vision for how faith and disabilities can make stronger social connections. Long ago, Al challenged me with this question: Is there something more for society to strive toward than making facilities 'accessible' to persons with disabilities? I knew that truth was 'Yes!' I also knew that I had no idea what that really meant. It has been nearly 20 years since that conversation, and Al has offered a powerful vision and deeper understanding for anyone interested in disability ministry. Take the time to read this!"

—RUSSELL HAM, ORDAINED ELDER in the East Ohio conference of the United Methodist Church

The Social Contexts of Disability Ministry

The Social Contexts of Disability Ministry

*A Primer for Pastors,
Seminarians, and Lay Leaders*

ALBERT A. HERZOG JR.

CASCADE *Books* • Eugene, Oregon

THE SOCIAL CONTEXTS OF DISABILITY MINISTRY
A Primer for Pastors, Seminarians, and Lay Leaders

Copyright © 2017 Albert A. Herzog, Jr. All rights reserved. Except for brief quotations in critical publications or reviews, no part of this book may be reproduced in any manner without prior written permission from the publisher. Write: Permissions, Wipf and Stock Publishers, 199 W. 8th Ave., Suite 3, Eugene, OR 97401.

Cascade Books
An Imprint of Wipf and Stock Publishers
199 W. 8th Ave., Suite 3
Eugene, OR 97401

www.wipfandstock.com

PAPERBACK ISBN: 978-1-5326-0770-7
HARDCOVER ISBN: 978-1-5326-0772-1
EBOOK ISBN: 978-1-5326-0771-4

Cataloguing-in-Publication data:

Names: Herzog, Albert A., Jr.

Title: The social contexts of disability ministry : a primer for pastors, seminarians, and lay leaders / Albert A. Herzog Jr.

Description: Eugene, OR: Cascade Books, 2017 | Includes bibliographical references and index.

Identifiers: ISBN 978-1-5326-0770-7 (paperback) | ISBN 978-1-5326-0772-1 (hardcover) | ISBN 978-1-5326-0771-4 (ebook)

Subjects: LCSH: Church work with people with disabilities | Disability—Religious aspects—Christianity | People with disabilities in the Bible | Disability studies.

Classification: BV4460 H40 2017 (print) | BV4460 (ebook).

Manufactured in the U.S.A.   SEPTEMBER 11, 2017

Portions of this work appeared in *Disability Advocacy among Religious Organizations: Histories and Reflections* originally published in 2006 by the Haworth Pastoral Press, now a subsidiary of Taylor and Francis. Used with permission.

Portions of *The Disabled God* authored by Nancy L. Eiesland, published in 1994 by Abingdon Press. Also, "Liberate Yourselves by Accepting One Another" by Jürgen Moltmann from *Human Disability and the Service of God: Reassessing Religious Practice* also published by Abingdon in 1998. Both are used with permission.

Scripture quotations are from New Revised Standard Version Bible, copyright © 1989 National Council of the Churches of Christ in the United States of America. Used by permission. All rights reserved worldwide.

To Phyl and "the Boys"

Contents

Acknowledgments ix

Abbreviations xi

Introduction: Disability and Religious Practice 1

1. Disability in Society: An Overview 17
2. The Rise, Fall, and Rebirth of Disability Advocacy in the Church 42
3. Congregational Movements and Disability Ministry 66
4. Ministry among People with Physical Disability and Chronic Illness 92
5. Ministry among People with Sensory Disabilities 101
6. Ministry among People with Developmental Disabilities 113
7. Ministry among People with Mental Illness and Dementia 126
8. Disability and the Christian Biblical Heritage 140
9. The Church and Disability across the Ages 163
10. Theology and Disability 183
11. Life Worth Living: Christian Ethics and Caregiving 208
12. Where Do We Go from Here? 225

Bibliography 231

Subject Index 249

Scripture Index 253

Acknowledgments

Many hands and eyes assisted in bringing this project to fruition. Russ Ham, Dan Church, and Bill Swatos reviewed early drafts. Allison Carey was the first sociologist to take a good first look at the entire draft. I owe a hearty thanks and indebtedness to R. Stephen Warner, who reviewed the final draft with an eye to publication, and in the process taught me to "own the narrative." His eye to what publishers look for in a manuscript helped to turn it toward an audience that needs to learn about disability and its connection to the life of the church. And while the subtitle embraces the pastoral and seminary community, it is hoped that more sociologists of religion and other religious researchers will read and be stimulated to include disability in their own research.

I am indebted to the staff of Wipf and Stock for their exceptional editorial assistance in turning the manuscript into book form, especially with the help of K. C. Hanson, Jeremy Funk, and Heather Carraher.

Over the years it has taken to turn ideas, into research, to drafts and finally into a complete manuscript, my wife, Phyllis (Phyl), has given me the freedom and space to work on this "labor of love." It is hard to believe that when I began this project, my son was an undergraduate. Now he has his doctorate, and has two sons. Hence, the dedication to "Phyl and 'the boys'"!

Abbreviations

ACC	Accessible Congregations Campaign
ADA	Americans with Disabilities Act
ADNet	Anabaptist Disabilities Network
APCM	Association of Physically Challenged Ministers
CAN	Connecting, Advancing, and Nurturing
CBU	California Baptist University
CCD	Confraternity of Christian Doctrine
CCPD	Christian Council on Persons with Disabilities
CDC	Centers for Disease Control and Prevention
CHIP	Children's Health Insurance Program
COPD	Chronic obstructive pulmonary disease
CPA	Cooperative Publication Association
CRC	Christian Reformed Church
DAYL	Disabilities Advocates Youth Leadership
EAHCA	Education for All Handicapped Children Act
EDN	Episcopal Disability Network
ELCA	Evangelical Lutheran Church in America
IDEA	Individuals with Disabilities Education Act
IEP	Individual educational program
IYDP	International Year of Disabled Persons
JSSR	*Journal for the Scientific Study of Religion*

LDS	Latter-day Saints
MCC	Mennonite Central Committee
MMA	Mennonite Mutual Aid
MMHS	Mennonite Mental Health Service
MRDD	Mental Retardation and Developmental Disabilities
NAE	National Association of Evangelicals
NAMR	National Apostolate for the Mentally Retarded
NAfIM	National Apostolate for Inclusion Ministries
NBDC	National Black Disability Coalition
NCC	National Council of Churches of Christ
NCPWD	National Committee on Persons with Disabilities (UCC)
NCPD	National Catholic Partnership on Disability
NIDCD	National Institute of Deafness and Other Communication Disorders
NOD	National Organization on Disability
PDCC	Presbyterians for Disability Concerns Caucus
RCA	Reformed Church in America
RDP	Religion and Disability Program
SDA	Seventh-Day Adventists
SSDI	Social Security Disability Insurance
SIPP	Survey of Income and Program Participation
SSI	Supplemental Security Income
UCC	United Church of Christ
UMC	United Methodist Church
UMCD	United Methodist Conference on the Deaf

Introduction

Disability and Religious Practice

For over sixty years, Christian churches throughout the United States have been engaged in a movement to place people with disabilities and their concerns at the heart of what is communicated, taught, and practiced. The sources of this movement stem from the absence of people with disabilities in the life of the church, from the marginalizing of disability concerns in the church including various forms of access, and from the failure of the church to explore its negative response to disability as expressed in its biblical, historical, theological, and ethical heritage.

The efforts to address these concerns have coalesced into what today is referred to as disability ministry. A generic term emerging from the work of evangelical churches and agencies, *disability ministry* has defused to point where mainline Protestant, Catholic, and Orthodox communions have adopted many of its emphases, especially that disability ministry should be focused on the local church. Disability ministry emerges from, and functions within, a wide variety of social contexts that include (1) how society responds to people with disabilities in a particular time and place; (2) how specific disabilities are shaped based on current societal views towards disabled people and the care they receive following advances in education, rehabilitation, and civil rights; (3) how the church responds to societal issues, including disability issues; and (4) the church's biblical, historical, theological and ethical response to issues of disability.

Many contexts of disability ministry will be discussed throughout this book. However, this is not a "how to do it" book with step-by-step instructions by which any congregation can add a disability ministry. Rather, this work delves into the contexts that must be considered when undertaking *any* disability ministry. No disability ministry exists apart from its social context. Social contexts change over time and the church has developed its response to disability accordingly. Secular agencies that focus on particular disabilities, such as multiple sclerosis or mental illness, have a role to play in how persons with these impairments live out their lives. They represent the context in which the church considers its response. In turn, by creating a response to a disability group the church establishes a social context from which the church considers future involvement with people with disabilities within the church and in society. For example, at one time mental health agencies were loath to seek the aid of churches for fear of negative attitudes held by parishioners. Today, these same agencies are seeking and affirming a role for the church in mental health in recognition of a congregation's access to communities where many people with mental health issues live. This is truly a tale of two contexts!

General Argument of This Book

We live in an age with the ubiquitous presence of disability. Disability is the end result of advanced medical care (e.g., to save severely injured people); the widespread availability of educational, vocational, and other community resources; and the increased presence of people with various disabilities living in the community. It is also the result of civil rights legislation, which insists, however imperfectly, that people with disabilities must be treated as having inherent rights that enable them to live in a "least restrictive environment." In a larger sense, "Disability is an enigma that we experience but do not necessarily understand. While some people are born with or experience disability as children, most of us become familiar with disability later in life. For the majority, then, what was once deemed as foreign, something outside of our bodies and experience, frequently becomes an intimate part of our lives as we age."[1]

Therefore (as I argue in this book), even religious institutions have had to consider what it means to have people with disabilities in their midst and how best to be inclusive in worship, education, fellowship, and service. Indeed, in recent years, scholars have begun to recognize the importance of religion in the lives of people with disabilities. Special issues of such journals as the *Disability Studies Quarterly* and *Disability and Society* have appeared devoted to the interface between the church and disability. The *Journal of Religion, Disability & Health* has focused on the interaction of disability and religion on a consistent basis. Religious scholars including theologians, ethicists, and pastoral care professionals have produced a plethora of books and articles that attempt to understand and explore the many facets of this interface.

---

1. Albrecht et al., "Introduction," 1.

Throughout this volume, I seek to provide a sociological perspective, which adds to the work of disability studies in religion. For what will follow in these pages is a description and analysis of the many contexts out of which churches have responded to people with disabilities. These include the use of materials from the Christian tradition, people who have spoken prophetically about the need to include people with disabilities in the life of the church, and, most important, the life experiences of those with disabilities, their families, and their friends.

Interactions between Disability and Christianity

The interactions between Christianity and disability in the United States are numerous, varied, and significant at all levels of church life. For example, the Harris Poll and the National Organization on Disability *Americans with Disabilities* survey conducted in 2000 and again in 2004 reported that while the disabled and nondisabled were almost identical in expressing the importance of religious faith, religious participation in worship and other church activities is lower for those with more severe disabilities.[2] Gerry Hendershot, in a study using data from the National Survey of Family Growth, showed that "persons of reproductive age with disabilities are not only less likely to attend religious services but also less likely to regard religion as important in their lives."[3] A survey of ninety-one congregations found that while self-reported accessibility to worship was "increasing," the majority of congregations studied were less likely to engage in serious discussions of what the inclusion of people with disabilities means in terms of removing attitudinal barriers, including people with disabilities in church leadership, and advocating for disability rights and reaching out to people with disabilities living in the community.[4] It is easier to make church facilities accessible to persons with mobility impairments (i.e., those who use crutches, walkers, wheelchairs, or scooters) than to address the issues of acceptance and belonging for all disability groups. Such findings merit a more nuanced discussion of the issues and effects of promoting the inclusion of people with disabilities in the church.

It is not that Protestant and Roman Catholic denominations and para-church organizations have refused to expend personal, theological, and financial resources to further inclusion people with disabilities into the

2. National Organization on Disability and Harris Interactive, *2000*; and National Organization on Disability and Harris Interactive, *2004*.
3. Hendershot, "Statistical Note."
4. LaRocque and Eigenbrood, "Community Access," 55–60.

Christian churches outright. Beginning around 1950, numerous denominational and interdenominational groups have sought to address issues related to disability, including architectural access, Christian education, and other programs designed to promote greater awareness of disability issues as they relate to the church and society.[5] Disability ministry represents a new paradigm toward which denominational and interdenominational organizations have shifted in order to better assist local congregations in responding more effectively to people with disabilities.

It is my hope that the program reviews and critiques in the pages to follow will be liberating and insightful, not only for those who have struggled to move from the margins to the center of the church, but for seminary students, pastors and laity. A host of materials has been collected that document the efforts of churches to advocate for the inclusion of people with disabilities. In addition, recent scholarship has focused on disability in the Bible, incorporating a disability studies perspective. Moreover, considerable theological and ethical reflection on disability and Christianity merits the close attention of all who are or intend to be church leaders.

The Marginalization of People with Disabilities in the Church

People with disabilities have been, and still are, located at the margins of congregational life. This can be seen at various times and places. Nancy Eiesland states that "Stories of religious abuse are ubiquitous in the disability movement. At most gatherings of people with disabilities I attend individuals recount detailed, personal, stories of discrimination or insult at the hands of religious folk."[6] Her conclusion derived from several face-to-face interviews reveals "the prevailing view among activists that Judeo-Christian interpretations of disability account for the negative cultural representations of people with disabilities."[7] My own research uncovered families with disabled children being denied religious education. In one Texas congregation, parents of a child with a disability were told that they were welcome anytime, but not to bring their child.[8] In addition, Harold Wilke has argued that while in the Roman Catholic Church men with disabilities are prohibited by canon law from entering the priesthood, in Protestantism there is an unwritten doctrine which "has historically deterred physically disabled

---

5. Herzog, ed., *Disability Advocacy among Religious Organizations*.
6. Eiesland, "Barriers and Bridges," 219–20.
7. Ibid., 221.
8. Herzog, *Analysis of the Disability Rights Movement*.

persons from entering the ministry, since it is of course admitted that some forms of disfigurement could cause discomfort or distraction within the congregation."[9]

When attention turns to the inclusion of various minority populations at the national, judicatory, and congregational levels, the financial, personnel, and material resources dedicated to assisting people with disabilities have been meager compared to other issues affecting the church. Thus, while many activists point to the fact that people with disabilities form the largest numerical minority, the voices of people with disabilities are often not heard or heeded. The issues that disability raises for the church are dealt with in a manner that results in marginalization, as when disability groups are allowed to do their work (i.e., hold workshops, occupy booths at church conferences, and publish resources), but those in powerful positions are unmoved by their efforts.

At a much deeper level, and despite a general rise in interest in disability, the church "doesn't get it." A lingering set of assumptions indicates a lack of awareness of what having a disability entails, especially at the deeper levels of acceptance and affirmation, where people with disabilities would be welcomed as an essential constituency of the church. People with disabilities and their families and friends are marginalized by the church. Parents and friends are often viewed as totally responsible not only for their members with disabilities in terms of personal care but also for their Christianization!

As a sociologist of religion with a disability (cerebral palsy since birth), an ordained minister in the United Methodist Church, and a disability advocate, I see the Christian church as lacking the commitment and understanding to thoroughly embrace people with disabilities as people of God. I see the church, in general, as inept at relating to people with disabilities. Churches fail to recognize the full humanity of disabled persons, viewing them as ones who need to be served, but not being able to provide ministries to others. This lack of awareness, welcome, and inclusion of people with disabilities extends even into theological education where little or no time is set aside for consideration of the many biblical, theological, and ethical issues related to disability.

As readers can tell, I am not neutral about this issue. I desire to provide an analysis that will be useful for those working in the field as well as one that is theoretically sound in keeping with the canons of the sociology of religion and disability studies. My position on this issue is well within the cannons of disability studies, which has an activist component as well as an

---

9. Wilke, *Creating the Caring Congregation*, 33.

emphasis on scholarship and writing.[10] This book brings together materials from biblical studies, church history and theology and studies of various ministries to and with people with disabilities. In addition, my own analysis of recent developments in the Roman Catholic Church and in Protestant denominations and in parachurch and other organizations, contained in a previous volume, calls for a larger, more theoretical analysis than I was able to provide at that time.

Toward a More Theoretical Base—Basic Concepts

Some basic terms require definitions, as they are either used frequently in this book or assumed as background for the discussion that unfolds as various topics are discussed.

Disability

An individual with a disability is a person who "(1) has a physical or mental impairment that substantially limits one or more major life activities, (2) has a record of such impairment, or (3) is regarded as having such impairment."[11] According to the report *Americans with Disabilities: 2010*, 56.7 million Americans (18.7 percent of the population) had some level of disability.[12] According to the report, disabilities can be classified in one of three domains: communication, physical, or mental.[13] People aged fifteen years and over were identified as having a disability in the communication domain if they met any of the follow criteria: (1) were "blind or had difficulty seeing," (2) were "deaf or had difficulty hearing," or (3) "had difficulty having their speech understood."[14]

People fifteen years and older are defined as having a disability in a physical domain if they met any of the following criteria:

1. Used a wheelchair, cane, crutches, or walker.
2. Had difficulty with one or more functional activities (walking a quarter of a mile, climbing a flight of stairs, lifting something as heavy as a 10-pound bag of groceries, grasping objects, getting in or out of bed).

---

10. Davis, "Introduction," in *Disability Studies Reader*.
11. Steinmetz, *Americans with Disabilities: 2002*, 1–2.
12. Brault, *Americans with Disabilities: 2010*.
13. Ibid., 1.
14. Ibid., 2.

3. Identified one or more related conditions as the cause of a reported activity limitation (arthritis or rheumatism; back or spine problems; broken bone or fracture; cancer; cerebral palsy; diabetes; epilepsy; head or spinal cord injury; heart trouble or hardening of the arteries; hernia or rupture; high blood pressure; kidney problems; lung or respiratory problems; missing legs, arms, feet, hands or fingers; paralysis; stiffness or deformity of legs, arms, feet, or hands; stomach/digestive problems; stroke; thyroid problems; or tumor, cyst or growth.[15]

People fifteen years and older were classified as having a disability in the mental domain if they met any of the following criteria:

1. Had one or more specified conditions (a learning disability, mental retardation or another developmental disability, Alzheimer's disease, or some other type of mental or emotional condition).
2. Had any other mental or emotional condition that seriously interfered with everyday activities (frequently depressed or anxious, trouble getting along with others, trouble concentrating, or trouble coping with day-to-day stress).
3. Had difficulty managing money/bills.
4. Identified one or more related conditions as the cause of a reported activity limitation (attention deficit hyperactivity disorder; autism; learning disability; mental or emotional problems; mental retardation; or senility, dementia or Alzheimer's).[16]

The report assumes that both the cause and the manifestations of disability are primarily internal, or located within the body. However, this "medical model" has been challenged as being generally limited to conditions amenable to clinical or surgical procedures designed to restore, to the extent possible, the physical, mental, or emotional health of an individual to what is considered "normal."[17] By contrast, the social model of disability locates disability in society as a consequence of social oppression, a perspective directly opposed to the medical model or individual model, as Michael Oliver puts it.[18] The contrasts between these models include the following: (1) the individual model focuses on the personal tragedy of disability whereas the social model focuses on social oppression; (2) the individual model focuses on disability as a personal problem needing individual treatment, whereas

15. Ibid., 2.
16. Ibid.
17. Oliver, *Understanding Disability*, 34–37.
18. Ibid., 37.

the social model views disability as a social problem necessitating social action; and (3) disability viewed from the individual model requires individual adaptation as opposed to social change as mandated by the social model.[19]

While not discounting the important role medicine plays in responding to illness and injuries with disabling consequences, disabled people according to Oliver's view are

> increasingly demanding acceptance from society as we are, not as society thinks we should be. It is society that has to change, not individuals, and this change will come about as part of a process of political empowerment as a group and not through policies and programs delivered by establishment politicians and policymakers nor through individualized treatments and interventions provided by the medical and para-medical professions.[20]

In the United States, a focus on social oppression and social barriers is encapsulated in the "minority group model," which places highest priority on barrier removal and other social changes rather than on medical or rehabilitation interventions.[21] *Minority* here refers not to a numerical body of people, but rather to a group whose power is diminished because they are not "able-bodied." In this case, functional limitations (as determined by the medical establishment) are only one aspect of disability: people with disabilities experience discrimination, oppressive attitudes and social relationships. It also acknowledges, along with other minority groups, that people with disabilities can celebrate their "disability identity, cultural distinctive[ness], and disability pride."[22]

This book is written from the perspective that human disability can only be viewed as embedded in social contexts. Medical categories, rehabilitation protocols, and professional conduct rest within socially constructed settings that are enabled through power relations granted by society. Architectural barriers, educational and community programs, and attitudes toward people with disabilities are also socially constructed which vary according to the time and place in which they emerge. Legislation and large-scale schemes such as Social Security and the Americans with Disabilities Act (ADA) emerge when social activists have the power, not only to lobby for legislation and policy, but also to employ cultural symbols which strike

19. Ibid.
20. Ibid.
21. Hahn, "Minority Group Model of Disability," 4.
22. Shakespeare et al., "Models," 1104.

at the heart of a society's understanding of disability and to articulate the "meanings" that are salient to a sufficient number of individuals and groups interested in their well-being. In sum, I am employing the term social context as a specific application of the social approach to understanding disability, and particularly, as a way to frame the mobilizing of programmatic efforts to include groups of people with disabilities in the life of the church.

The topics and analyses contained in this book center on the disabled as a group that has been marginalized in the church today as well as in the past. As the term *marginalization* implies, it is a form of oppression that shoves a group to the outer edges of a society or an organization (e.g., the church) and that flows out of the social contexts in which disability is situated. Marginalization is commonly referred to in social-science discussions of race, gender and social class but can be applied to other groups, including people with disabilities. Iris Young argues that people who are marginalized are "expelled from useful participation in social life and thus potentially subjected to severe material deprivation and even extermination."[23]

Disability Studies

Sharon L. Snyder asserts that "Disability studies functions as the theoretical arm of disability rights movements." It is an interdisciplinary field encompassing "study and scholarship" that analyze "the meanings attributed to human corporeal, sensory, and cognitive differences."[24] Disability studies scholars "examine the role that disability serves in expressive traditions, scientific research, and social science applications. They study the status of disabled persons, often by attending to exclusionary scholarly models and professional structures," and the "privilege that accrues to nondisabled persons within built environments."[25]

Disability studies as a field emerged well after the disability rights movement had won several victories that included the passage of legislation, the establishment of community living arrangements, and new programs emphasizing self-direction and care by persons with disabilities. Disability studies with its books, courses, and programs began to develop in the late 1980s and has seen rapid growth since, especially in the United States, Canada, the United Kingdom and Australia.[26] The term *disability studies* is meant to distance itself from conventional studies of disability, which are

---

23. Young. *Oppression, Privilege and Resistance*, 53.
24. Snyder and Mitchell. *Cultural Locations of Disability*, 1.
25. Ibid., 4.
26. Snyder, "Disability Studies," 1:478–79.

seen as being too closely allied with the "megalithic operation of management interests and government surveys that were frequently answerable to the goals of nondisabled persons at the expense of their disabled clients, family members, or neighbors."[27]

In keeping with a general trend, disability studies affirms the "growing appreciation of the body and embodiment in modern sociology and that the sociology of the body can make important contributions to the study of impairment and disability."[28] Studies of the body emphasize the "materiality of lived experience," and body theory provides a means to study the body and its performance "without having to validate (nor necessarily refute) medical findings."[29] In "embodied analysis," for instance, physical disabilities "are perceived as a private room in a public space—and that ideologies of disability assume a transparency to the motives and psychic life of physically disabled subjects." The focus on the body and the way disabled bodies are treated and pigeonholed constitutes another approach for understanding those who are oppressed because of their real or apparent lack of physical, cognitive, and sensory abilities.[30]

A number of other themes that are found in the current disability studies literature are directly relevant to the scholarly study of disability and the Christian church. History plays a prominent role in tracking down the origin of many contemporary practices and attitudes concerning disabled persons. The need to assemble a "new disability history" is mandated if for no other reason than to uncover the "experiences of cultural devaluation and socially imposed restriction, of personal and collective struggles for self-definition and self-determination [that] recur across the various disability groups and throughout their particular histories."[31] The emphasis uncovering the history of people with disabilities has come through in numerous articles on various topics from ancient through modern times. The emphasis on history has also been exemplified in monographs such as Stiker's *A History of Disability* and Metzler's *Disability in Medieval Europe* as well as an edited volume by Paul Longmore and Lauri Umanski titled *The New Disability History: American Perspectives*.[32]

---

27. Davis, "Introduction," in *Disability Studies Reader*, 1.
28. Turner, "Disability and the Sociology of the Body," 253.
29. Snyder, "Bodies, Theories of," 1:194–95.
30. Ibid., 195.
31. Longmore and Umanski, "Introduction," 4.
32. Stiker, *A History of Disability*; Metzler. *Disability in Medieval Europe*; and Longmore and Umanski. *New Disability History*.

Sociology of Religion

The sociological perspective (and in particular that of the sociology of religion) probes taken-for-granted assumptions, both exploring their basis and understanding specific social contexts (whether personal or cultural and social) from which religious views of disability and responses to disability emerge. Examining the church's historical and theological response to disability by taking a systematic and objective stance, using insights derived from both the discipline of disability studies and the field of sociology, has the potential to provide the basis for a serious consideration of disability and its place in the life of the church.

The use of perspectives from within the field of the sociology of religion has both positive and negative implications for the study disability and religion. On the positive side, the sociology of religion (1) entails studies "which further the understanding of the role of religion in society," (2) analyzes religion's "significance in and upon human history," and (3) seeks "to understand the social forces and influences that in turn shape religion."[33] As Grace Davie states, "A single assumption is, however, embedded in all three statements: The sociologist of religion is concerned with religion *only insofar as it relates to the context in which it inevitably exists*. It is this relational quality that distinguishes the strictly sociological from the wide variety of other disciplines that have interests in this area."[34]

However, the use of sociology of religion as an approach to study disability employed in this book is not without an awareness of its limitations. For one thing, the sociology of religion's track record with respect to disability is decidedly abysmal. Over the years, relatively few peer-reviewed articles on disability-related topics have appeared in the major sociology of religion journals. *Sociology of Religion*, the journal of the Association of the Sociology of Religion, and its predecessors (the *American Catholic Sociological Review* and the *Sociological Analysis*) listed one article on mental health professionals and two articles on psychiatry in its *50 Year Index [of the] American Catholic Sociological Review and Sociological Analysis*.[35] Since then, no articles have appeared that address even a tangential relationship to religion and disability.

A similar finding is derived from an examination of the index of the *Journal for of the Scientific Study of Religion (JSSR)*, the leading American interdisciplinary journal that contains sociological and other social-scientific

---

33. Davie, "Sociology of Religion," 483.
34. Ibid. (italics original).
35. Association for the Sociology of Religion, "50 Year Index," (1989).

studies of religion. Its *20-Year Index* contains a few entries on mental health, psychiatric patients, and mental-hospital chaplaincy, but none on other disability issues in its first twenty volumes from 1961 to 1981.[36] Since then, the *JSSR* has continued to include articles on mental health, culminating in Hackney and Sander's article "Religiosity and Mental Health: A Meta-Analysis of Recent Studies."[37] However, with the exception of "Religion and Attitudes toward Physician-Assisted Suicide and Terminal Palliative Care,"[38] articles on the interface between religion and disability from the sociology of religion perspective have been nonexistent in the *JSSR*.

The *Review of Religious Research*, which is the "official journal of the Religious Research Association," has sought to include articles which appeal to the practitioner as well as the scholarly community. Recent issues have included articles on various issues pertaining to religion and health and religion and the elderly, in addition to the well-worn topic of religion and mental health. These articles often appear in symposia of other related topics, and while encouraging, they tend not to be focused specifically on religion and disability. However, two recent articles have approached the topic in a more direct fashion: David C. Dollahite's article on "Fathering for Eternity: Generative Spirituality in Latter-day Saint Fathers of Children with Special Needs"[39] and my own 2004 article on disability advocacy among Protestant judicatories.[40]

Putting It All Together

Despite the depth and scope of the concepts involved in defining disability, the employment of the social model in analyzing the way society responds to sensory, physical, developmental, and mental impairment, and the tools provided by the sociology of religion, there is a need to develop a perspective that centers on the relationship between disability and the Christian church. The preceding sections have put forth numerous strands that can be assembled into a tentative theoretical approach to the study of Christianity's relationship to people with disabilities. The analyses contained in this book focus on the disabled, as a group, who have been, and still are, marginalized by the church. Only recently have churches begun to entertain the idea that its stand with respect to disability may not only contradict its biblical

36. Society for the Scientific Study of Religion, *Twenty-Year Index*.
37. Hackney and Sander, "Religiosity and Mental Health."
38. Burdette et al., "Religion and Attitudes toward Physician-Assisted Suicide."
39. Dollahite, "Fathering for Eternity."
40. Herzog, "Spires, Wheelchairs, and Committees."

and historical traditions but require a complete rethinking of its disability ministry. As will be shown in the pages to follow, the church often embraces the dominant medical/individual model while failing to understand newer approaches such as the social model or more nuanced models that embrace both impairment and disability. I am arguing here that one way of going about understanding and redirecting the church's approach to people with disabilities is to study the social contexts by which disability issues emerge in the church. As will be seen, these contexts often involve contacts with the surrounding societal environment with regard to disability ministry, and change according to time and place.

If marginalization implies a form of oppression that shoves a group to the outer edges of a society or an organization (e.g., to the edges of the church), then the chapters following must not only document the church's efforts but seek to offer critical reflection of both actors and acted upon. This implies that disability ministries, no matter how sincere and carefully planned, may have unintended consequences that further place people with disabilities on the fringes the church's thought and action. The analytical tools provided by sociology will assist in understanding how church bodies at the national, judicatory, and congregational levels respond to people with disabilities. However, what is important to keep in mind is that various disability ministries are not the same in different contexts of church life. A declaratory statement adopted by a national denomination may not affect a congregation's response to disability. On the other hand, activists at the local level may influence denomination-wide agencies to become actively involved in advocating for disability rights.

Because of my activist leanings, I also must necessarily ask whether there is anything derived from this book that actually advances the capacity of people with disabilities to overcome their marginalized position. In my view, to place the various disability ministries of churches in their respective social contexts constitutes the baseline upon which any "liberating" observations can be made. I am well aware that a significant amount of the actions described in the following chapters (even the recent work in biblical and historical theology and ethics) has been done at the instigation of people with disabilities and their families and friends. The question then becomes whether these actions and people can be recognized as essential to the church, and whether the center can recognize the need to be more inclusive of the disabled marginalized. Hannah Lewis argues (in the context of d/Deaf ministries in the UK) that people with disabilities must take the lead in bringing about ministries that enable them to fully function within the church.[41] Can it be the case that people with disabilities, their families, friends, and advocates can demand not only more voice in support of their programs but also to have a say in how the church incorporates disability into its life at all levels? Can they teach other people (i.e. the nondisabled) some of the insights gained as a result of their position in the church? These issues will be examined in the chapters that follow.

Outline of the Book

Following this introduction, chapter 1 provides a more detailed and nuanced overview of the nature of disability, strongly emphasizing the social contexts out of which disability categories are constructed as well as how certain disabilities rise to prominence over others. Medical dominance is an essential feature of this process, although society's tendency to marginalize people with disabilities also plays a significant role. The chapter also provides an overview of the various contexts that shape the social experiences of people with disabilities, and interrogates their tendency to marginalize the very people they seek to serve.

Chapter 2 provides an overview of disability advocacy in the Christian churches since 1950. I present the various models of disability that have been employed over these years and how these were shaped by the social contexts out of which they emerged. I demonstrate the importance of these models for analyzing the relationship between religion and disability, including the social construction of disability, body theory, and the relationship between disability and culture. Much of the data for this chapter is more macro than micro in concept and context, especially with regard to materials from mainline Protestantism and the Roman Catholic Church.

Chapter 3 examines how Christian congregations have responded to people with disabilities. I start with the concept of "disability ministry" as emerging from congregations, especially among evangelical circles, and its spread to other Christian groups. The chapter also includes a discussion of parachurch organizations (including Joni and Friends and the McLean Bible Church) that have sought to push congregations to do disability ministry. The chapter continues with a discussion of how mainline Protestant congregations, Roman Catholic parishes, and other church traditions have approached the concept of disability ministry, and concludes by providing an overview of studies that have sought to evaluate congregational ministries among the disabled.

---

41. Lewis, *Deaf Liberation Theology*.

Beginning with chapter 4 through to chapter 7, I provide a more detailed and nuanced overview of disability groups in their social contexts and what is entailed in providing a disability ministry that is inclusive and cancels out marginalization. Chapter 4 covers physical disability and chronic illness. Its subtopics include basics, disability experience, and a discussion of accessibility and its limits. Chapter 5 reviews the criteria involved in defining developmental disabilities, including intellectual disability, cerebral palsy, and autism. The chapter concludes with a discussion of people with severe intellectual and physical disabilities and the work of the L'Arche communities in establishing communities of care. Ministry among people with sensory disabilities is the topic of chapter 6 and includes discussions of deafness, blindness, deaf-blindness, and hearing loss. Chapter 7 covers several mental health topics including responses to mental illness and dementia.

Beginning with chapter 8, I explore Christianity's past, present, and future with respect to disability. Because the biblical tradition contained in both the Old and New Testaments forms a backdrop to contemporary responses to disability, the tradition's content with respect to disability must be interrogated, especially its role in promoting the marginalization of people with disabilities. Contemporary biblical disability scholarship is introduced and employed to examine critical biblical passages pertaining to disability.

Chapter 9 continues the threads identified in the previous chapter by interrogating the historical traditions of the church up to modern times. Disability studies scholars and church historians can shed light on critical representations of disability across the centuries. This will entail a critical analysis of Christian charity (from ancient times through to its secularization beginning in early modern times) as a source of marginalization.

Chapter 10 presents an overview of the various theological strands and major works that have been developed in response to disability. Theological thinking is required if for no other reason than that Christianity has to do as much with thinking as with doing. In the case of both disability advocacy and disability ministry, theology seeks to provide an underpinning that is directed at clergy and laity. Recent books by Yong, Reynolds, Betcher, Reinders, and Creamer are particularly aimed at the theological community by way of attempting to incorporate disability advocacy and ministry into seminary curriculums. Theological reflection also raises questions about who does theologizing—people with disabilities or nondisabled theologians?

Chapter 11 discusses ethical issues involved when the meaning and purpose of life for people with disabilities is challenged, especially from the view of medicine and secular ethics. In addition to theological reflection on disability, there is an extensive body of ethical reflection on disability. This reflection covers issues such as whether an infant with disabilities should be born and receive extensive neonatal treatment, whether society can afford to care for people with severe disabilities, and whether the aged with disabilities should be allowed to live until their natural deaths. As chapter 11 will show, these questions indicate that society continues to marginalize people with disabilities. The church continues to struggle to integrate people with disabilities into its life and itself marginalizes people with disabilities either through indifference, or (in the case of Roman Catholics and evangelicals) through disrespect for efforts to promote the value of those living with disabilities. The chapter concludes with a brief examination of caregiving.

Under the title "Where Do We Go From Here?" chapter 12 highlights key issues with respect to future of the Christian church's relation to disability. At issue are both practice and research, including the ubiquitous presence of disability in society, the advocacy of disability issues in the church, the relationship between disability advocacy in the church and disability advocacy in society, and the importance of theological reflection on disability for the future of the church. Special emphasis is placed on the need for the inclusion of disability-related topics in seminary curriculums, not as electives but as topics *required* of all students.

1

Disability in Society: An Overview

The social context of disability in the United States sets the stage for any discussion about how the church has responded to disability. Whereas an obvious case for understanding the social context of disability can be made in relation to including people with disabilities in the church's life, discussions of disability in Scripture and in church history as well as disability theologies and ethics have also emerged as contemporary developments because of efforts to include people with disabilities in the church's life. They are also products of the current environment in which disability is situated.[1]

Three Levels of Analysis

In order to produce a thorough analysis of the social context of disability, I will discuss disability as interfacing three levels of social life—the individual level, the social level, and the societal level; these levels come from the work of Barnes, Mercer, and Shakespeare[2] in the wake of work of Bryan S. Turner.[3] While Turner's aim is to provide an analysis of health and medicine at each of these levels, Barnes, Mercer, and Shakespeare apply Turner's model to disability.[4]

At *the individual level*, Turner analyzes the "illness experience" using "phenomenology (the analysis of everyday life to establish its underlying assumptions) and symbolic interactionism (the study of social life as a system

---

1. Altman, "Sociology."
2. Barnes et al., *Exploring Disability*.
3. Turner, *Medical Power and Social Knowledge*.
4. Barnes et al., *Exploring Disability*, 35.

of communication of symbols)."[5] In turn, Barnes, Mercer, and Shakespeare suggest that phenomenology and symbolic interaction might be employed to analyze the experience of disability and impairment in terms of challenges to self-identity, to look at disability not as a

> permanent position but as a 'career' which is affected by changing personal and social circumstances and texts, and interactions with others, including, most significantly, professional experts. The outcome may be compliance and reciprocity or conflict, but the crucial aspect for micro-level approaches is that the outcome is part of a negotiated and emergent, rather than fixed or determined, social process.[6]

At the social level, "medical sociology," according to Turner, "would focus on the social construction of disease categories ('illness', 'sin' and 'deviance') whereby individuals are classified and regulated by professional groups." Turner also maintains that at this level there is an "attempt to explore the emergence of institutions with a special responsibility for the sick and the deviant (asylums, hospitals and clinics)" as well as "the concept of the sick role."[7] In contrast, Barnes, Mercer, and Shakespeare argue that in addition to the specific concept of the sick role, attention should turn to "social roles and norms, and the social construction of concepts, such as disability, impairment and stigma, through which individuals are classified and regulated by the main institutions of social control." They believe that the sociology of disability at the social level should be extended to include "the perception of the 'disabled body' itself as the product of social and cultural practices."[8]

It is at the third level where disability is related to *the overall structure of society*. For Turner's medical sociology, this level of analysis "concerns the societal organization of health-care systems, their relationship to the state and the economy, and the problems of social inequality both within and between societies."[9] Barnes, Mercer, and Shakespeare specify their analysis to include "the overall organization of systems of health, education and social welfare of disabled people, [and] how these link to the state, economy and social policy." This extends to "issues of conflict and power, social disadvantage and discrimination," as well as to the ways advantaged groups dominate and "force or persuade weaker social groups into a subordinate

---

5. Turner, *Medical Power and Social Knowledge*, 5.
6. Barnes et al., *Exploring Disability*, 35.
7. Turner, *Medical Power and Social Knowledge*, 7–8.
8. Barnes et al., *Exploring Disability*, 34–35.
9. Turner, *Medical Power and Social Knowledge*, 5.

position." People with disabilities are viewed as belonging to a "weaker social group"that is socially dominated, with the dominant group having "access to disproportionate power, economic resources and knowledge." Nevertheless, "social domination may be achieved by persuasion, overt control and constraint, as well as by more covert manipulation, or 'ideological domination.'" At the same time, it is important to examine how far social order and relations are destabilized through individual resistance and collective mobilization."[10]

Barnes, Mercer, and Shakespeare seek to employ political economy models in analyzing societal responses to disability. They use neo-Marxism or materialist analysis, particularly in reference to the structural relationship between capitalism, power, and inequality. This raises specific questions about the institutional and policy links between the state and organized medicine, especially since medical practitioners "enjoy power, status and material rewards that rank them within the dominant class."[11]

Because of the general tendency to reduce various phenomena that are social in nature to the personal level, I will start with an examination of disability at the societal level. Then, I will discuss the individual level and the social level as one unit because both are influenced by society's response to disability, and because individual level responses to society are normally reflected in the immediate social context. In my view, this is a logical follow-up to what Barnes, Mercer, and Shakespeare have outlined.[12]

Disability and the Overall Structure of Society

Joseph Stubbins once commented that "The toughest item on the agenda of disability is that modern America has no need for most disabled persons."[13] This forthright statement probably exceeds what most people would regard as an acceptable critique, and while most people who work in various rehabilitation fields would label Stubbins's comment unthinkable, the statement does force the question, are we as good a society as we claim to be? That depends on one's perspective. If one has received benefits from the "system," then perhaps one can develop a positive view of it and how it works. On the other hand, if a person with a disability has not received a good response in terms of understanding and service, then disappointment, even outrage are both possible and necessary. Most programs offered through the state,

10. Barnes et al., *Exploring Disability*, 34–35.
11. Ibid.
12. Ibid.
13. Stubbins, "Politics of Disability," 35.

either directly or through agencies contracted by the state, are not designed to change society's attitudes and treatment of people with disabilities. Indeed, they are often engaged in making do with what is, often so as not to endanger financial support for their services.

In order to understand the system's offerings and benefits in larger context, both historically and presently, I will discuss four areas of action that have shaped how society has responded to disability: medicalization, education (including special education), program and supports, and disability rights.

Medicalization

Historically, industrialization and medicalization of previous centuries brought about "a significant intensification of the commercialization of land and agriculture, and the growth of industrialization and urbanization." This included radical changes in community and family life as well as changes in how and where people worked. The "speed of factory work, or working to the rhythms of machinery, often undertaking complex, dexterous tasks, the regimented discipline, and production demands" disadvantaged people with disabilities who had previously been integrated into the work of family farms and family home-based industries. In effect, they "were no longer easily integrated into the economic system and a potential drain on social welfare."[14]

The rise of scientific medicine led to the medicalization of society and later to the establishment of related occupations with a social/scientific/medical base, including physical therapy, psychology, social work, and rehabilitation counseling. Illness and disability were gradually brought under the control of the medical establishment, which defined and labeled sick and disabled people and prescribed treatment. This resulted in new forms of surveillance and discipline for people with disabilities, and the development of a wide range of techniques that sought to "identify, classify, and regulate sick and disabled people." Moreover, the rise of what is referred to as the "therapeutic state" resulted in "polarized conception of normal and abnormal, sane and insane, healthy and sick."[15]

In the nineteenth century, medicine was heavily involved in establishing residential institutions and schools designed to both treat and contain persons with various impairments. Braddock and Parish indicate that by 1850, there were 4,730 individuals with various disabilities residing

14. Barnes, et al., *Medical Power and Social Knowledge*, 35.
15. Ibid., 18–19.

in institutions in the United States. Thereafter, separate institutions were established for people with intellectual disabilities.[16] They also report that "Between 1850 and 1890, 55 state psychiatric institutions were opened," and that the number of residents rose to 74,028 in 1890 and to 187,791 by 1910. Beginning in 1830, the decennial census counted a number of disabilities, the reports of which were used to justify increases in institutionalized populations as well as a rationale for sterilization measures and state laws prohibiting the "marriage of persons with mental disabilities and epilepsy."[17]

Around the turn of the twentieth century, numerous medical programs and concepts helped to establish medical dominance in the treatment of people with disabilities. From 1890 to 1920, institutions referred to as "hospital-schools" were opened as "the first programs for the vocational training of 'cripples,' [and] an approach to the problem of disability emerged that became known as *rehabilitation*."[18] These programs were designed to eliminate dependency by fostering work behaviors and skills and by correcting physical problems through surgery and other forms of therapy. They solidified the medical model as the dominant approach to dealing with disability, especially after orthopedic surgery became established as a respected field of medicine.[19]

From 1920 on, rehabilitation became a widely accepted approach to disability. Veterans wounded in World War I and successive wars were incorporated into the systems already developed to provide medical care and vocational training. World War I made disability into a contested category where physicians "who approached disability in terms of diagnosis, prognosis, and treatment, became gatekeepers to benefits."[20] The "codification, institutionalization, and reification" of the medical approach to disability was accomplished through veterans' benefits legislation.[21] This legislation also benefitted nonveterans when they were incorporated into these programs beginning in 1920 with the passage of the Smith-Fess Act. This was followed by the Social Security Act of 1934, which "established state-federal VR [vocational rehabilitation] as permanent programs that could be discontinued only by an act of Congress."[22] Over the years since, additional legislation has broadened both in terms of coverage (especially mental health) and the

16. Braddock and Parish, "Institutional History of Disability," 34–35.
17. Ibid., 35.
18. Byrom, "Pupil and a Patient,"133 (italics original).
19. Ibid.
20. Hickel, "Medicine, Bureaucracy, and Social Welfare," 236–37.
21. Ibid., 237.
22. Bruyere, "Vocational Rehabilitation: Law and Policy," 4:1613.

amount of funding available for civilian as well as veteran rehabilitation programs.[23]

While medical dominance has led to the perspective that disability is largely viewed in hard-science terms, it is necessary to concede that, however we wish to critique and reduce its social power over the lives of people with disabilities, medicine stills plays an important role in determining and treating various disabling conditions. First of all, the road to disability often begins with an acute illness (e.g., a stroke), injury (e.g., traumatic brain injury), or the development of symptoms and signs of a chronic illness (e.g., rheumatoid arthritis). From there, the response to these acute illnesses can involve any number of treatments designed to provide immediate remedies, long-term care, and management. Medicalization also involves responses to additional disabilities which are either caused by the initial impairment or a new impairment adding additional complications. In addition, medical progress and the ability of the medical profession to expand has resulted in an increase in the number of people diagnosed as having a disability (especially among the elderly), as well as fostering advances in clinical treatment and health care delivery.[24]

Special Education

In 1856, the Columbia Institution for the Instruction of the Deaf and Dumb and the Blind was opened on a donated estate in Washington DC. This was later to become Gallaudet University, named after the Reverend Thomas Gallaudet (1787–1851), who pioneered use of sign language for the education of the deaf in the United States. Gallaudet University became the college where graduates from state schools for the deaf matriculated after high school. The use of sign language at these schools led to the development of a deaf culture with its own set of customs and organizations. However, the use of sign language for educating the deaf was challenged by the "oralists," who insisted that the deaf learn to lip read and speak English as taught in regular schools.[25]

In the nineteenth century, specialized institutions were the places to gain an education if you were blind, intellectually impaired, or deaf. As American society became more industrialized, the demand for such schools increased, primarily as a form of rescue, which included the themes of "protection, separation and dependence." However, Margaret Winzer suggests

23. Frontera, "Medicine."
24. Ibid.
25. Lane, *When the Mind Hears*.

that "the emergence of specialized institutions marked a significant shift in attitudes toward, and treatment of, disabled individuals, and their development illuminates rapidly changing perceptions of the role of disabled persons in an industrializing society." A broad view of this change is indicated by the fact that the residents were at first "seen as supplicants depending on private philanthropy" but "were next viewed as dependents on official charity, and finally, by the opening decades of the twentieth century, as individuals deserving of educational rights similar to those ceded their nonexceptional counterparts."[26]

The expansion of special education was solidified in the post–World War II period when special education began to be viewed as "an equal member of the educational family." Whereas institutional settings remained important for a small population of individuals with disabilities, "from the firm establishment of segregated classes in 1910 until well into the 1970s, the education of learning and behaviorally disordered children was generally equated with special class models of service delivery" in public schools.[27] During this same era, advances in medicine led to the development of new techniques in prevention, intervention, and care of various disabling conditions, as well as "technological advances [that] improved the functioning of scores of disabled people." Indeed, "while just over 1.2 percent of American school-aged children were enrolled in special education" in 1948, by 1958, it rose to 2.1 percent, and by 1978, to "8.2 percent."[28]

These trends helped to establish special education as a profession, resulting in a shift toward the "technical problems of assessment, pedagogy, classroom management, and curriculum."[29] In addition, segregated classes were promoted enthusiastically, with strong impetus coming from parents, who demanded special facilities and noninstitutionalized programs for their children. Gradually, this led to increased funding and the availability of community-based facilities, and set the stage for a series of dramatic changes to come.[30]

While the quality of special education continued to improve dramatically well into the 1960s, especially for children with intellectual disabilities, by the 1970s, in Winzer's view, "a more humanistic movement" emerged

26. Winzer, *History of Special Education*, 79.
27. Ibid., 363.
28. Ibid., 354.
29. J. G. Carter, "Sociology and Special Education," 38.
30. Winzer, *History of Special Education*, 364.

representing "a gradual but positive change in society's attitudes toward exceptional persons."[31] Winzer continues:

> The traditional notions that exceptional children should be educated separately from their peers or that mentally handicapped people should be herded into large institutional settings were now rejected. A key goal of society became the normalization of all exceptional individuals, which meant regarding exceptional people as individuals and treating them fairly and individually. As segregated facilities that were once taken for granted were seriously challenged, many institutionalized people moved from large institutions into more normal living environments.[32]

During the early 1970s, child advocate Marian Wright Edelman discovered that many children with intellectual and other developmental disabilities were being excluded from schools based on deep-seated rationales. This led to Edelman's founding of the Children's Defense Fund, "to help establish the right of all students to a public education."[33] In 1975, the combined efforts of several groups led to the passing of the All Handicapped Children Act, "the first separate federal legislation authorizing special education for children and youth."[34] This legislation emerged during a period of advocacy for civil rights for various groups in addition to those with disabilities. The legislation also resulted in a changed role for special education in meeting the educational needs of children with disabilities: it introduced into law the concept of "mainstreaming" and the associated concept of "least restricted environment." According to Linda Ware, mainstreaming

> aimed to promote the social acceptance of students identified for special education services. However, the context was one in which students identified as needing special education services were typically removed from the general education classroom and, depending on need, reassigned to resource rooms for 21 to 60 percent of the school day or to disability-specific classrooms when student needs exceeded placement for more than 60 percent of the school day.[35]

Mainstreaming did not eradicate the labeling of difference: indeed, teachers assigned to regular classrooms have claimed that they are

---

31. Ibid.
32. Ibid.
33. Stroman, *Disability Rights Movement*, 161.
34. Albrecht, "Chronology."
35. Ware, "Mainstreaming," 3:1052–53.

ill-prepared to work with students with disabilities. In addition, these labels have resulted in a "naive interpretation of the law" which, in turn, has fostered "controversy and contested practice by both general and special educators."[36] Ware and Allan contend that "Special education continues to be preserved, while inclusive education discourses are silenced, not least of all by professionals in the United States who hold a vested stake in protecting their own interests in segregated education by issuing dire warnings about the 'inclusion' of full inclusion."[37] Nevertheless, the law has required schools to prepare an individual educational program (IEP) for each child with a disability, involving input from teachers, principals, counselors, medical professionals, community agencies, and parents. The IEP must be kept on file and reviewed annually.[38]

Programs and Supports

It is not enough to have medical programs and special education for people with disabilities. They must be organized, implanted, and funded. In addition, children with disabilities become (quite frequently) adults with disabilities. Some people with disabilities have needs that must be tended to because they cannot live on their own without supervision or personal assistance.

When families who have children with disabilities need financial or other kinds of interventions, some assistance is available through the federal Maternal and Child Health Bureau, which seeks to identify children with special health care needs. In recent years, there has been an attempt to define what is referred to as an "ideal medical home," which among other things, stresses accessible, family-centered, and coordinated care that is community based and provided in a culturally competent manner.[39] In addition to private medical care insurance, families may receive financial support through Supplemental Security Income (SSI), Medicaid, the Children's Health Insurance Program (CHIP), Title V, and provisions of the Individuals with Disabilities Education Act (IDEA). Each of these programs has specific criteria for coverage depending on family income and the child's age.[40]

---

36. Ibid., 3:1053.
37. Ware and Allan, "Special Education," 4:1492.
38. Simeonsson and Lollar, "Individuals with Disabilities Education Act of 1990," 2:945–47.
39. Giardino, "Health Care Delivery Systems," 624–25.
40. Ibid., 628.

Programs for adults with disabilities vary considerably depending on the type and severity of impairment and financial resources. Beginning no later than age sixteen, the IEP must contain a statement outlining transition plans from school to "post-school" activities. These include postsecondary education, vocational training, integrated employment, adult services, independent living, or community participation.[41] From this position, any number of programs can assist adults with disabilities, including vocational rehabilitation, enrollment in sheltered workshop and activity programs, placement in a group home or other spaces of independent living, and the provision of various forms of financial assistance, including Social Security Disability Insurance (SSDI), workers' compensation, and private disability coverage.

Disability Rights

During the last decades of the twentieth century, Americans have witnessed an increased emphasis on the rights of persons with disabilities, culminating in the enactment of the ADA. This was and remains the most important piece of disability rights legislation, shaping numerous interfaces between persons with disabilities and the larger social arena. Yet, the road to ADA's passage in 1990 was a struggle, which continues as policies are shaped and those parties involved (i.e., consumers, service providers, government agencies, and various corporate entities) contest its implementation.[42]

The struggle leading up to the ADA can be traced to a number of factors. One of them was the rise of Social Darwinism's notion of the survival of the fittest, which from the late 1800s on provided part of the ideological underpinning for programs that sought (for example) to link sexual and criminal deviance to "abnormal intellectual impairment." According to Steven Gelb, Darwin "described persons with intellectual disability as evolutionary stand-ins for missing ancestral forms." However, the careful observation and reasoning that characterized [Darwin's] work on pigeons, worms, and barnacles was notably missing in his discussions of the evolution of human beings.[43] Nevertheless, in the United States and in most modern societies, the eugenics movement sought to assert that mental and intellectual disability was the root cause of social problems such as crime, alcoholism, and pauperism. They also claimed that those with low mental

---

41. Wehman and Walsh, "Transition from School to Adulthood," 5.
42. See Albrecht et al., "Introduction."
43. Geib, "Darwin, Charles (1809–1882)," 1:343.

ability turned to antisocial behaviors because of their inability to cope in an increasingly complex society.[44]

Yet, despite the clamor for laws and policies favoring institutionalization and numerous restrictions for people with disabilities living in the community, there is also a history of activism championing disability rights. In the United States, early work among persons who were deaf and blind enfranchised some to advocate on their own behalf. In 1880, the National Association of the Deaf held an organizational meeting in Cincinnati under the leadership of persons educated in state schools for the deaf and the National Deaf-Mute College (the precursor of Gallaudet University).[45] Later, such organizations as the Disabled American Veterans of the First World War (later known as the Disabled American Veterans) and the American Foundation for the Blind were established to "contest" societal attitudes that had ruled out the participation of people with disabilities in the American mainstream.[46]

The period before, during, and after World War II also set the stage for the disability rights movement of the 1960s and beyond. In addition to several pieces of legislation including the Smith-Sears Veterans Rehabilitation Act of 1918, the Smith-Fess Vocational Rehabilitation Act of 1920, and the Social Security Act of 1935, the presence of Franklin D. Roosevelt in the White House and the establishment of additional disability advocacy groups fostered a gradual recognition that the presence of people with disabilities was not going to go away. Also, the activism of parents of children with disabilities (described in the section on special education, above) had a profound effect on the provision of services in addition to education.[47]

A major force for civil rights among people with disabilities was deinstitutionalization. Deinstitutionalization occurred mainly among two populations: the mentally ill and the developmentally disabled. In 1959, over five hundred thousand persons lived in psychiatric residential institutions in the United States. By the year 2000, this population was reduced to sixty thousand patients.[48] Deinstitutionalization was fostered by several overlapping developments, including press exposure of overcrowding and inadequate treatment afforded at public institutions,[49] and the development of new briefer therapies to deal with neuropsychiatric problems involving

---

44. Allen "Biological Determinism," 1:173.
45. Fleischer and Zames, *Disability Rights Movement*, chapter 2.
46. Ibid.
47. Stroman, *Disability Rights Movement*, 122–23.
48. Ibid., 126.
49. Ibid.

the use of early intensive treatment, group therapy, sedation and even hypnosis, The combination of each of these led not only to an increase in efforts to search out better care options, but especially to the use of "pharmacotherapies" and community outpatient care.[50]

Many of the causes of for the deinstitutionalization of mental health patients also applied to those living in institutions housing people with intellectual and other developmental disabilities, except that there was no "drug revolution." Duane Stroman identifies six "intertwined and mutually reinforcing causes of deinstitutionalization and what was to replace it—a continuum of community services." These are (1) the indictment of the poor quality of life in large public institutions; (2) the advocacy movement; (3) the spreading of new treatment policies involving integration, normalization, and inclusion; (4) the support of President Kennedy for deinstitutionalization and community care; (5) the growing cost institutional placement and the opportunity for the states to shift costs to the federal government for community care programs; and (6) the judicial and legislative responses to the first five forces listed in an era of reform, protest, and the expansion of civil rights.[51]

Today these treatment trends for persons with mental illness as well as for those with developmental disabilities are taken for granted. They have become the standard way American society has responded to these persons, complete with a system of federal, state, and local agencies. Yet, it took a considerable amount of effort to acknowledge such persons' needs and to come forth with the needed funding and organizational infrastructure. Even now, these organizations must compete for dollars offered by various granting agencies as well as asking the voting public for endorsement of taxing schemes used to match state and federal funds.

Deinstitutionalization and community care were underpinned by advocacy for the ideas of integration, normalization, and inclusion. In the early 1950s, parents of children with intellectual disabilities began to actively change society's structural response. Their advocacy gradually led to the development of the organizations referred to above and their associated ideas.[52]

The move toward disability rights was also fostered by the rise of centers for independent living, especially among physically disabled people who could articulate their own needs. Independent living can be conceptualized as "the emancipatory philosophy and practice that empowers

---

50. Paraphrase of Stroman, *Disability Rights Movement*, table 5.6.
51. See Stroman, *Disability Rights Movement*, chapter 5.
52. Hasler, "Independent Living," 2:930.

disabled people and empowers them to exert influence, choice, and control in every aspect of their lives."[53] The movement was born in Berkeley, California, where a group of students with physical impairments at the University of California "rebelled against the notion that they should accept living in a nursing home and united to demand the right to an accessible living environment and paid aids to give them the personal assistance necessary for them to lead normal lives."[54] This group, called the Rolling Quads, essentially worked to support other disabled students at Berkeley. They also developed and extended the centers for independent living concept throughout the United States and Europe through "the work of a few well-traveled disabled activists."[55]

While there are many aspects to the independent-living concept, it was the specific actions of the Berkeley group that empowered a new wave of advocacy and action for disability rights. For several years after the passage of Rehabilitation Act of 1973, the federal government failed to issue rules and regulations implementing the law. Finally, on April 1, 1977, disabled activists from cities around the United States organized protests at the federal offices of the Department of Health and Human Services. It was the protest staged in San Francisco that "stands out in history due to its length and the impact it had on social and political change:"

> Wheelchair users, people who were deaf or blind, and people with developmental and other disabilities organized themselves to exercise their collective power and political might. The protesters held the regional offices hostage for 28 days, gaining national attention and resulting in an agreement with federal officials for the rapid establishment of the rules and regulations to implement Section 504 of the 1973 Rehabilitation Act.[56]

The events of 1977 not only mandated the civil rights of people with disabilities as they participated in educational institutions and social programs receiving federal funds (Section 504) but served as the propellant toward the Americans with Disabilities Act of 1990 (ADA). As early as 1984, an American Bar Association publication presented a "'statutory blueprint" for such a law. It should provide a definition of discrimination on the basis of disability and should explicitly impose obligations to make reasonable

---

53. Ibid., 2:931.
54. Ibid.
55. Balcazar and Luna, "Activism," 1:25.
56. Burgdorf, "Americans with Disabilities Act of 1990," 1:94.

accommodations, to remove architectural, transportation, and communication barriers, and to eliminate discriminatory qualification standards.[57]

Subsequently, these ideas took shape through the work of the National Council on the Handicapped, whose presidential appointees issued a report titled *Toward Independence* based, in part, on the results of sponsored forums across the country. Finally, after a series of preliminary efforts, the Americans with Disabilities Act passed both houses of congress and signed into law by President George H. W. Bush on July 26, 1990.[58]

The ADA is divided into five sections or titles. Title I, pertaining to employment, prohibits discrimination in hiring on the basis of disability on the part of employers having fifteen or more employees. It also specifies that people with disabilities shall not be discriminated against with regard to such issues as compensation, employee benefits, and promotion. It also requires that employers make "reasonable accommodations" to the known limitations of a qualified individual with a disability.[59]

Title II prohibits discrimination by any public entity with regard to providing benefits or services to people with disabilities. Title II includes detailed provisions applicable to "public transportation systems, Amtrak, and community transit authorities."[60]

Title III of the ADA addresses "public accommodations" defined very broadly to encompass most types of privately owned businesses, including

> places of lodging, establishments serving food or drink, places of exhibition or entertainment, places of public gathering, sales or rental establishments, transportation terminals and stations, places of public display or collection, parks and other places of recreation, schools and other places of education, social service establishments, and places of exercise or recreation.[61]

Title III also includes what Robert Burgdorf refers to as a "sweeping 'general rule' that prohibits discrimination 'on the basis of disability in the full and equal enjoyment of the goods, services, facilities, privileges, advantages, or accommodations of any place of public accommodation.'"[62]

Title IV "establishes requirements regarding telephone transmissions and television public service announcements." These companies must provide services to people with deafness in their covered area, including

57. Ibid.
58. Ibid.
59. Ibid., 1:95–96.
60. Ibid.
61. Ibid.
62. Ibid.

telecommunications devices for the deaf (TDDs) as well as closed captioning of public service announcements on television. Title V of the ADA "contains various provisions related to procedural and enforcement issues."[63]

Since its passage, the ADA has resulted in numerous enforcement and legal cases that have been taken all the way to the United States Supreme Court. Burgdorf notes that "by the end of its summer 2004 term, the Supreme Court of the United States had decided 19 cases interpreting and applying the ADA." He concludes by stating,

> It is difficult to draw many firm conclusions from these decisions, but they suggest some general patterns or trends. Examining the results according to which title of the ADA was at issue reveals that the Court decided cases under Title III (public accommodations) in favor of litigants with disabilities, ruled about evenly for and against litigants with disabilities [while] in cases under Title II (activities of state and local governments), and came down against litigants with disabilities in a significant majority of the cases under Title I (employment).[64]

Looking into the future, the ADA's limitations are being addressed on at least two fronts. The National Council on Disability has issued reports that have documented matters pertaining to "federal compliance, enforcement, technical assistance, and public information activities for Title I through IV" of the ADA. In 2004, the council issued *Righting the ADA*, in which it provided, among other items, a draft of what was to become the "ADA Restoration Act of 2004." This act was designed to (1) reinstate the scope of protection the act affords, (2) restore previously available remedies to successful ADA claimants, and (3) repudiate or curtail certain inappropriate and harmful defenses that have been grafted onto the carefully crafted standards of the ADA.[65]

The fact that the ADA has fallen into a pattern of contestation has implications for how disability is viewed, culturally as well as socially. The ADA Amendments Act of 2008 was passed and signed into law in September 2008. It seeks to clarify and reiterate who is covered by the law's civil rights protections, revising the definition of *disability* to make explicit which impairments substantially limit a major life activity.[66]

---

63. Ibid., 1:100.
64. Ibid.
65. National Council on Disability, *Righting the ADA*.
66. Ibid.

Disability and the Individual

In keeping with the focus of disability studies, most of the discussion in this chapter has concerned the wider aspects of disability. However, there is both a personal side to disability and more localized social settings from and into which these wider aspects unfold. It is in these arenas that the societywide phenomena of medicine, special education, programs and supports, and disability rights are mostly experienced by the disabled. The stories of individuals with disabilities and of their interactions with their immediate environment are being told by people with disabilities, researchers, and writers. The cases to follow are drawn from a growing literature as well as from my own knowledge base.

Living with Lifetime Intellectual Disabilities

Ken, Jim, Tom, and Karen are four people with intellectual disabilities known to me (but whose names have been changed to protect their identities). While Karen is in her early twenties, the three men were born between thirty-five and fifty-five years ago and their circumstances are different. They were born in the post–World War II period when community services taken for granted today were either not available or (if they were available) relatively limited. In fact, parents of the three men fought and obtained services that benefited not only their children but the children with intellectual disabilities who came after them (including Karen).

Each has been involved in educational programs that are available, by law, up to age twenty-two. Each of them has accomplished a great deal. Tom works as a janitor for his local school system, drives a pickup truck, is responsible for his own personal grooming and hygiene, and handles his own money. The same is broadly true for Ken, although he is not as independent as Tom. He is employed at a workshop operated by his county board of mental retardation and developmental disabilities. His involvement in this adult program extends to various recreational activities such as membership in a choir that is well regarded in his community and participation in a church program for young adults with developmental disabilities. Jim works in a program that trains and supervises a community placement for him at a local fast-food restaurant. Karen works in a workshop program four days each week; on the other day she goes riding in an equestrian program operated by the conference camps program of the United Methodist Church.

Older adults with adult children who have developmental disabilities face a number of challenges. Jim has developed Alzheimer's disease, a condition that has been found among older people with Down syndrome.[67] This has put an additional strain on his parents, who are in their early eighties and have their own health issues. The issues of providing care and protection for Jim and the others whose parents are approaching retirement, foreshadows their own incapacitation, their eventual death, or both. In most cases, elderly parents work to develop a plan for care and protection often involving their siblings and the local Mental Retardation and Developmental Disabilities (MRDD) program as well as other agencies that operate group homes and other independent-living options.

With specific reference to community living challenges arise that should be of concern to all people, especially those active in religious communities. Katherine McDonald argues that "a serious challenge of community-based options persists, with great disparities in resources within and across countries. Although worldwide the majority of children and many adults with intellectual disabilities live in family homes, many people in Western countries with disabilities now reside in community living arrangements."[68] She points to several issues that are problematic for efforts to attain inclusive communities: (1) attitudes toward residents with disabilities living in the community taking the form of "not in my backyard," as well as problems with local zoning and land use restrictions; (2) recent research calling into question whether group homes are able to significantly improve the quality of life for people with disabilities; and (3) questions about whether "the current system often wrongly associates a need for high levels of support with restrictive environments, thereby leaving many people with significant support needs seldom considered for community living arrangements."[69]

Living with Lifetime Physical Disabilities

Diane DeVries is a "woman born with all the physical and mental equipment she would need to live in our society—except arms and legs."[70] Diane's development (which is traced in Geyla Frank's anthropological biography *Venus on Wheels*) was rather slow compared to that of "normals." When she was about one year old, she learned to pick up and drop "large round plastic pick-up beads," more or less instinctively, which caused her parents to give her other objects with which to play. She learned to "sit up by herself by age one or two," and walked across a room on her own and without

---

67. Holland, "Alzheimer's Disease."
68. McDonald, "Community Living and Group Homes," 1:286.
69. Ibid.
70. Frank, *Venus on Wheels*, 1.

much coaching shortly thereafter. By the time Diane was old enough to go to school, "she took with her a background of accomplishment in everyday occupations." She was fitted with her "first lower prosthesis at the age of three and artificial arms at five," but had some difficulty using them for kindergarten activities.[71] A major event for her each year between the ages eight and eighteen was her attendance at a summer camp specifically geared to develop the abilities of children with a variety of disabilities in "swimming, archery, horseback riding, arts and crafts, and sing-alongs by the campfire—in short, all the activities that a child from the city or suburbs could want at a sleep-away camp."[72]

Just before turning fourteen, Diane entered a rehabilitation center "to provide her with functional lower prostheses so that she could walk."[73] Yet, despite efforts to impose "medical discipline," Diane eventually eschewed all prostheses in favor of using a motorized wheelchair, thus giving her increased mobility. Much of her resistance to the medical imposition of artificial limbs was facilitated by her participation in the "distinctive underground culture" of the rehabilitation facility, which fostered "a set of strategies to manage the impression she made on others."[74] By the time Frank and Diane met, Diane had developed a "positive attitude toward her body" despite the awareness that her body would give her trouble as she aged. Socially and politically, Diane was decidedly a person "come of age," who finished school, sought and obtained a job, fought discrimination, and faced limitations imposed on her by state and federal rules in order to obtain money to live on as well as to garner the services of attendants. Indeed, Diane has worked hard to achieve the ideals of self-esteem and independence that feminists advocated. However, "because Diane must rely on various kinds of helping systems to achieve her goals, the line between independence and dependence is not clear cut."[75]

Escaping for a While—The Case of Polio

Lauro S. Halstead, MD, acquired polio at age eighteen, just after he completed his freshman year in college. He describes his own experience as having taught him "the mixed blessings of denial." From his point of view, he "had recovered and yet did not feel disabled, nor did I grieve." And, "even

71. Ibid., 28.
72. Ibid., 30.
73. Ibid., 31.
74. Ibid., 34.
75. Ibid., 37.

though my arm remained largely paralyzed, I did not think of myself as handicapped."[76] From then until he was much older, his contacts with the medical establishment (as a patient) were relatively infrequent, and when he did make contact, it was mostly for minor issues such as a brace adjustment. Then, when the symptoms of postpolio developed, there were no records of how individual cases had progressed over the years: this set of circumstances he refers to as "the legacy of being forgotten." Part of this "forgotten legacy" may result from the extensive hospitalization required at the onset of polio—a hospitalization that emphasized the importance of intake records but not updated records, and (more important) a hospital stay full of negative memories for many patients (memories to be forgotten). Indeed, for Halstead, "Returning to the hospital—even as a visitor—would have reminded me of an illness I wanted to forget and one I thought I had conquered. Therefore, just perhaps, another visit would have reminded me that I was disabled."[77]

Acquiring a Disability during Life's Active Years

Nancy Mairs was twenty-nine when doctors confirmed that she had multiple sclerosis (MS). The diagnosis was made after a series of physical and mental illnesses could not be easily explained and tests ruled out a brain tumor. From that point on, she began what I choose to call an "articulated journey" because of her well-known books *Ordinary Time, Voice Lessons, Plaintext, Carnal Acts,* and *Remembering the Bone House.* In another book, *Waist-High in the World: A Life among the Nondisabled,* Mairs documents how "what had begun as an uphill struggle turned into a long slow slide downward, actually as well as metaphorically." The journey she describes involves a steady series of declines followed by "an increasingly intricate set of exercises in problems solving," as when faced with an inability to go and get groceries and other items, she hired a "shopping service."[78] This has led her to the conclusion that

> Virtually every activity, no matter how automatically most people would carry it out, has necessitated for me this sort of attention, resourcefulness, and adaptability. Like many young women of my generation, the first to aspire to "have it all," I vastly overextended myself when I was younger, and by the time of my diagnosis, I wore so many hats I could hardly hold my

76. Halstead, "Lessons and Legacies of Polio," 200.
77. Ibid.
78. Mairs, *Waist-High in the World,* 200.

head up: wife, mother, teacher, graduate student, political activist, not to mention cook, house-keeper, family correspondent, redecorator, needlewomen, digger of pet graves . . . Over the years, I've had to pare down this list, and relinquishing, or at least revising, each role has wounded and shamed me.[79]

People with a History of Mental Illness

In the aftermath of deinstitutionalization and the development of community services, programs have emerged that are "run entirely by mental health consumers for their peers—adults with schizophrenia, bipolar disorder, major depression, and other serious mental illnesses."[80] Underlying these programs is the idea that "rehabilitation is not enough." In other words, they seek to address the needs of people with mental illness because of the associated life crises, medical conditions, and disabilities. These include the need for rehabilitation programs that address training in life skills, the need for socialization into the outside world, and the need to accommodate emerging movements for various civil rights, including antipsychiatry and consumer/survivor alternatives to traditional mental health treatments.[81]

Peer-run support programs offer a combination of emancipatory and caring functions. Emancipatory functions are referred to as "empowerment, [and] the struggle for rights and advocacy services at the individual, interpersonal, organizational, and societal level of society."[82] Caring functions turn "away from the psychiatric systems and mutual support groups" to emphasize "personal contact, communication, and concern." They are based on a number of assumptions. (1) "Peer support programs cultivate an atmosphere that is entirely different from that of professionally provided services." (2) "Most of the problems facing mental health consumers/survivors are purely practical ones—where to live, how to get a job, or how to obtain welfare." (3) "A diagnosis of mental illness permeates all aspects of a mental health consumer's life, constricting the ideological, material, and emotional resources that give people meaning in life and allow them to act as the historical subject of their own lives."[83] In the final analysis,

---

79. Ibid., 33–34.
80. Clay, "About Us," 1.
81. Campbell, "Historical and Philosophical," 15.
82. Ibid., 34.
83. Ibid., 37–38.

Peer support allows autonomous moments for people to control their lives with acts of affirmation and resistance and to find legitimacy and hope in their own ways of experiencing. The interaction between peers proves a way for consumers to reclaim mental subjectivity by producing native wisdom. Such wisdom is not developed for the sake of abstract knowledge but to transcend one's condition.[84]

Living Longer, but with a Disability

As was emphasized in the previous chapter, the longer one lives the more likely one will have some type of functional limitation, a condition that places one among the disabled. There are a number of works which document the personal and social implications of developing a disability during one's later years. One of them is *My Mother's Hip: Lessons from the World of Eldercare* by Luisa Margolies. At the time of the book's publication in 2004, Margolies was Clinical Research Director of the Hip Fracture Project of South Florida.[85] In telling her story of what happened when her mother broke her hip, Margolies blends two issues encountered among the elderly with disabilities. The first revolves around the problems that arise from medical progress and associated technologies. Throughout her narrative, Margolies documents countless decisions, including what therapies to pursue, what drugs to take and what effects will they have, and what types of care (such as hospital care, nursing home care, and in-home care) should be provided.

More relevant for our use is the second topic: the relationship between providing care and the roles the children of the disabled elderly play in providing that care, often directly. Margolies's situation is somewhat unique in the sense that while she provided some direct care, she acted as a go-between, and often from outside the country or from across the country (California to Florida). However, caregiving has become a major activity in American society as more people live longer, which has been confirmed by recent studies sponsored by the United Hospital Fund, the Visiting Nurse Service of New York in collaboration with the Harvard University Survey of Public Health and other surveys.[86] Among the many findings of these studies are that (1) caregiving is "usually assumed to be, and in many respects remains 'women's work'"; (2) "most care recipients were female (65.3

---

84. Ibid., 39.
85. Margolis, *My Mother's Hip*.
86. Levine, "Introduction."

percent)"; (3) almost two-thirds were older than 64, and almost half that group were 80 years or older"; (4) "care recipients were most often (41.8 percent) a parent of their caregiver; another third were grandparents, aunts, uncles, cousins, siblings, or other relatives"; and (5) "the great majority of care recipients (73.9 percent) had one or more health problems . . . including heart disease, osteoarthritis, diabetes and/or cancer."[87]

Focusing on caregiving, especially with reference to the elderly, heightens the fact that nearly every American family will have to face disability in some form even if no family members face disability early in life.[88]

Disability at the Social Level

This level of analysis is where societywide views and individual experiences take shape through "social institutions, roles and norms."[89] It is where the label is applied as to who is "normal" and who is "disabled," thus giving meaning to a diagnosis from the medical establishment. It is also the level at which decisions are made about schooling, work potential, and one's ability to live independently. Such activities occur in everyday interactions often unacknowledged but powerful enough to stand for a considerable amount of time, even a lifetime. For example, when a youngster is labeled as being "developmentally disabled," a host of implications are applied, such as that the child needs special education, close supervision, and parental guidance. Connected to this is the stigma of being viewed by others, and by her-/himself, as "different."[90]

Of course, labels and their associated stigma can be resisted or negotiated or both; persons who acquire a disability later in life after years of living nondisabled do this.[91] This implies that the social interaction that takes place within institutions such as the family and the Christian congregation, can be viewed in any number of ways. Thus, when a person with autism serves as a greeter in church every Sunday, he or she is breaking the social role of disability-as-dependent and embracing the notion that "everybody belongs, everybody serves."[92]

---

87. Ibid., 8–9.
88. Levine, *Always on Call*.
89. Barnes and Mercer, *Exploring Disability*, 7.
90. Goffman, *Stigma*.
91. Barnes and Mercer, *Exploring Disability*, 7.
92. This phrase has become common use in churches working to respond more effectively to people with disabilities. It originated in Christian Reformed churches.

Implications and Conclusion

From the standpoint of the church, there has never been a range of disability responses and ministries equal to the breadth and depth of need. The following explains, at least in part, why this is the case.

Pervasiveness and Scope

To say that disability is pervasive in American society is to understate the issue. Among every age group, in every racial or ethnic category, and within both genders, significant numbers of lives are impacted by some type of disability. In addition, families, relatives, and friends are involved in numerous ways, providing support and encouragement and major portions of caregiving: those affected go far beyond the 20 percent who are identified as having disabilities. This impact is felt in numerous institutions, including the families, governments at all levels, and institutions that provide health care and education. Today, a significant portion of our legislative, administrative, and judicial activity is devoted to issues and programs centered on numerous manifestations of disability. As Gary Albrecht has described in his book *The Disability Business*, providing services and care for people with disabilities is a major sector of the U.S. economy, employing millions and involving billions of dollars.[93]

Still, churches approach the issues of disability in a piecemeal fashion. While congregations seek to make their facilities accessible and meet the specific needs of known children, youth, and adults with disabilities, the broader issues of disability tend to be ignored. This is so even when denominational and ecumenical agencies provide resources and services and witness to the presence of people with disabilities in their communities and in the larger society. The number of people with disabilities involved, even in larger congregations, would not come near to the number of persons with disability living in the surrounding community.

A related issue is the realization that the presence of disability within a community is not distributed equally. Some gender, age, racial/ethnic, and social groups have a disproportionate share of people with disabilities as opposed to others, although all social groups have a share. Thus, the number of persons with disabilities, the form of disability in terms of functional limitations, and the presence of certain types of disability are dependent on the community setting of the congregation. For instance, a congregation situated in a low-income community would probably find a higher proportion

---

93. Albrecht, *Disability Business*.

of persons with back injuries related to having worked in occupations requiring strenuous and repetitive movements, while a congregation located in an upper-income community might experience a number of disorders related to emotional stress.

Who Is Disabled?

The Survey of Income and Program Participation (SIPP) and follow-up studies include people with developmental, mental, and learning impairments among the population with disabilities as well as those with sensory and physical impairments.[94] This, on the one hand, results in a larger proportion of the population having a disability. Yet, on the other hand, their inclusion provides a more complete picture of the groups covered by the ADA and, most importantly, alerts us to those who fall under the umbrella of disability ministry. Also important to consider is that the SIPP points to large segment of the population with impairments in more than one disability domain, leading to the conclusion that many people with disabilities are challenged in various ways that are complex and emotionally demanding.

Visibility

Some forms of disability are more fixed in the public's view because well-known persons have been impacted. When the late Christopher Reeve fell from his horse severely injuring his spinal cord, media attention was immediately fixed on his subsequent rehabilitation, and later on, on his attempts to gain political and financial support for developing medical and technological devices to enable him and others with spinal cord injuries to walk.[95] A similar series of events unfolded when it became public that Michael J. Fox had Parkinson's disease. His admission to the media resulted in numerous articles, interviews, and appearances, including a series of committee hearings in both houses of the U.S. Congress.[96]

However, other forms of disability do not receive nearly the same level of exposure. One example is fibromyalgia. According to Kristin Barker, "Fibromyalgia, strictly speaking, is not a disease. Rather, it is a clinical 'syndrome' representative of a collection of symptoms, such as chronic and widespread pain and a host of associated symptoms, including fatigue,

---

94. Steinmetz, *Americans with Disabilities: 2002.*
95. Goffman, *Stigma*; and also Davis, *Enforcing Normalcy.*
96. Fox, *Lucky Man.*

headaches, sleep irregularities, irritable bowel syndrome, irritable bladder syndrome, cognitive and mood disorders, and increased sensitivity to stimuli, to just name a few."[97] Its impact is heightened by the inability of the medical community to make it visible and the medical community's debate (often vocal) as to whether fibromyalgia even exists. It, nevertheless, impacts the lives of between 2 and 5 percent of the general population, with rates far higher for women than for men and with a disproportionate share coming from the lower classes. One may ask if one has read or heard of anyone such as Christopher Reeve or Michael J. Fox appearing before legislative bodies or making the talk-show circuit on behalf of those living with fibromyalgia.

In addition, the wider society tends to understand the term disability as applying to conditions that are visible but not to conditions that are invisible. Responding to needs of people with physical disabilities by installing ramps, elevators and accessible bathrooms results in part from the visibility of physical disabilities and from the recognition that a congregation's elderly members have begun to experience disability. It is more difficult to recognize people with developmental and emotional disabilities because their functional limitations are not obviously apparent. Yet they are counted as being among people with disabilities, and their various functional limitations have a significant impact as they, their families, and their caregivers live out their lives in the communities served by their congregations.

---

97. Barker, *Fibromyalgia Story*, 3.

2

The Rise, Fall, and Rebirth of Disability Advocacy in the Church

Advocacy is a very important concept for persons with disabilities, as it pertains to their ability to obtain or increase their rights. "Advocates, [who are] people who take advocacy actions, may focus their actions on themselves, other individuals, families, organizations, communities, and/or public policies."[1] In terms of the mainline Protestant churches, disability advocacy refers to actions taken within the church to achieve increased participation by and integration of persons with disabilities into the life of the church.[2] Ideally, such efforts should foster the self-advocacy of people with disabilities as they "pursue, obtain, and, if necessary, demand particular things they need in their daily lives to attain and exercise their rights."[3]

In this chapter, I focus primarily on the rise and current state of disability advocacy within American mainline Protestantism and Roman Catholicism. In the following chapter, I focus on disability ministry of the congregation, which is the primary approach taken by evangelical Protestants. As will be shown, these two forms as they are practiced in various Christian congregations and organizations are not mutually exclusive. Many mainline Protestant churches, while advocating for the rights of people with disabilities within society (and within churches) also emphasize programs of ministry to or with people with disabilities at the congregational level. Similarly, many evangelical Protestant churches and interdenominational programs not only provide various forms of disability ministry, but advocate for disability rights. The Roman Catholic Church has traditionally

---

1. Colon et al., "Advocacy," 1:42.
2. See Herzog, ed., *Disability Advocacy among Religious Organizations*.
3. Colon et al., "Advocacy," 1:42.

integrated disability advocacy and disability ministry. In addition, churches from the Orthodox, Anabaptist, and the Reformed traditions have also made efforts at disability advocacy and ministry.

What will also be documented in this chapter is the churches' dependency on outside contexts for resources to construct their approach to advocacy. Since 1950, churches, at all levels, have shaped responses to people with disabilities by what was happening in secular society. In fact, some of the statements that the movement produced quoted verbatim from secular sources even when they were attempting to garner support for their efforts *within* churches. Again, as I mentioned in the introduction, only recently (with some exceptions) have the churches probed for resources within their own Judeo-Christian heritage to buttress their actions on behalf of people with disabilities.

Disability Advocacy in American Mainline Protestantism

The National Council of Churches

In the early 1950s, state councils of churches and chaplains at institutions for the disabled began to ask the newly formed National Council of Churches of Christ (NCC) for help in ministering to people with various disabilities.[4] The NCC's response was in keeping with its general purpose as the "instrument through which American churches now work together in all common tasks."[5] It subsequently published eight articles in volume 30 (from September 1953 through July-August, 1954) of the *International Journal of Religious Education* that called for congregations to respond to the needs of people with disabilities. Under the banner of "unhandicapping the handicapped," the church should play a role in preventing accidents and crippling diseases as well as providing aftercare. Persons with disabilities were presented as spiritually and socially isolated from churches and other communities; thus their marginality was acknowledged.[6]

The NCC began formal attempts to develop a response to disability in 1957 by convening a consultation on "the Churches' Responsibility for the Christian Education of Exceptional Persons." The participants were from several secular fields, including medicine, its allied therapies (physical, occupational, and speech therapies), and especially special education.[7] The

---

4. Ima Jean Kidd, personal communication (2011).
5. Marty, *Under God, Indivisible, 1941-1960*, 111.
6. Herzog, "The Disability Advocacy of the National Council of Churches," 12.
7. Ibid., 13.

meeting yielded suggestions from different work groups devoted to serving people in separate disability categories, including people with physical disabilities, the "socially disabled," people with cognitive and developmental disabilities (labeled then "mental retardation"). This group also focused on ministry to parents and families caring for a child or adult with cognitive disabilities.[8]

In the aftermath of the conference, the NCC established a Commission on Christian Education of Exceptional Persons, including a Committee on Mental Retardation. Like the consultation, the commission included working groups on "persons under custody of the law," physical handicaps, and persons with emotional disturbances. The use of words such as "handicaps" and "the exceptional person" were reflective of terms used in the secular contexts at the time.[9]

In 1960, the Committee on Mental Retardation conducted a survey of programs for persons with mental retardation under denominational auspices. This led to the publication of a study titled *The Church's Mission and Persons of Special Need*. Additional information was gathered for special educators in 1961 and 1962, which led to the preparation of the manual *Christian Education for Retarded Children and Youth* published by Abingdon Press in 1963.[10]

Much of the work during this time was accomplished through the Cooperative Publication Association (CPA), which included representatives from the publishing organizations of fourteen cooperating denominations. At the height of its operation (in the 1950s, '60s, and early '70s), the CPA acted as sounding board, clearinghouse, and facilitator for various publications having to do with persons with special needs (usually through a committee on mental retardation). These representatives would meet annually to discuss needs. Once the need for a particular publication was identified, one of the representatives would solicit the writing and oversee all matters pertaining to the publication's preparation. Upon completion, the article would be made available for use in publications of member denominations.[11] Work also began on designing a church school curriculum suitable for children and youth with developmental disabilities, later titled the Adventure Series.[12]

---

8. Ibid., 13–15.
9. Ibid.
10. Ibid.
11. Ibid., 17.
12. Ibid.

From 1969 through 1973, the NCC Committee on Mental Retardation expanded its activities in a number of areas, including publishing a manual *Camping and the Mentally Retarded*, holding exploratory sessions with the American Bible Society on making the Scriptures more useful for persons with retardation, and conversing with leaders in black denominations to discuss special education needs and opportunities. During this time the articles "We Visited Leon Today," "New Directions for Parents of Persons Who Are Retarded," and "Let's Do More with Persons with Disabilities," and the Adventure Series curriculum were among the resources produced by the NCC and cooperating denominations.[13]

During the period from the early 1950s to the early 1970s, the work of the NCC and its member denominations was constructed and shaped to a large degree in a secular context that focused on cure or treatment, or both, along medical/individual lines. Strong emphasis was placed on special education in keeping with the profession's rise in American public schools. Special education models employed during this era were closely linked to the medical model, which focused on the individual with a disability. Special education models were also closely tied to the emerging field of mental retardation with its emphasis on providing educational and other community-based services.[14]

Nevertheless, the NCC's efforts fulfilled a genuine need for a contemporary Christian response to disability issues by generating resources of use to member communions. While it is difficult to determine the exact impact on the local, community level, it is important to recognize that during this period state and local councils of churches were alive and well staffed—many with religious educators. This, of course, is difficult to appreciate today since the context has changed in that ecumenical agencies at all levels have experienced a significant downsizing in both staff and funding.

Mainline Denominational Responses

Toward the end of the 1970s, several mainline denominations moved toward an advocacy role and away from focusing on merely Christian education resources. In 1976, the General Conference of the United Methodist Church referred two petitions expressing concern for the "problems of the handicapped" to its Board of Global Ministries, which organized a "Task Force on Ministry to the Handicapped and Retarded" and hired a staff person the following year. These forces successfully lobbied the 1980 General

---

13. Ibid.
14. Ibid., 17–18.

Conference of the United Methodist Church to add a statement on disability to the denomination's Social Principles.[15]

A similar course was followed by the Presbyterian Church (U.S.A.). Its 189th General Assembly (1977) adopted a resolution titled *That All May Enter: Responding to the Concerns of the Handicapped*, and also organized a task force similar to the United Methodists. The Presbyterians for Disability Concerns Caucus (PDCC) was formed "to act as a clearinghouse for information concerning disabilities, as well as questions of architecture and attitude; to serve as a place for persons with disabilities to join together and express their concerns, and, as a caucus, to advocate for changing society's, and the church's, approach to disability."[16]

In the United Church of Christ (UCC), the national program began as a grassroots effort. In 1971, the Metropolitan Association of the UCC's New York Conference established a Task Force on Exceptional People. From 1971 to 1976, the Task Force educated UCC congregations in the New York City area on the needs of people with disabilities. In 1976, the Task Force decided to present a resolution to the New York Conference calling for greater awareness of the needs and gifts of people with disabilities across the denomination. Adopted unanimously, it was referred to the next General Synod of the United Church of Christ, which also adopted the measure, by then, was widely supported.[17]

The UCC resolution was indicative of the interfacing between disability issues in the church and disability issues in society. The resolution's "Background Statement" was constructed with reference to the U.S. Rehabilitation Act of 1973, noting that "one-tenth of all Americans were physically or mentally handicapped."[18] The resolution was also ecumenical in that it referred specifically to "The Handicapped and the Wholeness of the Family of God," adopted by the 1975 General Assembly of the World Council of Churches, and employed often in defense of Christian disability advocacy and ministry. It affirmed the concepts of equality, mutuality, and human worth and personal dignity with specific reference to persons with disabilities:

> The church cannot exemplify the full humanity revealed in Christ, bear witness to the interdependence of humankind, or achieve unity in diversity if it continues to acquiesce in the social isolation of disabled persons and to deny them full participation

15. Herzog, "Disability Advocacy in American Mainline Protestantism."
16. Ibid.
17. Ibid., 81–82.
18. Quoted in ibid.

in its life. The unity of the family of God is handicapped where these brothers and sisters are treated as objects of condescending charity. It is broken where they are left out.[19]

Soon, most of the Protestant mainline churches passed similar measures, including the American Baptist Church, the Disciples of Christ, and the main Lutheran bodies that later formed the Evangelical Lutheran Church in America. In 1978, the General Board of the American Baptist Churches called upon American Baptists "to recognize persons with disabilities as integral members of the Christian fellowship and to take immediate affirmative action to enable their full integration into society, the local congregation, and in church organizations."[20] Beginning in 1979, the General Assembly of the Disciples of Christ voted in favor of resolutions including affirmations of its "commitment to the principle that full acceptance of persons with disabilities within the life, witness and service of the church [as] a requirement for the wholeness of the family of God." This was followed by a "Resolution of Concern for Persons with Conditions of Impairment" in 1985 and a "Resolution Concerning the Rights of Handicapped Infants" in 1989.[21] In 1982, the General Convention of the Episcopal Church established the Presiding Bishop's Task Force on Accessibility. From its inception, the Task Force was charged with including persons with disabilities into the full life of the church community and with providing resources for those needs. It worked to establish a Committee on Disability Concerns in each Episcopal diocese.[22]

Response from the NCC

In 1977 as part of the move to a greater emphasis on disability rights and advocacy across American society, the Governing Board of the National Council of Churches adopted an extensive statement titled "Resolution on the Church and Persons with Handicaps," which used the World Council of Churches statement (cited above). Thus, its first resolution, called upon member communions to "increase efforts at all levels of church life (national, regional, local) toward full participation by persons with handicaps, through such means as providing appropriate educational programs, making necessary architectural modifications, being sensitive in the building of

---

19. World Council of Churches, "Unity of the Church."
20. Herzog, "Disability Advocacy in American Mainline Protestantism," 82.
21. Issued by the Disciples of Christ, 1985 and 1989, respectively.
22. Herzog, "Disability Advocacy in American Mainline Protestantism," 82.

new structures to the needs of handicapped persons, overcoming attitudinal barriers, and developing advocacy programs in the church and society."[23]

In 1978 the United Nations declared 1981 to be "The International Year for Disabled Persons" (IYDP). As part of a yearlong event, the NCC and numerous American faith traditions were called upon to identify and implement projects which would draw attention to the need for the inclusion of persons with disabilities in all areas of social life, including participation in religious groups.[24] By 1980, a consultation was held with the goal "Toward Full Participation of all Disabled Persons in Church and Society" with projects in three areas: (1) finding jobs for disabled persons who were presently unemployed, (2) providing for adequate transportation in each community, and (3) lifting up educational opportunities.[25]

The auspicious beginnings of disability advocacy in the Mainline Protestant denominational structures were to be followed by years of limited success in terms of institutionalizing disability advocacy at the grass roots. The NCC took steps to keep in line with secular developments in special education, medicine and rehabilitation, and by attempting to grapple with serious issues impacting the disability community, including deinstitutionalization, mainstreaming, citizen advocacy, and human sexuality. However, the gap between decisions and programs made at the national level and the local level still remained, and problems encountered at the congregational level were only indirectly addressed. It is safe to say that in addressing the marginality of disability in the churches, those involved were unaware of their own marginalization within their respective organizations.[26]

In 1987, a transition to a new era began as the Committee on Developmental Disabilities of the NCC pursued a list of goals for 1988–1991, including (1) to advocate for the active participation of persons with developmental disabilities in church and society; (2) to broaden the information base for ministry with persons with developmental disabilities through sharing and evaluating resources, program models, research studies and denominational priorities and policies; and (3) to enable denominational representatives to participate in joint projects, such as leadership programs and media development.[27]

At its 1991 annual meeting, the NCC Committee on Disabilities selected five areas where the church could have an impact: (1) fostering

23. Ibid.
24. Herzog, "Disability Advocacy of the National Council of Churches."
25. Ibid., 19–26.
26. Ibid., 23.
27. Ibid., 26–28.

inclusive education, (2) preparing people with disabilities for work, (3) providing educational advocates besides the parents for children with disabilities in regular or special church-school settings, (4) thinking of ways for Christian institutions of higher education to comply with "the same standards of inclusiveness as secular institutions of higher education," and (5) brainstorming on how to bring young people into professions in the field of disabilities.[28] The committee gradually identified itself as the leading ecumenical group where representatives from member communions, from other nonmember religious organizations, and from secular agencies gathered to share developments within each participating group and to receive support for their work among other groups advocating for people with disabilities.[29]

Beginning in 1995, the committee began to prepare an NCC policy statement on the inclusion of people with disabilities intended to be enacted by the NCC governing board. The committee sought to bring issues of concern to people with disabilities to the NCC, member communions, and the larger society. It remained an active body, which attracted one of the largest contingents of noncommunion representatives of any NCC committees. Trends in diminishing funds and staff had not dampened enthusiastic participation at annual meetings, at which issues and ideas were shared, and program thrusts (such as seminary education) were kept on task.[30]

However, in 2013 the committee was eliminated as the result of the NCC's downsizing in the face of declining financial resources. In response, members of the committee have proposed that its work be continued via an organization outside of the NCC. This organization would continue the communication and information sharing in operation under the NCC. Some of the members are unsure about the necessity of an organizational structure but are convinced that the functions of the former committee can be continued informally. As of this writing, no such committee has emerged.[31]

Roman Catholicism

While some of the earlier Roman Catholic work with people with disabilities began well before World War II, it was in 1961 that a group of Catholic teachers of religion (mostly priests and members of religious orders) "spoke

28. Ibid., 29.
29. Ibid.
30. Ibid., 30–31.
31. Ibid.

publicly for the first time about their feelings of inadequacy and isolation in their diocesan programs or private apostolates for persons with mental retardation." They were "outraged" that children and adults "were excluded from full participation at Eucharist and other sacraments because of their cognitive and intellectual abilities." This led to the formation of the National CCD (Confraternity of Christian Doctrine) Apostolate for the Mentally Retarded to "promote religious instruction for mentally retarded persons." Early input from teachers, parish centers, and institutions identified the need for religious education, inclusion, and hospitality. As training programs developed to equip people to work with persons with mental retardation, grass-roots support was built for "the idea for a national apostolate to honor their rights as people of God." A business meeting and conference was held in August 1967 culminating in the establishment of the National Apostolate for the Mental Retarded (NAMR).[32]

The NAMR began by meeting on a yearly basis and by publishing a newsletter. In 1976 the U.S. Catholic bishops created an Advisory Committee on the Ministry to the Handicapped. This was followed in 1978 by the issue of a *Pastoral Statement of U.S. Bishops on Handicapped People*,[33] which contained numerous "constructions" linking faith statements to the needs of people with disabilities. The statement was subsequently used by the Apostolate in garnering support for its advocacy in parishes and dioceses. Meanwhile, the NAMR monitored issues such as the stories of abuse of people with mental retardation at Willowbrook State School in New York, and the passage of the Education for All Handicapped Children Act (EAHCA). It issued resolutions calling for at least one parish in each deanery to be architecturally accessible and "that each parish begin to remove all barriers that hinder persons with disabilities from full participation in parish life."[34]

As mainline Protestants did, the NAMR too partnered across religious groups and within the Catholic Church. It has continued to work on inclusion and keeping the Church informed about current issues affecting people with disabilities and assisting workers involved in the various disability ministries in the dioceses across the United States. It has also studied Catholic schools' response to IDEA, work reflected in the change of its name to NAfIM: National Apostolate for Inclusion Ministries.[35]

The National Catholic Office for Persons with Disabilities (NCPD) was founded in 1982 and was renamed National Catholic Partnership on

32. Lampe, "Story of the National Apostolate for Inclusion Ministry," 58.
33. United States Conference of Catholic Bishops, "Pastoral Statement."
34. Lampe, "Story of the National Apostolate for Inclusion Ministry," 62–63.
35. Ibid.

Disability in 2002. Its initial mission was to ensure "further implementation of the directives of the 'Pastoral Statement,' which insists that disabled Catholics must be able to participate in the celebration and obligations of their faith," and to ensure that the church fosters "access, providing training, creating resources, and holding workshops and conferences." It hired an executive director who spent time traveling to meet with bishops and staff in each diocese and with parish personnel who had been working with disabled people in their various capacities. Work began on such projects as *Guidelines for the Celebration of the Sacraments for Persons with Disabilities* and *Opening Doors to Persons with Disabilities*. The latter serves as a "guidebook for developing programs, and provides ministry models, bishops' documents, essays, access surveys, and fact sheets."[36]

Since its establishment, the NCPD has advocated for secular legislation and for change within the Catholic Church. In cooperation with such groups as the Religion and Disability Program of the National Organization on Disability (see below), it supported the passage of the Americans with Disabilities Act (ADA) and other legislation defending the civil rights of all persons with disabilities. In 1991, Mary Jane Owen became its executive director and promptly set a new tone for the NCPD by saying that "'disabilities are the normal expected and anticipated outcome of the risks, stresses and strains of the living process itself. Disability is not something that happens only to the unlucky few but is an event that can be anticipated by us all.'" Owen's presence at local, national, and international church and secular events enabled the NCPD to express in concrete terms the significance of Roman Catholic policy statements, actions, and resources. More recently, the NCPD has established working relationships with several disability groups within the Church as well as secular groups, in recognition of its need to operate in an environment of scarce personal and financial resources.[37]

Conservative Protestantism

Disability advocacy among conservative Protestants is more difficult to pinpoint, in part, because conservative Protestant denominations are not organized from the top down and many paradenominational groups carry the weight of the work beyond the local church. The Christian Council on Persons with Disabilities (CCPD) was organized in 1998 when Joni and Friends (see below), under its charismatic leader Joni Eareckson Tada,

36. Baum and Benton, "Evolution and Current Focus," 47–48.
37. Ibid., 49.

sponsored the National Congress on Disability. The gathering brought together "over 700 people with disabilities, advocates, family members, friends, and disability ministry workers."[38] During this event, "30 key leaders in the Christian disability community met at Tada's invitation to develop an action plan." It was Tada's conviction that a strong voice was necessary to gain the needed attention of national leaders and to "encourage them to work in the area of disabilities," a goal which she believed "could come only from a united front."[39] This they did by organizing the CCPD, whose bylaws clearly outlined its stated goal, which was to "further advance Christ's gospel in the disability community" and to (1) promote the biblical perspective on persons with disabilities and the church, (2) offer the church an evangelical position on issues related to disabilities, (3) establish standards that will advance the ministry gifts of persons with disabilities, and (4) encourage Christian leaders to take initiatives that will enable persons with disabilities to actively and fully participate in the life and ministry of the church.[40]

From the beginning, the CCPD board adopted the Statement of Faith of the National Association of Evangelicals (NAE) and "determined that membership in CCPD would be 'open to individuals and organizations that support our evangelical Statement of Faith.'"[41] Its board later adopted a statement of "Principles of Ministry," which included five statements of confession and five implications following from the confessions. Among the confessions was included the affirmation "that all people are made in God's image in order to serve Him in all arenas of life," and the further affirmation that "Jesus Christ bears our grief, carries our sorrows, and heals our brokenness in body and spirit."[42]

Immediately upon adopting the confessions, the CCPD won the support of both the board and membership of the NAE. In 1989, the CCPD met to develop separate position papers on "key disability concerns relative to the church," including "Church Attitude and Responsibility," "The Role and Responsibility of the Pastor," "Everyday Accessibility," "Political Issues," and "Evangelism, Discipleship, and Missions."[43] Over the intervening years, the CCPD has sponsored annual education conferences on such themes as job access, euthanasia, life worth living, a theological framework for ministry, independence, and integration and mainstreaming. More recent topics have

---

38. Taege, "Christian Council on Persons with Disabilities," 142.
39. Ibid.
40. Ibid., 143.
41. Ibid.
42. Ibid., 143–44.
43. Ibid., 144.

included Alzheimer's disease and its impact on the family with a disabled member, power and control, AIDS, Christian camping, and disability and suffering. It has also developed services including media contact, a mentoring program, and speakers bureau; it has supported the ADA and other legislation. Through newsletters and journals as well as a series of Caring Church Awards, it has sought spread its concern for people with disabilities. In 2005, the CCPD embarked on a new initiative CAN: Connecting, Advancing, and Nurturing Disability Ministry.[44]

Anabaptism

Paul Leichty notes that four "interlocking themes formed the core of the Mennonite response to persons with disabilities:

1. An unconditional and redemptive *love* for people with special needs, based on the Biblical mandate to love all people, especially the poor, the sick and the hurting.
2. A mandate to *serve*, acting in the name of Christ to minister healing and hope to those in need, first within the community of faith and then to the larger world.
3. A commitment to be agents of God's *peace and justice* to the earth, bringing healing to individuals, families, and nations and treating all persons with dignity and respect.
4. A sense of *community*, in which young and old, rich and poor, and those with more or less abilities could live together, experience God's love in an environment of safety and regard, each for who he or she is.[45]

These themes grew out of service in institutions for the mentally ill and the developmentally disabled by Mennonites with conscientious objector status during World War II. By the early 1960s, mental health centers were opened under Mennonite sponsorship, and from this developed "an awareness of the needs of persons with developmental disabilities."[46]

In 1963, a "Retarded Study Committee" was convened, and two years later, its first program was established—a camp to serve people with developmental disabilities and their families. The success of the camping program led to the formation of a "Resource Committee on Mental

44. Ibid., 144–49.
45. Leichty, "Mennonite Advocacy for Persons with Disabilities," 196.
46. Ibid., 197.

Retardation," which considered the development of resources, workshops, and consultations to local churches. Later, the committee became known as the "Developmental Disabilities Council." Initially, this work was "loosely coordinated" by the Mennonite Mental Health Service (MMHS) of the Mennonite Central Committee (MCC). But in the late 1970s, the council became an administrative and policy-setting board with advocacy ministries as well as service provision parallel to that of mental health.[47] Beginning in the 1990s, however, a series of forces led to the downgrading of these groups, and in 2002, a "unilateral decision" by Mennonite Mutual Aid (MMA) eliminated the advocacy program on short notice. After a small group of parents lobbied its national headquarters, the Anabaptist Disabilities Network (ADNet) was formed; MMA agreed to turn over to the fledgling group its disability and mental illness resources and to provide some initial funding. Since then, ADNet has established a national board, raised funds to hire a half-time director, prepared new resources, published the newsletter *Connections* and other bulletins, and established a website.[48]

The Reformed Tradition

In spite of the fact that the Americans with Disabilities Act (ADA) exempted churches, the Christian Reformed Church (CRC) made the decision to comply with the law by advocating for "full inclusion of people with disabilities in all aspects of CRC life."[49] Its Committee on Disability Concerns noted that "compliance with the ADA is not a matter of conforming to civil law; rather, it is a matter of seeking social justice by extending God's righteousness and justice to all people regardless of their handicapping condition."[50] The decision to adopt the ADA provisions and guidelines within the denomination was the culmination of a decade of work that made the denomination "cognizant of the indispensable gifts and abilities offered by persons with mental and physical disabilities." Leaders of the CRC contend that "though American religious institutions are largely exempt from the ADA, the church's willingness to meet the provisions of the Act should be greater than that of secular institutions."[51] This has resulted in the creation of educational, technical, and financial resources in order to implement the provisions of the ADA. It not enough to "make theological and biblical

47. Ibid.
48. Ibid., 200–206.
49 Pridmore, "Christian Reformed Church," 95.
50. Ibid.
51. Ibid., 97.

arguments for the inclusion of disabled individuals"; rather, the CRC "has gone the next step by providing ecclesiastical support and information" to enable compliance.[52]

The CRC has also sponsored Friendship Ministries, a program that works with congregations to set up "Friendship groups, which center on group worship and one-to-one Bible study in the context of mentoring relationships." In addition, "Friendship Ministries advocates for the inclusion of people with cognitive impairments in the full life of their faith communities, encouraging full church membership and opportunities for people with cognitive impairments to share their gifts."[53] Friendship Ministries appeals to the nonevangelical mainline, and even non-Protestant congregations because of its approach of ministering directly to adults with developmental disabilities. In this respect, it is similar to Joni and Friends, which appeals to evangelicals and evangelical congregations in mainline denominations.

Parachurch Organizations

One of the most widely known disability advocacy programs targeted at religious bodies is the Religion and Disability Program (RDP) under the auspices of the National Organization on Disability (NOD). The NOD's founding followed the 1981 International Year of Disabled Persons, which, among other goals, had a strong religious component. Its board recognized early that religious institutions played a key role in the integration of people with disabilities into the mainstream. Under the leadership of board member Rev. Dr. Harold Wilke RDP sought to establish "a concentrated effort to promote and expand the participation of disabled persons in the religious life of their communities, emphasizing greater accessibility of places of worship and the involvement of disabled persons in the activities of their places of worship."[54]

Following the intent "to make religious participation of people with disabilities a major priority," RDP hired Ginny Thornburgh as its director. Its first publication of *That All May Worship: An Interfaith Welcome to People with Disabilities* "became known not only for what it says about accessibility, but how it says it." Its fifty-two pages contain lists describing how a congregation—of any faith—can develop a program of inclusion, and offers "short bullets of information designed to grab the reader's attention,

---

52. Ibid., 104.
53. Genzink, "Friendship Ministries Story," 163–64.
54. Herzog, "Working Interfaith," 209.

thereby encouraging creative responses tailored to specific congregational needs."[55] In addition, the RDP sponsored "That All May Worship" conferences in eight cities across the United States during 1993 and 1994 as pilots for stimulating interest in disability issues in congregations. The knowledge gained from these events led to the publication of *From Barriers to Bridges: A Community Action Guide for Congregations and People with Disabilities*.[56]

Another individual actively involved in the disability advocacy of the NOD as well as in interfaith, ecumenical, and denominational circles was Harold Wilke (1914–2003). Born without arms, Wilke, with the active support of his mother, learned to dress and care for himself and to otherwise live independently. Educated to become an ordained minister in the UCC, he served two pastorates, as chaplain in the army during World War II, as a hospital chaplain, and as a denominational executive (in the evangelical and Reformed side of the UCC), and as disability advocate. He formed the Healing Community, which functioned as a base operation for his disability work; the community assembled a board of notables, including psychiatrist Karl Menninger and violinist Itzhak Perlman. From this base Wilke shared his ideas on disability across the United States and around the globe. He was a staunch supporter of the ADA and gave the blessing at its signing on July 26, 1990. Wilke often signed his autograph using one of the pens employed to sign the ADA and given to him by President George H. W. Bush (from hand to foot!).[57]

Another parachurch organization is the Religion and Spirituality Division of the American Association on Intellectual and Developmental Disabilities, whose membership consists of chaplains, religious educators, and others interested in the furthering the role of religion in working with persons with developmental disabilities. It functions within the larger association by fostering "(1) interfaith dialogue and interdisciplinary collaboration; (2) the development of resources to support the practice of religion and the spirituality of persons with intellectual disabilities; and (3) efforts to support professionals in ministry with people with disabilities."[58] Among its activities is the Cooperative Resource Exhibit at its annual meetings, which is open to the entire association. In 1988, it sponsored the founding of the *Journal of Religion and Developmental Disabilities*, which after three years of negotiation became the *Journal of Religion in Disability and Rehabilitation* published by the Haworth Pastoral Press. The journal ceased publication

---

55. Ibid., 211.
56. Ibid., 214–20.
57. Anderson, "A Look Back."
58. Schurter, "Religion and Spirituality Division," 109.

after two volumes but was revived as the *Journal of Religion, Disability & Health* in 1999 and has since published numerous volumes of relevance to the general area of religion and disability with application to the present study.[59]

Addressing issues of disability among African American denominations, the National Black Disability Coalition (NBDC) acknowledges that "African Americans with disabilities are subject to discrimination and stigmatization both as people of color and as people with disabilities."[60] The NBDC points to exclusion and stigmatization of black people with disabilities that often occur within "their own cultural communities," including within the church. It also calls for research into "the disability experience within the African American Community," and in particular "the relationship between African Americans with disabilities and their churches."[61]

The Orthodox Tradition

In recent years, the Orthodox communions have shown considerable interest in responding to, and including, people with disabilities in the life of their congregations. In 2009, its statement "Disability and Communion," called upon clergy and laity in the "Holy Church throughout the Americas" to "embrace people with disabilities within the Church."[62] The language in this document employs the social model of disability in that "a person is not necessarily handicapped except through physical and attitudinal barriers created by others." It emphasizes that human life is "characterized and defined by communion or interdependence, not exclusion or independence." The denomination (also in 2009) produced an "Eastern Orthodox Christian Edition" of the *Inclusion Awareness Day Workbook* originally published by Pathways Awareness of Chicago.[63]

Moving On: Toward and Into the Twenty-First Century

It is interesting to note that disability advocacy arose at the very time when mainline denominations were declining and when there was a backlash

---

59. Ibid., 118–25.
60. National Black Disability Coalition, *Disability Inclusion Toolkit for Black Faith*.
61. Ibid., 2.
62. Canonical Orthodox Bishops in the Americas. (2010).
63. Ibid. See also Pathways Awareness, *Inclusion Awareness Day Workbook*. Note: Participating denominations are free to develop their own edition.

against social programs and debate concerning the effectiveness of social statements.[64] As these bodies moved into the 1980s, there was a decline in funding in general, and programs such as disability work and advocacy were sharply reduced or eliminated. In most cases, persons who advocated for disability rights were caught off guard because they didn't foresee the need to fight political battles for funding, staff support, and the support of the church in general. While it is generally assumed that cuts were made "across the board," disability advocates did not have the organizational and ideological resources that women and other minority groups brokered to assure their programs' continuance.

Nevertheless, denominational and ecumenical downsizing has not curtailed the advocacy of disability rights in society and in the churches. Committees, caucus groups, and parachurch organizations have continued to work, legislate, and push congregations to do more, rather than less, with disability issues. This can be seen in a number of areas, including support of the ADA, the updating and expansion of statements on disability by denominations and ecumenical bodies, new efforts to inform and otherwise influence congregations to include disability advocacy in their ministries, and the rise of new theologies of disabilities along with an emphasis on the need for exposure to disability issues in theological education.

Above, I pointed to the Christian Reformed Church's commitment to follow the letter and spirit of the ADA. This has also been the case for the United Church of Christ, which has called its congregations "to embrace the spirit of the Americans with Disabilities Act (ADA) and hold themselves morally bound by the provisions of the act." Acting as a member the UCC's National Committee of Persons with Disabilities, Harold Wilke stated that the UCC should support the ADA "not for the many compelling psychological, social, and economic reasons—there are many—but for the Biblical and theological reasons which compel an affirmative vote." Such support was indicative of Wilke's well-honed ability to bridge the theology of the church to secular contexts of disability. On the other hand, several religious groups moved to opt out of its provisions, a position heavily influenced by a letter-writing campaign from fundamentalist bodies that believed the ADA would violate the separation of church and state.[65] And even now, after more than twenty-five years, there remains skepticism as to whether churches should or should have not opted out of the ADA despite strong support of the measure by American mainline Protestant denominations.

---

64. Herzog, "Disability Advocacy in American Mainline Protestantism," 89.
65. Adapted from Wilke, "Signs of Liberation and Access."

Nevertheless, the passage of the ADA in 1990 does seem to act as a major historical line for disability advocacy among Christian denominations and ecumenical groups in America. While the emphasis on disability rights has continued, and many Protestant denominations took their stand on the ADA *after* its passage; many religious groups shifted their emphasis toward the grass roots, the congregation. Even the committees and other previously created structures (described above) began to recognize that among congregations was a great field of need requiring a response. Also, events within denominations in the early 1990s saw some interesting developments that not only challenged but extended the work of previous groups.

Two United Methodist–sponsored groups emerged during this period: the Association of Physically Challenged Ministers (APCM) and the United Methodist Task Force on Developmental Disabilities. The APCM was formed to address the recruitment, training, ordination, and placement of ordained ministers with disabilities across the denomination. With the generous support of the United Methodist General Board of Ministries and the General Board of Higher Education and Ministry, several consultations were held to discuss disability-related issues.[66]

Another group formed by the United Methodists during the early 1990s was the United Methodist National Task Force on Developmental Disabilities, recently renamed the United Methodist Committee on Disability Ministries. Its origins stem from the activities of a small congregation in Leavenworth, Kansas, and the formation of the Gateway Club, which was designed to meet the religious and social needs of adults with developmental disabilities. It was the success of this ministry and involvement in church-related camping that led to lobbying of the United Methodist General Board of Global Ministries to establish a denominationwide task force on developmental disabilities.[67]

The reorganization of the national structure of the UCC resulted in a crisis when it was proposed that the National Committee on Persons with Disabilities (NCPWD) be located under what was named Wider Church Ministries (WCM) with its emphasis on health and welfare ministries. This plan in the view of the NCPWD would have perpetuated the medical model of disabilities. The NCPWD argued successfully that

> Persons with disabilities have felt alienated and separated under the medical model. When the medical model is the paradigm, persons with disabilities have been made to feel that their disabilities are what defines them. When that is the paradigm,

66. Herzog, "Disability Advocacy in American Mainline Protestantism," 90.
67. Ibid.

persons with disabilities, as a group, are "done to and for" and not expected to take charge of their own lives or to contribute to society. The medical model perpetuates the stereo-type that persons with disabilities are "*unable*."[68]

In contrast, the NCPWD strongly advocated for a "minority empowerment model," which they hold to be instituted in the passage of the Americans with Disabilities Act of 1990 (ADA). The NCPWD "has repeatedly advocated for coordination of ministries by, for, and with persons with disabilities under the Local Church Ministries, recognizing that the most important issue for people with disabilities in the United Church of Christ is full inclusion in all aspects of church life, for both lay and clergy."[69]

In 1998, the National Organization on Disability's Religion and Disability Program launched the Accessible Congregations Campaign with the goal of recruiting two thousand committed congregations by the year 2000 "that include people with disabilities as full and active participants." The campaign was supported by eighty-five organizations, including the National Down Syndrome Society, the Jewish Educational Service of North America, and the National Council on Independent Living. Its theme, "Access: It Begins in the Heart," was aimed directly at "congregations of all faiths" and was based on "the scriptural understanding that people, with and without disabilities, are created in the image of God."[70] Congregations were asked to sign a "commitment form" that the church, synagogue, or mosque was willing to work toward the full inclusion of people with disabilities. In turn, the congregation received a certificate quoting Isaiah 56:7, "for my house shall be called a house of prayer for all peoples." In addition, the certificate contains "three principles concerning the congregation" as it committed to be accessible to people with disabilities:

1. In this congregation, people with disabilities are valued as individuals, having been created in the image of God.

2. This congregation is endeavoring to remove barriers of architecture, communications, and attitude that excluded people with disabilities from full and active participation.

3. People, with and without disabilities, are encouraged in this congregation to practice their faith and use their gifts in worship, service, study, a leadership.[71]

68. Herzog, *History of Disability Ministry*.
69. Ibid.
70. Herzog, "Working Interfaith," 216.
71. Ibid., 217.

In recent years, the Religion and Disability Program has moved from the NOD to the American Association of People with Disabilities. Under this new umbrella, the Religion and Disability Program has continued to advocate for inclusive policies on the part of congregations, theological seminaries, and secular agencies seeking to integrate people with disabilities. One of it most recent publications, "Grounded in Faith: Resources on Mental Health and Gun Violence," seeks "to ensure that the ongoing debate on gun control does not do great harm by stigmatizing people with mental illness or depriving them of their rights and freedoms."[72]

If there is a cutting edge among disability advocacy within mainstream religious denominations in the United States at the time of this writing, it is the attempt to link disability issues into the very heart of the respective denomination's identity. In November 2010, the Evangelical Lutheran Church in America (ELCA) adopted "A Message on People Living with Disabilities."[73] This comprehensive document begins by stating that: "As a church committed to the gospel of Jesus Christ, the Evangelical Lutheran Church in America (ELCA) is called to welcome all people into full participation as baptized members of the body of Christ in all its congregations and ministries." It reminds its readers that the ELCA as a church "believes that God, as creator and sustainer, intends that society regard all people as of equal worth and make it possible for all—those without and those with disabilities—to participate freely and fully as members of society in all important aspects of common life."[74]

The statement continues by discussing several issues under the general title "Perspectives of Christian Faith:" "Creation in the Image of God," "The Human Condition and Disabilities," "Sin and Injustice," and "Jesus Christ and Human Disabilities."[75] Part III of the ELCA's 2010 "Message" is titled "Confession." Its argument is that Christians need to examine themselves, individually and corporately, in the hope that they may be led to confess ways in which they have viewed and acted negatively toward people with all types of disabilities under the assumption that they are fundamentally different or inferior.[76] Part III also extends the litany of confessions to include the "ways in which congregations and other local ministries" have not been welcoming and have been unwilling to accept "people living with dis-

---

72. Interfaith Disability Advocacy Coalition, 2013. *Grounded in Faith*.

73. Evangelical Lutheran Church in America, "A Message on People Living with Disabilities" (2010).

74. Ibid., 1.

75. Ibid., 2–5.

76. Ibid., 5.

abilities as partners in a common ministry." The Confessions are extended to make the point that congregants "have not actively opposed—or even encouraged—religious explanations that teach or imply that disabilities and impairments are punishment for individual sins or for those of parents and family members or sent as a test from God meant to bless, refine or redeem." Part III concludes with a series of statements calling readers to confess the individual and corporate ways society (and culture) makes the lives of people with disabilities difficult, including the ways in which "society idolizes the perfect body."[77] It cautions that

> Such confessions are not ends in themselves. By the power of the God who creates all and who makes us alive in faith, such confession becomes the occasion for all people to recommit themselves in freedom, hope and joy to one another. It becomes the occasion to articulate the commitments and courses of action that could better conform this church to the ways of Jesus in the treatment of people living with disabilities. It becomes the occasion to seek justice and fuller participation in both church and society.[78]

From this bold statement (which is more theological than practical), the paper moves on to outline what it views as necessary measures for the ELCA to commit its congregations, synods, churchwide organizations and ministries, seminaries, and social ministry organizations "to the full inclusion and equitable participation within its own life of all people along *the entire spectrum of abilities and disabilities.*" In each area, the statement commends work that has already taken place and calls for additional measures to be taken.[79] The paper concludes by affirming the opportunities for people with disabilities in society noting that "Society has a long history of mistreatment of people with disabilities ranging from discriminatory to demeaning to even cruel." It also acknowledges that such history "began to change when people with disabilities and other concerned individuals began to speak out publicly on behalf of people with disabilities."[80]

It is obvious that this "message" is comprehensive, affirming and challenging, and aimed directly at all levels of the church. It links the church and society in using the patterned ways that have been developed over the period from after World War II to the present. Moreover, the "message" brings to the surface many issues concerning the ways in which the content of such

---

77. Ibid., 6.
78. Ibid., 7.
79. Ibid. (italics original).
80. Ibid., 13.

THE RISE, FALL, AND REBIRTH OF DISABILITY ADVOCACY   63

a statement can be operationalized through concrete action at all levels of the denomination. At the of time of this writing, it is too early to tell, but it seems apparent, that its implementation will depend on effective strategies (including people) that bring the various points of the "message" home to the people and entities involved at every level.

The Presbyterian statement is just as detailed as the ELCA "message," with a focus on what it means for the Presbyterian Church (U.S.A.) to be the body of Christ inclusive of people with disabilities. Its pages contain not only the usual biblical references, but also direct references to liberationist ideas under the civil rights slogan, "nothing about us without us."[81] It emphasizes and reaffirms past efforts at inclusion, calling attention to the book *That All May Enter,* which is a denominational adaptation of the NOD Religion and Disability Program's *That All May Worship*. It notes the civil rights progress made by people with disabilities and calls upon the church, not only to recognize these rights, but to assure that churches "seek to satisfy the requirements of the [ADA] law in providing accessible facilities and reasonable accommodations to all persons living with disabilities."[82]

Conclusion

The disability actions described in this chapter provide a rough outline of what has transpired over the past sixty-five years to open the doors (literally as well as symbolically) of the church and society to persons with all types of disabilities. The resources and programs created over these years have resulted in some gains, but one has to look carefully at what has been accomplished, at the congregational as well as the denominational level. We can only determine the impact indirectly, as there are few studies of disability ministry at the congregational level. Therefore, I offer some observations based upon my firsthand experience as an advocate involved in many of the issues raised in this chapter.

First, at no time in this history have denominations or the NCC made disability advocacy a top priority. At the height of the NCC's involvement, staff portfolios contained other duties not directly concerned with disability ministry. This was also the case for most staff of denominational agencies. While at times national personnel were devoted full time to the effort, either these positions were cut entirely, or other tasks were added to their work. Some denominations, such as the ELCA, had as many as three and a half positions devoted to disability ministry, but they were slashed when lack

---

81. Presbyterian Church (U.S.A.), *Living into the Body of Christ,* 13.
82. Ibid., 16.

of funds impacted the denomination.[83] However, the Christian Reformed Church employs one person whose entire portfolio is devoted to disability ministry, who is the only full-time staff person so assigned according to my knowledge. Still, despite the lack of full-time staff at the national level, there is a great deal of current activity in congregations with significant involvement of lay and clergy who have really done more with fewer resources.

A second issue is that except for a few committed staff, the work of these ministries is performed by people who are directly involved with disability. That is, these volunteers either have a disability themselves or have family members with disabilities. Over the years, staff members have come and gone. Parents and family members have come and gone as well, but they have been the mainstay of disability activism in the churches. Their personal interest (often expressed in a high level of intensity) is what drives disability advocacy. Therein lies the source of the problem touched on in the introduction. Because denominational executives, staff, pastors, and other congregational personnel do not normally view disability action as a priority, people with disabilities as well as their parents, family, and friends are left to pursue the movement's goals, with little support, and often with few financial resources. Hence, when workshops or other programs are offered to get nondisabled people "on board" there are few takers, and the disability activists who are present end up "preaching to the choir." Over time, this process repeats itself, via either the same people or a mixture of new and older disabled activists or an entirely new group who may or may not know what has previously transpired.

Third, there doesn't appear to be much general knowledge at the congregational level about the disability-related materials produced at the ecumenical, denominational, or parachurch level. Many of the materials produced over the years are unknown to most pastors and church workers, except where specific individuals have taken on the task of locating them and using them. Conversely, those that are aware of and have attempted to use these materials often find them difficult to use in their particular settings.

More important for this analysis is to place disability advocacy in the churches within the wider perspective associated with sociological analysis and disability studies. First, it is quite clear that much of the work described in this chapter has happened *in response to* outside events, rather than as a unique response from within the church. In most cases religious disability advocacy follows society rather than leads society. This was the case in the early 1950s when professionals or college professors in the field of special

83. See Eiesland, "Barriers and Bridges."

education and rehabilitation, or both, guided the NCC to develop articles and resources for congregations and local ecumenical organizations. The church also jumped on the bandwagon when mental retardation became important in the early 1960s, following secular agencies who advocated deinstitutionalization and the establishment of community programs.

The rise of disability advocacy among mainline Protestant churches in late 1970s is likley a classic case of response based upon the disability rights movement. After all, the late 1970s were the years when people with disabilities from around the country demonstrated the need for disability rights, and specifically for implementation of Section 504 of the Rehabilitation Act of 1973. Additional legislation, including the Individuals with Disabilities Education Act (IDEA), fostered a culture in which segregation of people with disabilities in institutions, schools, and federally funded programs would no longer be tolerated or, at the very least, done only after careful analysis determining no other options.

3

Congregational Movements and Disability Ministry

No discussion of the relationship between Christianity and disability is complete without a discussion of congregational responses to people with disabilities. Congregations form the backbone of American religious life. As R. Stephen Warner states, "It is in the congregation that religious commitment is nurtured and through them that most voluntary religious activity is channeled." In fact, he argues that "the significance of congregations is *increasing*."[1] Mark Chaves argues a more generic consideration that has a direct impact on how people with disabilities are received and included in the church. Congregations are "social institutions in which individuals who are not all religious specialists gather in physical proximity to one another, frequently and at regularly scheduled intervals, for activities and events with explicitly religious content and purpose, and in which there is continuity in the individuals who gather, the location of the gathering, and the nature of the activities and events at each gathering."[2]

Hence, a logical conclusion is that if disability ministry is to become a major aspect of the ministry of the church, it must be in, and through, the context of the congregation. However, one cannot rely on sociologists of religion to supply information regarding the participation by, and inclusion of, people with disabilities in congregational life. That literature simply does not exist, and if such references do exist, it is only in passing, and the topic isn't indexed. Indeed, what follows is a description and analysis of what has been done to foster the inclusion of people with disabilities into the life of the local church. Using congregational websites on the Internet or information provided by denominational and parachurch organizations, or both,

---

1. Warner, "The Place of the Congregation," 145 (italics original).
2. Chaves, *Congregations in America*, 1–2.

will aid in providing a picture of what is being done to assist congregations in fulfilling their ministry to and with persons with disabilities.

This chapter, therefore, seeks to pull together the body of current information on the disability ministry by congregations. I am using the term "disability ministry" as defined and implemented by evangelical churches in the lead on this issue. I begin by describing the concept of disability ministry as it has emerged from within evangelical circles, then I describe how mainline (i.e., nonevangelical) congregations have embraced disability ministry, and I conclude the chapter by providing an analysis and interrogation using sociological and disability studies tools.

Before continuing, however, I need to point out that the issue of congregational responses to disability is currently receiving its due, and for a variety of reasons. First, even though most of the action with regard to disability and Christianity documented earlier has been at the denominational level and above, over the years the congregation has received emphasis through the development of curriculum such as the Adventure Series, and the printing of a number of publications aimed at integrating people with disabilities into the church. Harold Wilke's book *Creating the Caring Congregation* was specifically aimed at congregations that missed opportunities to minister and be ministered by persons with disabilities.[3]

Second, the current emphasis on congregations is partially a response to the limitations placed upon denominational programs due to lack of financial and staff resources. Moreover, the studies of congregations referred to earlier indicate that the congregation, especially in America, is the place were Christianity is nurtured and enacted for the vast majority of nonprofessional adherents. If there is any hope that the church will show hospitality toward persons with disabilities and integrate them to the point where people with disabilities make an indispensable contribution to the church, it will be in and through the congregation. That, after all, is where the message of their acceptance must be proclaimed and implemented.

Disability Ministry

In recent years, disability ministry has emerged as a new form of Christian response to disability. Its emphasis is on responding directly to people with disabilities and their families, placing advocacy aside to meet immediate needs. These include Christian education, respite care, support groups, and to some degree providing a theological voice different from that of mainline churches. Pierson maintains that the term "disability ministry" is not as

3. Wilke, *Creating the Caring Congregation*.

important as its purpose, which is to assure that "people with disabilities are not excluded from the mandate of the Great Commission (make disciples and teach them). In short, we do the same for people of all abilities. We tell them who Jesus is. After they accept Him, we nurture them in the life of faith. Disability ministry, special needs class, or whatever name we attach to our service is not as important as the eternal result."[4]

However, disability ministry has certain components that require description. At the outset, disability ministry happens at the congregational level, so it acknowledges the existence and presence of people with disabilities, and the need for persons with disabilities to be included in the life and work of the local church. This involves a formal response from the congregation in terms of specific programs providing opportunities to hear and learn about God and his plan of salvation, usually in a special classroom and with a particular curriculum—both of which meet specific needs of class members. For example, Hope in God Ministries of Bethlehem Baptist Church in Minneapolis has as its mission to include people with disabilities in the life and work of the church, while building supportive relationships of love to reach out and help families and individuals find a place in the congregation where they can use their gifts.[5]

Disability ministry, for the most part, is underpinned by an evangelical point of view that leaves disability as a larger social issue unchallenged. Churches such as Bethlehem Baptist Church embrace conservative points of view, including the inerrancy of the Bible and Jesus Christ as the only way to salvation. Nevertheless, there is considerable theological depth to their disability ministries. For example, the disability ministry program at Bethlehem Baptist Church argues for "the supremacy of God in disability and suffering." The vision statement for its ministry argues that "a church filled with 'strong' people coasts," while "individuals with disabilities, and their families, do not have the luxury of coasting." It acknowledges the ongoing issues faced by people with disabilities and their families, including surgeries, therapies, doctors, social workers, and even outright discrimination, that create a daily, never-ending struggle. The temptation to lose hope and give up is strong as the statistics on divorce and depression show. The members of the congregation are invited to "embrace children with disabilities in a variety of ways, and by allowing their entire families to experience the God-centered, life-affirming teaching of Bethlehem. As God moves,

---

4. Pierson, "The Term – Disability Ministry" (2009).
5. Bethlehem Baptist Church, Hope in God Ministries, "Ministry Outline" (2010).

we desire to see people of all ages, all kinds of disability, serving and being served."[6]

Bethlehem Baptist Church is just one of many evangelical congregations in the United States that have embraced disability ministry as part of the context of their life and work. By searching the Internet, one can find a number of such congregations. I did so by entering the search terms "disability ministries" and "disability ministry" into the search engine. This produced 2,190 results, which I subsequently reduced to 438, or 20 percent of the first total, from the top of the list; these I assumed would be the most relevant entries. The vast majority of these listings were not congregational ministries but other categories relevant to entries that referred to either "disability ministry" or "disability ministries." These included articles, resources, and denominational, judicatory, and educational programs. There were twenty-five congregational entries with four duplicates. What follows are descriptions of some disability ministries that can be found on the Internet. While these descriptions are by no means complete, they are adequate to the task at hand, which is to provide an overview of the recent trend to provide a Christian response to people with disabilities, and their friends and families.

Patmos Church, a Seventh-Day Adventist congregation in Winter Park, Florida, offers a full range of ministries, including a disability ministry that seeks to provide for the full inclusion of people with disabilities in this congregation's programs and services. Patmos Chapel also seeks to provide facilities and programs designed to meet the needs of people with disabilities. The website encourages pastors and members to be sensitive to the needs of people with disabilities and to foster interaction among members and visitors with disabilities. Finally, the website encourages its local conference to include people with disabilities when seeking to fill jobs in the churches. The webpage also states that Patmos Church seeks to enable people with disabilities to be involved in providing "service to the cause of God [by] using their talents and skills in the wonderful work of inviting others to accept to love of Jesus."[7]

The Evangelical Free Church of Newbury Park, California, also lists a full range of programs as part of its disability ministry, which reaches out to people with disabilities within its membership and in the surrounding community. The ministry at the EV Free Church of Newberry Park offers specially trained buddies for children who want to attend Sunday school while their parents attend church. This program is designed so that parents "do

---

6. Horning et al., "A Vision for Disability Ministry" (n.d.).
7. Patmos Chapel, Website. http://www.patmoschapel.org/.

not have to worry about their child causing a disturbance." Adults with disabilities are invited to attend a weekly Friendship Class (see below), where teens and adults with developmental disabilities meet for song, lessons, and refreshments with a one-to-one friend/mentor. At the time this information was retrieved, the congregation was in the planning stages of hosting a "Disability Awareness Weekend" scheduled for the following February.[8]

The Christian and Missionary Alliance Church in Zanesville, Ohio, has organized Caring Hearts Disability Ministries, which includes a bus ministry, the conducting of Friendship Children's Parties, a Friendship Youth Group, and an adult Friendship class. Also listed are a caregivers' support group, a parents' night out and Friendship partners. The congregation is also linked to Wheels for the World which is an international program sponsored by Joni and Friends (see below).[9]

Park Street Church in Boston has been the site of many "historic events" and the scene of many "national and theological firsts," including the founding of the Handel and Haydn Society of Boston (1815), the comissioning of the first Protestant mission to Hawaii (1819), and an address by William Lloyd Garrison (an important figure in the antislavery movement) given on July 4, 1829. Dr. Harold J. Ockenga, pastor from 1936 to 1969, was cofounder and first president of the National Association of Evangelicals. Its disability ministry, Enable Boston, was funded in part by a bequest, and seeks to enable Park Street Church to become a congregation that ministers to and with people of differing and disabilities.[10] According to its statement "About Us," the ministry entails three goals, each affecting the entire congregation, composed of individuals with and without disabilities:

> **Educate:** We seek to educate others with a Christ-centered theology of disability. We want to teach children and adults with disabilities about the love of Jesus and to enable them to grow in their faith.
>
> **Equip:** We seek to equip members of the congregation to get to know and love people in our midst who have disabilities, as well as to equip those with disabilities to minister with and to the rest of the congregation.
>
> **Extend:** We seek to extend the Kingdom of God by reaching out to the greater community of people affected by disabilities and

---

8. Doyle, "Newbury Park Church Offers Disability Ministry" (2011).
9. Zanesville Christian Missionary Alliance Church, "Disability" (2017).
10. Park Street Church, "History" (2011).

sharing the good news of Jesus Christ. This community includes both individuals with disabilities and those that love them.[11]

From the listing provided by the congregation, it is apparent that the above goals are expressed in numerous programs, including a Bible study that meets on Thursdays, and Friday social activities for adults with cognitive or learning disabilities. The information available on its website gives the impression that these activities are built around the format provided by Friendship Ministries (see below). These programs as well as the fact that the congregation's facilities are wheelchair accessible help to enhance the belief "that the church is disabled without the presence and ministry of people with disabilities."[12]

The question of which churches conduct a disability ministry is difficult to answer at this time. It would seem that congregations with larger memberships and more abundant resources would be most likely to pursue disability ministry. This is certainly the case for three congregations: Willow Creek Church in suburban Chicago, Saddlebrook Church in California, and McLean Bible Church in suburban Washington DC.

Willow Creek's "Disability Ministries" offers a number of programs for "those with special needs." These include the Special Friends Community, which is a monthly outreach to adults with developmental disabilities who live in group homes in area communities; Living Stones, a Bible study group of more functionally independent young adults with developmental disabilities that meets on Wednesday evenings; and Friendship Club, which is an "alternative worship service for teens and adults with more significant developmental delays [that] meets on Sunday mornings." The congregation also conducts Eagle's Nest which provides spiritual support for parents of children with special needs, a gathering that meets every other Saturday while their children attend Eagle's Nest Kids, "a program for children with special needs whose parents attend Eagle's Nest small groups": the class for children offers "Bible teaching, worship, and creative play." There is also "Promiseland Inclusion," a program that matches kids who need the support of a one-to-one buddy with a consistent volunteer who can help them fully participate in Promiseland, Willow's children's ministry for infants through grade 5 available during weekend services.[13]

The Willow Creek Church's website on disability ministries asks, "Can I invite persons with special needs to Willow?" The answer given reveals the entire program's basic stance:

11. Ibid., "Enable Boston" (2011).
12. Ibid.
13. Willow Creek Community Church, "Disability Ministries" (2011).

Yes! Many families and individuals affected by disability are just waiting to be invited. Perhaps their experience with God's people hasn't been very good so far. At best, they've been ignored; or worse, they've never been invited because there were no programs to accommodate the special needs of their loved one. Willow welcomes and embraces all families affected by special needs or disabilities and has ministries to serve them.[14]

Rick Warren's Saddleback Church in Lake Forest, California, also has a disability ministry that consists of a weekend program for children ages two through twelve with "special needs," and Super Kids which is a program for teens also with the label, "special needs." Each of these meets on Saturdays as well as Sunday mornings with a curriculum that emphasizes "sensory and language enriched lessons," music and "social interaction with peers and adults."[15]

The disability ministry of McLean Bible Church, located in suburban Washington DC, explains its use of "Access Ministry" as a title. "Access Ministry is the 'disability ministry' of McLean Bible Church. While the word 'disability' is used, we prefer to think of Access as a ministry of 'possibilities" not defined by what can't be done but rather by what all individuals regardless of ability level can achieve in God's house." The Access Ministry of the congregation, therefore, fits into its total ministry based on the belief that "Access to God [is] for all His people and celebrate[s] our uniqueness and differences. It is our hope to develop all people into fully-devoted followers of Christ, integrated into the church."[16] Begun in 1997, Access has served over five hundred families of children with special needs in the DC area.[17] Its programs include Beautiful Blessings,[18] a Sunday school class geared toward children with special needs, respite care for parents who need a break from caring for their children with special needs, a Friendship Club, which is directed to adults who are in need of mentoring by adults,[19] and Soaring Over Seven, which is a "Summer adventure for campers of all abilities."[20]

For the past several years, the congregation has sponsored an "Accessibility Summit," a special conference "intended for families and caregivers, faith-based organizations, teachers, and other professionals connected to

---

14. Ibid.
15. Saddleback–Lake Forest, "Disabilities Ministries" (2011).
16. McLean Bible Church, "Access." (2017).
17. Ibid., "Access Ministry Wish List" (2017).
18. Ibid., "Beautiful Blessings" (2017).
19. Ibid., "The Friendship Club" (2017/2011).
20. Ibid., "Soaring Over Seven Summer Camp" (2017/2011).

disabilities." It features nationally known speakers as well as several breakout sessions devoted to care issues and other community programs, in addition to several sessions on aspects of disability ministry. In effect, the Accessibility Summit seeks to promote disability ministry in other congregations in the DC area and other parts of the country.[21]

From these congregation websites it is clear that disability ministry is one ministry among many with all kinds of ministry choices, for the non-disabled as well as disabled. Of course, there is the commitment and passion that is required for anyone, lay or clergy, to expend the time and energy to do the work of disability ministry. So, in many cases, these congregations are constantly searching for volunteers to do various activities associated with disability ministry. McLean Bible Church has a formal program to teach volunteers to function in Sunday school classes for the disabled by serving as helpers and apprentices.[22]

Some of the programs described above have a full- or part-time program director. Presumably intended to fill the need for training such persons, California Baptist University (CBU) offers a 100-percent online Master of Arts in Disability Studies with a Disability Ministry Concentration. CBU says about its program that "Students in this concentration complete specialized coursework that prepares them to establish, build and lead disability ministries within a congregational setting. Graduates will be agents for change within the Christian church around the world."[23]

The newness of disability ministries within American evangelicalism leads to the conclusion that these efforts form a social movement. Such a conclusion is based not only upon the number of evangelical congregations conducting various disability ministries (of which only a handful could be described above), but also upon the number of emerging parachurch organizations that have promoted disability ministry. These programs provide the social context out of which future disability ministries will emerge.

CCFH Ministries (hence CCFH) was chartered in the state of Kentucky in 1983. Its original title was the Christian Church Foundation for the Handicapped, and its focus was on establishing group homes for people with disabilities. Its ministries are not affiliated with any denomination and it is "sponsored by individuals, churches, and groups that God has led to partner with this ministry."[24] While still maintaining its residential program, it has developed a significant number of resources targeted toward disabil-

21. See the Accessibility Summit website: accessibilitysummit.org/.
22. McLean Bible Church, "Friendship Club" (2011).
23. California Baptist University (2011).
24. CCFH Ministries, "Mission Statement" (2012).

ity ministry in congregations. Jim Pierson, whose definition of disability ministry was referred in the opening paragraphs of this chapter, was its first director. He has relinquished his post in order to work for CCFH Ministries as coordinator of its educational component. He is also Associate Professor of Special Education and Director of the Certificate in Disability Ministry Program at Johnson Bible College.[25]

The connection between the congregational and parachurch levels is suggested by the fact that the coauthors of *Making Changes That Lead to Real Inclusion* are CCFH's Pierson and Jackie Mills Fernald, who is Director of Disability Ministry at McLean Bible Church. Their work entertains the possibility that it is time to move students with disabilities out of special classrooms and include them in general education classes. In their view:

> As the country has gone through a paradigm shift regarding persons with disabilities, education and community living, the church and its leaders began to follow suit with regard to their spiritual development. So often in the past, God's people did not do a wonderful job in making the church fully accessible, not only in the physical sense of building structure, but also in the attitude and condition of the heart."[26]

They also note that the movement toward integration in some congregations has already begun, but that more needs to be accomplished. They observe that in many congregations, programs like ministry to seniors and youth are well known and supported. However, disability ministry is not. It is time, they argue, "to rethink our approach to including people with disabilities in the life of the church." They are convinced that the mandate to reach all for Christ, including people with disabilities, should be on the minds and hearts of all church members, and not on those specifically assigned to work directly with people with disabilities: "Every community has people with disabilities" who need to be a part of the mandate to "go into the world community and take the message of Christ's love to everyone."[27] The booklet continues by urging the inclusion of people with different disabilities, acknowledging the significant rise in the number of children with autism. Within a given congregation, disability ministry should be viewed not as a sign that one church is keeping up with other churches; rather, disability ministry should be motivated by sharing the good news. In addition,

---

25. Ibid.
26. Mills-Fernald and Pierson, *Making Changes*.
27. Ibid., 11.

"A diagnosis does not alter the need for God's love."[28] The booklet ends with what amounts to a plea:

> Inclusive ministry is reciprocal. People with and without disabilities will learn from each other. We grow in our faith in a community of acceptance and respect. With myriads of abilities and gifts, God can use all of us in His church. All we need to do is to see our members with disabilities as worthy of God's love, recognize their gifts, and find them a place of service in the congregation ... Build an inclusive ministry in your church, and it will last a life time and make a difference to some wonderful people even in eternity. Take the Great Commission to heart.[29]

Special Touch Ministry is another effort within the evangelical camp that seeks to call attention to people with disabilities. It is organized into chapters across several states, mostly in the Midwest and the Southeast. Most of its work focuses on evangelizing people with disabilities and their families. Its beliefs are very similar to those of evangelical congregations, with an emphasis on conversion and "Regeneration by the Holy Spirit [which is] absolutely essential for personal salvation." The ministry is operated in a typical evangelical fashion. Its directors (who are appointed as missionaries) travel about the country encouraging congregations to join Special Touch Ministry in reaching out to people with disabilities. A major emphasis is placed on summer camping, including on the "annual Wisconsin Summer Get Away." An indication of connection between parachurch and denominational ministries is that Special Touch's executive director also serves as head of the National Center for Ministry to People with Disabilities of the Assemblies of God.[30]

Zachariah's Way is yet another parachurch organization that seeks to "help churches ... become more aware of and to better minister to special needs people and their families." Its website notes that many people in congregations are "fearful of these people" and that to remedy this, the staff of Zachariah's Way speaks and preaches in churches and conducts "very practical training seminars" using its own manual, *Disability Ministry for Dummies*. Accordingly, their focus is the local church and the average person sitting in church pews and pastors, who are, for the most part, "totally unaware of this world of special needs and the needs of families all around them." Zachariah's Way adds that such people "are unaware of the

---

28. Ibid., 14.
29. Ibid., 39.
30. Special Touch Ministries (2011).

tremendous blessing God has in store for them when they choose to get involved with these special people and their families."[31]

The theme of ignorance of the need for disability ministry is carried further by Zachariah's Way's latest project: P.U.R.E. The overall aim of this project is captured in the heading, "A Christian Awakening, a Nationwide Project to Increase Awareness of and Ministry to People with Disabilities and their Families in our Churches." The use of the word "pure" is actually the frame for an acrostic which follows:

> P – Perfectly created by loving sovereign God, designed for His Purposes.
>
> U – Unique in his or her own gifts, blessings, talents, and desires.
>
> R – Receptive and responsive to our communication, touch, and acts of love.
>
> E – Eternal- There are No Disabled Souls.[32]

It is difficult to say what level of success the P.U.R.E. project will have on the congregations that become involved. Nevertheless, evangelicals have begun to take a serious look at their institutions to see if there needs to be a seismic shift in their ability to respond effectively to those with disabilities. It is worth remembering that these entities are not engaged in critiquing biblical passages for their antidisability bias, or in developing new theological approaches to underpin radical changes in ministry to/with people with disabilities. The current focus/context of evangelical institutions is to encourage and sustain disability ministry in as many congregations as possible.

This may also be the case for parachurch organizations that service at the border between evangelical and mainline churches. I will examine three of these: Bethesda Lutheran Homes and Services, Joni and Friends, and Friendship Ministries.

Bethesda Lutheran Homes and Services originated in 1904 as a residential program of the Lutheran Church–Missouri Synod to serve people with disabilities. However, these institutions were not limited to providing residential services; they also afforded their residents an education, vocational training, and work. In the 1960s and '70s, the program expanded in response to the growing demand for disability rights and the provision

---

31. Zachariah's Way, "About Zachariah's Way" (2011).
32. Zachariah's Way, "The P.U.R.E. Project," (2011).

of services for people with disabilities, especially those with intellectual and other developmental impairments. While this led Bethesda to expand its residential services to include better medical care, vocational training, and community involvement, it was in the 1980s that the program spread to other areas. As a result, greater emphasis was now placed on providing support for community living and resources to help congregations understand the needs and gifts of community residents with disabilities and their families.[33]

As a multifaceted parachurch organization unaffiliated with any denomination, Joni and Friends has numerous programs designed to meet the needs of people with disabilities and their families. At the congregational level, Joni and Friends' Church Relations Program "equips, trains, and mobilizes the church to reach out and embrace people affected by disability" by providing training programs, information resources, and consultation to congregations desiring to start a disability ministry. It offers a "getting started" newsletter, and a "Through the Roof Program" with "a guide to developing effective disability ministry and outreach." Along with a handbook *Successful Models of Disability Ministry*, these materials are free upon request. They are designed to fit into regional training events, including "Through the Roof Conferences" or "Through the Roof Summits," or both. In addition, Joni and Friends offers programs such as family retreats, and internships for people interested in setting up and directing disability ministry programs.[34]

While the Church Relations Program focuses directly on the disability ministry of the congregation, additional Joni and Friends programs enable congregations to reach out to people with disabilities, internationally. Wheels for the World is a widely known program that takes donated used wheelchairs through its "Chair Corps," restores them in "restoration shops" and then ships them around the world. Each recipient receives a custom-fitted wheelchair and training in its use and upkeep. Team members also present each recipient with a Bible and gospel message.[35]

Joni and Friends also sponsors "Family Retreats" across the United States and abroad. Each retreat offers persons with disability and their families "encouragement and care in the comfort of a safe and accessible family and camp environment." Campers "enjoy fully-accessible and age-appropriate fun activities," and a time to "be nourished by hearty home-style meals,

---

33. Lutheran Disability Ministry, "Equipping the Church to Minister" (2011).
34. Joni and Friends, "Church Relations/Through the Roof Program" (2011).
35. Ibid., "Wheels for World" (2011).

and glean from meaningful conversations from a network of families who understand the challenges of life with disability."[36]

Friendship Ministries offers a program that works with congregations to set up Friendship groups, centered on group worship and one-to-one Bible study with mentors. It advocates for the inclusion of people with cognitive impairments in the full life of their faith communities by "encouraging full church membership and opportunities for people with cognitive impairments to share their gifts."[37] Friendship Ministries developed out of religious needs expressed by parents of a son with Down syndrome. Their approach to CRC Publications, the publishing arm of the Christian Reformed Church, sparked immediate interest since the need for materials was demonstrated. However, since no apparent model existed, a "model group" was formed at Third Reformed Church in Holland, Michigan. The model embodied what would become the defining characteristics of Friendship groups: meet first together as a group for fellowship, worship, prayer, and a lesson; follow this by pairing a student and a teacher one on one so that the two can form a relationship, and so that the lesson can be personalized and reinforced.[38]

At the same time, a parent also approached a faculty member from Western Theological Seminary with a request to start a ministry to youth and adults with intellectual disabilities. This led to recruiting a student who developed what became known as "the mentoring model." The program grew quickly as word spread to other parents of children with developmental disabilities. The ministry was guided by a board with financial support from the Reformed Church in America and the Christian Reformed Church. Having seen the endeavor's success, CRC Publications undertook the project of developing curricula, which included a three-year cycle of materials first published in 1982. However, it soon became apparent that a separate organization was needed, especially as the model attracted wider interest from different denominations. Since then, Friendship Ministries "has worked with churches and organizations in more than forty denominations (including most of the mainline churches in the United States and Canada), and in twenty-one countries in North and South America, Australia, Africa, and Asia."[39]

---

36. Ibid., "Family Retreats" (2011).
37. Genzink, "Friendship Ministry Story," 163–64.
38. Ibid.
39. Ibid.

Mainline Congregational Responses to Disability Ministry

Mainline churches have also developed the concept of disability ministries as more resources and programs are designed and targeted to meet the congregational needs of people with disabilities and their families. Some of these programs connect with such ministries as Joni and Friends and Friendship Ministries partly because of the conservative ideologies of these ministries. However, some large mainline congregations have disability ministries similar to those described above yet have different theological reasons for their actions. And, as this section will show, the concept of disability ministry has reshaped the way mainline denominations are approaching disability issues in the church.

In Overland Park a suburb of Kansas City, the United Methodist Church of the Resurrection offers Matthew's Ministry. The ministry grew out of a conversation between the congregation's pastor, Adam Hamilton, and the mother of Matthew, a boy with developmental disabilities. Upon learning the mother's problems with getting to and from Sunday services, Hamilton asked "what needs to be in place for you to worship on Sunday?" A ministry was formed around Matthew's needs. Matthew died a number of years ago, but today, Matthew's Ministry has grown to encompass eight offered "services," including a Bible study for "adults with special needs," Angel Care Services, providing "one-on-one and group assistance . . . for individuals with special needs during worship times," and Camp Sunflower a summer camp offered to all Matthew's Ministry participants. Also offered is Family Night Out, a special night of fun, crafts, games and movies (and a talent show when I was there) for individuals with special needs. Children with special needs are encouraged to participate in regular Sunday school classes but may request an angel care team to facilitate integration. Sunflower Ringers, a bell and chime ringers program, is conducted in collaboration with the congregation's music department, and Youth Small Group is a Bible study for youth with special needs. There is also a Sunflower Bakery for "Adults with special [needs who] prepare baked goods each week which are sold at the Spring Café as well as catering events" held in the congregation's facilities. This program helps adults who would normally work in sheltered workshops but do not attend because of issues related to client care and safety. Matthew's Ministry is an extensive program that grows as need is demonstrated, and that is underpinned by its mission statement: "It is Mathew's Ministry's mission to actively reach out and extend the love and message of Jesus Christ to all persons with special needs and incorporate them fully into life of the church."[40]

Following reductions in funding and staff at the national level (as discussed in the previous chapter), considerable attention has been placed on providing resources and training for congregational disability ministry. Mainline denominations have seen the need to encourage congregations to establish disability ministries. However, while they have also developed the term "disability ministry," in most instances it refers to a broader understanding of what it means for a congregation to respond to people with disabilities and their families.

Upon the dissolution of its Task Force on Accessibility, the Episcopal Church established The Episcopal Disability Network (EDN) to carry on its work. Under the direction of the Reverend Barbara Ramnarine, EDN has provided Episcopal congregations with resources and tools through serving diocesan committees on disability issues. EDN is also involved in coordinating the use of people with expertise in various disability ministries throughout the denomination. It loans various print and media resources and assists in conducting workshops in dioceses and congregations. While all disabling conditions "fall within the scope of the EDN," mental illness concerns are referred to the Episcopal Mental Illness Network.[41]

The United Church of Christ (UCC) has adopted the rubric of "Disability Ministries" and established an office that offers resources and programs designed to engage UCC congregations in various forms of response to people with disabilities. Recently, the UCC-sponsored "A National Gathering" titled "Widening the Welcome II: Inclusion for All." Its goal was to develop "the life of congregations to include persons with disabilities and persons with mental illnesses/brain disorders and their families." Literature for the "Gathering" reveals a high level of commitment from a number of "experts" both within and outside the denomination to promote inclusion at the congregational level. In fact, the workshop enlisted several session leaders with experience in various disability ministries in the local church. The UCC Disability Ministries has also produced a study guide for local churches, *Any Body, Everybody, Christ's Body*.[42]

The Evangelical Lutheran Church in America (ELCA) has continued to serve the needs of its local parishes as well as to maintain continuity with established programs. Perhaps the most successful of its efforts is the

---

40. United Methodist Church of the Resurrection, *Matthew's Ministry Pamphlet* (2010).

41. Episcopal Disability Network, "Accessibility: Together We Can" (2012).

42. United Church of Christ, *Disability Ministries* (2012).

"All-Lutheran Candle Lighting for Mental Illness" held in parishes around the country. The ELCA also gathers youth with disabilities in a program referred to as DAYL or Disabilities Advocates Youth Leadership. This program is held just prior to its triennial national youth event. In recent years, the ELCA has worked to establish a mentoring program for clergy with disabilities. Its website, under the heading "Disability Ministries," emphasizes inclusive congregations, accessible facilities, and ministries that target specific disability groups, including the blind and visually impaired.[43]

Since the early 1990s, The United Methodist Committee on Disability Ministries (formerly the United Methodist National Task Force on Developmental Disabilities) has sought to become more connected to the local church. It has recruited members from across the United States who have not only a passion for disability issues in the United Methodist Church (UMC) but hands-on experience with disability ministry in their local church or conference committees on disability concerns, or both. It has employed the use of denomination's websites to make available a number of resources for use in the local church. The Task Force has made a concerted effort to share resources developed by people at the grassroots level. For example, the Task Force has put a two-page document on its webpage titled "Why Should Your Congregation Start a Disability Ministry?," which was developed by the North Alabama Conference. This conference program is the most organized of any conference in the UMC, with committees at the district level, which is the closest judicatory to the local church. Other UMC congregations have become connected to the Task Force and its website. It has held its annual meetings at such sites as the Church of the Resurrection (see above) and the Methodist Theological School in Ohio.[44]

Among the UMC resources shared via the Internet is the Mentoring Program designed to provide assistance to persons with disabilities who are attempting to establish themselves in the local church. This program was created for the United Methodist Men and first presented at a national meeting of the Congress of United Methodist Men. It is now possible for any group in the church to use these materials under the title "How to Start a Mentoring Program at Your Church." The Committee has also sought to expand the emphasis on camping as a way to connect persons with disabilities to the life of church by providing fun, recreation, and spiritual formation in a retreat setting away from their home and work. The committee is also

---

43. Evangelical Lutheran Church in America, "Disability Ministries" (2012).
44. Herzog, Compiled from Minutes as member (2001–2012).

attempting to work closely with other UMC agencies and caucus groups that relate to the goals and programs it sponsors.[45]

In common with other mainline denominations, the Presbyterian Church (U.S.A) has sought to engage its congregations in effective responses to the presence of people with disabilities. Since the late 1970s, its various committees have published resources, conducted workshops, and advocated legislation in order to raise awareness and promote various disability ministries. In 1989, the PC (U.S.A.) called for all levels of the church (national, synod, presbytery, and congregation) to "advance the idea of invitation and communications with disabilities." To that end, the booklet *Living into the Body of Christ: Towards Full Inclusion of People with Disabilities* testifies that "We've Come a Long Way, But Still Have Far to Go." The statement includes a study guide designed to be used by Presbyterian congregations, and other materials which raise social aspects of living with a disability, in society, and in the church.[46]

What is also significant is that the Presbyterian Panel, a research program drawing on samples of three groups (members, elders [lay leaders] currently on session, and ordained ministers), has queried the church three times regarding disabilities: in 1983, 1993, and 2004. The detailed observations in the resulting reports cannot be covered here. However, the 2004 report is essentially a measurement of the denomination's progress with respect to disability issues over the periods covered by the previous reports. A few highlights of the 2004 report will serve to confirm this progress:

> 1. The vast majority of congregations have a sanctuary, fellowship halls, and restrooms that are fully accessible to persons with disabilities. Few, however, have fully accessible chancels or choir lofts.
>
> 2. When compared to other congregations, more of those that have one or more elders on session with a disability have taken action in the previous three years to make various programs more accessible.
>
> 3. One in six members and around one in ten elders and ministers has at least one disability. The most common types among them involve hearing and mobility, while among ministers the most common types involve learning disabilities, hearing impairments, and mental illness.[47]

---

45. Ibid.
46. Presbyterian Church (U.S.A.), *That All May Enter*.
47. Presbyterian Church (U.S.A.), *Living into the Body of Christ*.

When some answers to the 2004 Panel were compared to answers provided by the 1993 Panel (many questions from the 1993 Panel were used again in 2004), the 2004 report showed an increase in several accessibility-related features, including parking spaces and curb cuts, entrances to congregational facilities, and use of aids such as large print materials and supplemental sound systems. However, in contrast to the 1993 Panel, only 53 percent of the elders believed that the PC (U.S.A.) was a "'stronger advocate for the inclusion of persons with disabilities in the church,'" whereas 67 percent believed so previously. A similar decline was found for those who advocated holding presbytery meetings in facilities accessible to persons with disabilities.[48]

In the American Baptist Church as well as the Christian Church–Disciples of Christ there doesn't appear to be as strong a tradition of disability ministry as in the other mainline denominations. While the Disciples have undertaken some projects such as group homes and camping facilities and outings for those with special needs, the idea of providing resources to congregations seeking assistance in conducting their own disability ministries is relatively new. Under the Disciples national website is a listing "Children with Special Needs" under Family and Children Ministries. This listing describes Camp Lakey Gap for people with autism, which offers a "unique program approach of therapeutic recreation using visually structured programing [that provides] 1:1 and 1:2 positive support from well-trained college and graduate students."[49] Other Disciples organizations include Embracing the Spirit of the Child, which is dedicated to supporting parents, caregivers and faith communities involved with children with special needs. The Disciples also offer a Special Families Guide, an e-newsletter featuring helpful ideas for families and a resource guide for "faith-based communities to understand the needs of individuals with Autism Spectrum Disorders." The website on special needs also notes that congregations should do "all that they can" to respond to people with disabilities, "especially children," but does not appear to provide additional resources to assist Disciples congregations in their efforts.[50]

Even less is known about present efforts of congregations to provide disability ministries in the American Baptist tradition. The denomination's website refers to only one document, a resolution developed in 1978 that has been subsequently renewed and modified three times, most recently

---

48. Presbyterian Church (U.S.A.), The Presbyterian Panel: Disability Issues (2004).
49. Disciples of Christ, "Children with Special Needs" (2011).
50. Ibid.

in 2002.[51] However, in October 2012, the *Christian Citizen* (a periodical published by the American Baptist Home Mission Societies) devoted its entire issue to the theme "Disability Ministry: From Access to Inclusion." This theme has two thrusts. The first urges continuing efforts to make congregations not only physically accessible, but fully inclusive of all people, including those with disabilities. The second thrust is centered on providing employment opportunities in the community as well as in the church.[52] It is too early to gauge the impact of this theme on the congregations of the American Baptist Church, but this publication is significant in terms of its potential in getting them interested in disability ministry.

Disability Ministry in the Peace Church Tradition

Readers will recall that in the previous chapter reference was made to the Anabaptist tradition of disability ministry growing out of the work of conscientious objectors during World War II. From this position, the Mennonite Church evolved a response to people with disabilities that over the years has led to an emphasis on developmental disabilities—in some cases providing residential facilities, workshops, and day activity programs. In the 1990s, these ministries were placed within the denomination's Stewardship Education emphasis, which resulted in "a flurry of activity around the development of tangible disability and mental illness 'products' that could be marketed to families and congregations."[53] More recently, these ministries evolved into ADNet (Anabaptist Disabilities Network), which has provided resources to congregations. One of these is a monthly newsletter, *Connections*, which highlights several issues including living with a disability, stories of successful congregational disability ministries, and feature stories around the theme of hospitality and removing barriers. The work of ADNet spans disabilities from mental illness to multiple sclerosis (MS).[54]

Other Christian Groups

The recent merger of the Christian Reformed Church Disability Concerns and the Reformed Church in America into Disability Concerns, CRC & RCA, has continued both denominations' strong emphasis on inclusion.

51. Ramsey-Lucas, ed., "Communities of Care."
52. Ramsey-Lucas, "Disability Ministry."
53. Leichty, "Mennonite Advocacy for Persons with Disabilities," 204–5.
54. Anabaptist Disabilities Network, "Connections." November (2011).

The Inclusion Handbook's subtitle, *Everybody Belongs, Everybody Serves*, indicates its emphasis on disability advocacy as well as disability ministry. Effective ministry is argued as being "relational by nature and grow[ing] over time," the goal being to include all people, including people with disabilities, who "yearn for the church to embrace and to engage all God's people in ministry." The handbook emphasizes a relational approach to building disability ministries (i.e., people with disabilities come first, rather than formal programs) and offers numerous "tips" on how to carry out inclusion in congregations from both Reformed traditions.[55]

Stakes and wards in the Church of Jesus Christ of Latter-day Saints (LDS) have also come to terms with the need to include people with disabilities. The LDS website contains, among other related items, descriptions of various types of disabilities, a question-and-answer page from which members and leaders can gain help in solving problems such as how to adapt approved curricula and resources to "individual circumstances," and support for LDS families struggling with a child "with unique needs."[56]

As we saw earlier in the chapter, the Seventh Day Adventist Church (SDA) has responded to the goal of inclusion of people with disabilities at the local church level. Its North American Division offices have joined in support of these efforts by providing resources including coordinators of the Commission for People with Disabilities. These coordinators provide consultation services to local churches seeking assistance in making their facilities accessible; the coordinators also provide transportation solutions for people with disabilities, and the coordinators promote the involvement of people with disabilities in church leadership. The North American Division of the SDA makes available three separate resources that promote disability awareness: a "Handbook on Disability Ministries, Guidelines for Disability Ministries, [and] A Guide to Conducting a Disabilities Awareness Sabbath."[57]

Despite its small membership, the Evangelical Covenant Church has devoted considerable energy to developing programs and resources devoted to inclusive disability ministry. Currently there are numerous resources on its website. In 2011, an audio resource was added that is designed to provide a way of working through the denomination's confirmation process with persons with disabilities. Also reported was a series of webinars on various topics related to disability ministry. Representatives from the church have been active participants in the work of the Committee on Disabilities of

---

55. DeYoung and Stephenson, *Inclusion Handbook*.
56. Church of Latter-day Saints, "Disability Resources" (2011).
57. North American Division of Seventh-Day Adventists (2011).

the National Council of Churches. A few years ago, the committee met in Chicago and visited the denomination's North Park Seminary, conducting one of its worship services and an evening seminar.[58]

Roman Catholicism

Readers will recall from the previous chapter that the Roman Catholic Church in the United States has developed two organizations devoted to ministry among people with disabilities: the National Apostolate for Inclusion Ministry (NAfIM), and the National Catholic Partnership on Disability (NCPD). Both organizations have in recent years focused on the inclusion of people with disabilities in congregational life. In 2008, NAfIM sponsored "Winds of Change, Spirit of Inclusion," hosted by the Dioceses of Toledo and Cleveland. Its keynote address, "The Parish as a Welcoming Community: Fostering the Spirit of Inclusion," set the stage for a series of panels and workshops. These events provided attendees with several ideas and practical steps congregations can take to develop hospitable responses to people with disabilities and their families. Some workshops were devoted to families with disabled members while others focused on specific disabilities, including autism and mental illness. Still others focused on theology and ethics, and on the more practical side, how to integrate people with disabilities into the sacramental life of the church and how to enable people with disabilities to connect with God, with a specific focus on severe disabilities.[59] In 2010, the NAfIM *Messenger* highlighted the pastor's role in "Welcoming People with Intellectual/Developmental Disabilities" by providing a "Tip Sheet." The tip sheet included facts about disabilities and encouraged pastors to "consult . . . the parish counsel about making the parish hospitable" to people with disabilities in religious education programs, and called for "a personal commitment to making liturgy meaningful to persons with intellectual disabilities."[60]

The National Catholic Partnership on Disability has also moved toward a disability ministry concept by providing "Something to Consider for Every Parish: A Disability Advisory Committee." However, in this case there is more of an advocacy role than with NAfLM. According to the NCPD Internet post of November 2011, the parish disability advocacy committee should seek to "ensure that persons with disabilities in the parish are able to fully practice their faith, receive the sacraments and participate in parish

58. Evangelical Covenant Church (2011).
59. NAfIM, "Winds of Change" (2008).
60. Ibid., "Tip Sheet" (2010).

functions regardless of their disability or limitations." Thus, while using the same or similar words as NAfIM, NCPD's advocacy role is much more assistive by placing the bulk of advocating role for parish changes in the committee's hands. The online post also profiles a parish in the Archdiocese of Philadelphia that established such a committee, and details the process of advocacy that they took over a period of three years. This process involved drawing up a mission statement, making suggestions about how the parish facilities might become more accessible, and establishing a subcommittee to advise parishioners on mental health issues.[61]

Conclusion

It needs to be indicated, first of all, that the materials presented in this chapter are no substitute for hands-on empirical studies of the ministries described here. At best, we can indicate what the congregations and parachurch groups *said* about the programs they sponsor, taking their descriptions at face value. Disability ministries have developed out of concrete needs, especially from parents who want to attend a church that is welcoming to their child(ren) with disabilities. No parent needs to be told, "You are welcome here anytime, but don't bring your child with disabilities." Also, in areas where congregations are situated are group homes whose residents need to be acknowledged as full members of their communities wherever they go, including into a church.

It does appear that denominations and judicatories are responding. Disability ministries are now scattered throughout the United States. These ministries recognize people with various disabilities as valued members of the human community; they are appreciated and not taken for granted or ignored. Some congregations are motivated by the simple call to reach out because of the command to go and preach the good news of salvation in Jesus Christ. Others recognizing this call also want to extend their work to full inclusion in every aspect of congregational life. It is of no small significance that leaders in the disability ministries movement, even among evangelical disability ministries, are beginning to ask questions about their own programs in the realization that in doing their job well, they may have created their own ghetto. They sense that it is possible that the people they serve as well as the ones offering and conducting their programs may have become too isolated from the other arenas of congregational life. They may have thereby created a situation in which the remaining church programs are not

---

61. National Catholic Partnership on Disability, "Something to Consider for Every Parish" (2011).

benefitting from the presence of people with disabilities at the church. If people with disabilities are kept in separate programs, then they are robbed of the opportunity serve the church. The Reformed churches have acknowledged this issue with their catchy phrase, "everybody belongs, everybody serves."[62]

It is important to acknowledge that disability ministry has received some attention from the research community. In addition to the studies conducted by Research Services of the Presbyterian Church (U.S.A.), articles have appeared in journals related to special education and rehabilitation.[63]

I wish to highlight research appearing in the *Journal of Religion, Disability & Health,* because this publication combines the areas most connected to disability ministry as well as theological aspects of this topic, which will be extensively reviewed in the following chapters. Here, I simply want to provide some examples of what is being published in order to raise questions about the empirical study of disability ministry and mainstream religious scholarship.

In 2005, Karrie A Shogren and Mark S. Rye published "Religion and Individuals with Intellectual Disabilities: An Exploratory Study of Self-Reported Perspectives."[64] Using semistructured interviews and instruments such as the Intrinsic Religious Motivation Scale developed by the late Dean Hoge, and a religious coping scale developed by Pargament and others, Shogren and Rye were able to determine that participants scored high on measures of intrinsic religiosity and used positive religious coping strategies, and individuals with mild intellectual disabilities identified significantly with more abstract religious representation.[65]

In 2007, Jeff McNair and Michelle Sanchez published "Christian Social Constructions of Disability: Church Leaders," an article that reported findings from a sample of church leaders whose congregations participated in the National Organization on Disability's Accessible Congregations Campaign.[66] McNair and Sanchez determined that persons with disabilities "(1) were not expensive to the church, (2) do not drive potential members away, and (3) do not take excessive time away from other potential areas of service." However, they were able to identify confusion among church leaders with respect to the causes of disability and a lack of knowledge of "the life experience of persons with disability."[67]

62. Young and Stephenson, *Inclusion Handbook.*
63. Presbyterian Church (U.S.A.), *Presbyterian Panel.*
64. Shogren and Rye, "Religion and Individuals with Intellectual Disabilities."
65. Ibid.
66. McNair and Sanchez, "Christian Social Constructions of Church Leaders."
67. Ibid.

Jeff McNair also published an article that addressed "Christian Social Constructions of Disability" among "church attendees," using the same database. His analysis determined that (1) there was a gap between church leaders' advocacy of disability ministry and the provision of such ministries, (2) more than half the church leaders surveyed perceived women as being more accepting of the birth of a child with a disability than men, and (3) that according to church leaders, people in the pews perceive children with mental retardation through a variety of images, including angels and heroes. The last finding left the author with questions about the influence of some popular books circulating in Christian circles.[68] McNair also found some reasons to be suspicious of theological responses to disability and indicated a need for more work to be done "to increase understanding among churches and their leaders about persons with disability."[69]

Finally, Angela Amado, Megan DeGrande, Christina Boice, and Shannon Hutcheson coauthored a University of Minnesota study titled "Impact of Two National Congregational Programs of the Social Inclusion of Individuals with Intellectual/Developmental Disabilities." The two programs are (1) the National Organization on Disability Accessible Congregations Campaign (ACC) and (2) the Befrienders Ministry of Bloomington, Minnesota. The ACC focused on congregations that indicated a willingness to include people with disabilities. The Befrienders Program is much broader in focus, including people in need of support, such as the unemployed, those struggling with addiction, and victims of trauma, in addition to the groups normally associated with disabilities.[70]

The report discusses each program separately. The Accessible Congregation Campaign survey sought to uncover the actual impact on people with disabilities in the life of the congregation. The number of people with developmental disabilities who had been involved in or impacted by the campaign was 127, with a range of between 1 and 30 in any one congregation. Among the impacts reported were (1) the establishment of friendships between congregation members and those who have developmental disabilities, and (2) and the seeking of additional assistance outside the congregation as needed either through denominational assistance or from community-based agencies.[71]

However, the bulk of the information from the Accessible Congregation Campaign survey was derived through a content analysis of open-ended

68. McNair, "Social Constructions of Attendees."
69. Ibid.
70. Amado, et al., "Impact of Two National Congregational Programs."
71. Ibid., 10.

questions. Six "major themes" were identified: (1) "specific physical characteristics of the church and/or accessibility to areas of the church," which gave indication of change "in terms of how accessible the church was to individuals with disabilities"; (2) "welcoming/including/accepting people with disabilities in the community"; (3) increased awareness of and education about disabilities as well as an appreciation of the "value of diversity"; (4) references to a lack of resources "such as time, money and/or volunteers, how they influenced the accomplishments of the ACC"; (5) "relationship/emotional ties with reference to friendships forming, or any strong emotional connections between those with disabilities and those without disabilities"; and (6) "I don't know" or "did not share a common theme with the other responses."[72]

The study provides more data than can be possibly reviewed here. Yet, the responses to specific goals achieved as a result of the congregation's participation in the Accessible Congregations Campaign is hard to ignore, especially with regard to welcoming people with disabilities. The authors indicate that participation was not only beneficial to people with disabilities in terms of their "relation to feeling more welcomed and accepted into the community," but to the members of the congregation as well. The latter is especially case even though some of the disabled were still stigmatized.[73] Thus, while most ACC respondents indicated that their major goal planned was increasing physical accessibility, the greatest benefits were seen in the areas of "welcoming/including/accepting, increased awareness, and relationship/emotional ties."[74]

In turning to the Befrienders part of the report, the researchers were provided a list of 730 names and addresses. These included 165 distinct congregations with a total 288 contacts related to these congregations. Also, "there were an additional 442 persons with addresses without a specific congregation listed."[75] All 730 were contacted with 142 surveys (19 percent) returned. Ninety-two (65 percent) of the returned indicated "Befrienders" who were "participating with people with disabilities, and 31 (21% of all returned) of these were participating with people with developmental disabilities."[76] The summary of the open-ended questions reflected the same themes as the ACC survey, with results emphasizing welcoming/including/accepting people with disabilities in general, and the develop-

72. Ibid., 11.
73. Ibid., 12.
74. Ibid., 16.
75. Ibid., 18.
76. Ibid., 20.

ment of relationships "most commonly discussed." The study acknowledges that "the nature of the Befrienders program as a one-to-one match or link between particular individuals resulted in many benefits in the area of relationship[s], understanding, and acceptance," and concludes that "there were many benefits to those who were befriended, the people who were Befrienders also gained tremendous benefits from getting to know individuals with disabilities."[77]

Two critiques can be made after reviewing the findings of this study. The first is directed at those who study religion, in general, and at those who study religion from a social-scientific perspective. It is the question, where are you? If the number of people with disabilities represents nearly one-fifth of the population (not to mention the number of families, friends, and professionals impacted), then where is the research equal to the major societal phenomenon that disability presents? Why is it the case that when a call for papers on religion and disability is issued for a session at a mainstream social-science annual meeting such as the Society for the Scientific Study of Religion or the Association for the Sociology of Religion, conveners are hard pressed to assemble a set of papers, let alone to find people who want to attend such a session? One can only say that this is a disgrace. The impact of disability on all segments of society, including religion, is increasing and will not go away even if medical science has given us the security of removing disability from public view. Stay tuned!

The other critique is that the reports and other materials discussed in this chapter point to just how difficult it is to conduct disability ministry, from the view of the people with disabilities, without creating ghettos. Work among people with intellectual disabilities, central to most of the programs described in this chapter, can lead to an us/them mentality. One may ask, is there a way to realize such ministries without assuming that participants cannot give, however limited? Even those congregational disability ministries from an evangelical base are beginning to ask if their efforts are in fact resegregating participants from the congregation's central programs of worship, education, fellowship, and service. The same level of critique needs to be aimed at secular programs including people with disabilities housed in group homes. For example, questions about group homes being a replacement for institutions have already been raised in terms of resegregation. A further critique has been raised by Amos Yong, who advocates for a much closer involvement by the church in community programs for people with disabilities.[78]

77. Ibid., 26–27.
78. Yong, "Disability from the Margins to the Center."

4

Ministry among People with Physical Disabilities and Chronic Illness

To the average person in the pew, defining physical disability or chronic illness may appear to be rather straightforward. A person with a physical disability uses a cane, crutch, a wheelchair or scooter. This presumes that (1) those who are physically disabled can be readily seen; and (2) those who can be seen constitute the entire population of those with physical disabilities. The same cannot be so easily said of chronic illness. In many cases, such as chronic obstructive pulmonary disease (COPD) or heart disease, there may not be any outward sign such as an oxygen tank to indicate an illness. However, a severe case of COPD may result in disability that is made visible by the use such an aid.

This chapter explores the many challenges that occur when physical disability and chronic illness are considered in relation to the ministry of the church. I emphasize the embodied nature of the numerous impairments that fall under these two broad categories. Such an analysis provides opportunities to develop both an in-depth knowledge of physical disability and chronic illness, and a base for evaluating and extending ministries to and with this population.

Basics

Physical disability is a very general category that refers to a "physical condition that significantly impacts one or more major life activities."[1] The *Americans with Disabilities: 2010* report produced by the United States Census Bureau provides a useful listing of what disabilities fall under the

1. Clause, "What Is a Physical Disability?" (2017).

"physical domain." People with physical disabilities include those who (1) "use a wheelchair, cane, crutches, or walker"; (2) "had difficulty walking a quarter of a mile, climbing a flight of stairs, lifting something as heavy as a 10-pound bag of groceries, grasping objects, or getting in or out of bed;" or (3) indicated having "arthritis or rheumatism, back or spine problems, [a] broken bone or fracture, cancer, cerebral palsy, diabetes, epilepsy, head or spinal cord injury, heart trouble or atherosclerosis, hernia or rupture, high blood pressure, kidney problems, lung or respiratory problems, missing limbs, paralysis, stiffness or deformity of limbs, stomach/digestive problems, stroke, thyroid problem, or tumor/cyst/growth as a condition contributing to a reported activity limitation."[2]

The people referred to above represent a mix of those who are disabled physically and those who have a chronic illness, which is "a long-lasting condition that can be controlled but not cured."[3] In many cases their conditions warrant membership in both groups. Most chronic illnesses are found among the elderly; these include arthritis, cardiovascular disease, cancer, diabetes, and epilepsy. Of course these may occur earlier in life, but what makes chronic illness different from physical disability is the constant, day-to-day medical attention and caregiving required throughout the life span. In addition, the trajectory of many chronic diseases such as multiple sclerosis (MS) or diabetes may be thought of as having a series of stages that may or may not involve increasing debilitation.[4]

One of the challenges associated with both physical disabilities and chronic illness is determining the number of people affected. The Centers for Disease Control (CDC) estimate that among noninstitutionalized American adults eighteen years and older, 17.2 million people, or 7.3 percent of the American population, either are unable to walk or find it very difficult walk, while chronic illness affects 88 percent of those age sixty-five and older.[5]

Some people's experience may lead them to embrace a disability identity; others may insist that they are not disabled. Also, some physical disabilities, especially in their early stages, may be invisible. Chronic conditions may be so at any age. A distinct identity may be embraced, especially after one has experienced prejudice and discrimination because of their disability, has contacts with other disabled persons, and sees the value of identifying with a disability group. It takes some effort to embrace a minority

2. Brault, *Americans with Disabilities: 2010*.
3. University of Michigan, "What Is Chronic Illness?" (2015).
4. MedicineNet.com, "Definition of Chronic Illness" (2015).
5. Ibid.

status when it is realized that contact with the medical establishment and rehabilitation agencies discourage a contested view of disability.[6]

The examples cited in chapter 1 should be sufficient to dismiss any conclusion that disability is entirely a personal matter. It clearly is not. Even though many aspects of being disabled are assumed to reside in the person, their origin stem from the environment. For example, a person who uses a pair of crutches for mobility is disabled when approaching a flight of stairs. On the other hand, the fact that the environment has stairs means that the disability has been and is socially excluded.[7]

In a study of thirty people with physical disabilities and chronic illnesses, Heather Ridolfo and Brian W. Ward found that the interviewees faced a range of barriers in the home and in the community. After becoming impaired, they found it difficult if not impossible to safely enter their homes, to move about their homes once inside, to use the toilet, to wash themselves, and to prepare meals. Adapting their homes to their needs was difficult for many because of cost or because they lived in rental properties whose landlords would not permit the installation of accessibility features.[8] Going out in the community for various activities, including medical appointments, shopping, and recreation may involve detailed planning, as buildings, sidewalks, and doors may not be accessible, or accessible features may be inconvenient. Sometimes able-bodied people offer assistance without ever asking whether the person with disabilities desires it.[9] In the workforce, architectural structures may cause difficulty in addition to attitudinal barriers. However, Ridolfo and Ward found that those persons who worked at a jobsite prior to becoming impaired often found it difficult to return to their original work because they could not maintain the same pace as they maintained before, or because the nature of the work demanded a level of dexterity they no longer were able to perform.[10]

Ridolfo and Ward's study also reported that people with physical impairments were unable to maintain ties to community activities, friends and relatives. Since many activities involve travel outside the home, excursions had to be planned. New activities involved scouting out their sites in advance and using a walker rather than a scooter until it was determined that the venue could safely accommodate its use. Many reported that going on too many excursions involved too much effort and resulted in selective

6. Ridolfo and Ward, *Mobility Impairment*, 3.
7. See Jaeger and Bowman, *Understanding Disability*.
8. Ibid., 42–50.
9. Ibid., 50–56.
10. Ibid., 65–68.

choice of outings in order not to cause additional physical problems that would make it difficult to maintain everyday tasks.[11]

Many also reported that friends and relatives found it difficult to understand their "new selves" often tied to their inability to maintain their previous physical abilities. They found it difficult to explain their current status to friends whose demeanor and ignorance often made them give up in frustration. Some gave up dating because they felt that few would be interested in someone with their level of physical impairment. In some cases, friends and families were overly accommodating. Making new friends was also difficult because of the effort required to socialize.[12]

For people with disabilities, a certain degree of apprehension comes when talking about what it is like to be disabled. Sharing one's disability experience can be rewarding, especially when one is asked in the spirit of seeking useful knowledge and understanding, and not in mere curiosity. However, one can never assume that the knowledge gained by sharing personal stories about any disability is sufficient to understand the entire field of disability, even the experience of having a physical disability.

However, exposure to the varieties of "disability experience" may assist churchgoers in approaching someone with a disability, especially for the first time.[13] No magic formula provides sufficient knowledge to be comfortable in every situation in which a person with a physical disability or chronic illness is present. The challenge is to learn how to approach someone with enough comfort to get to know about the person as one would learn about anyone. It is important to keep in mind that disability is multidimensional in character. Some people come to disability at birth, others during their adult or working years, and others as the result of old age.

Accessibility and Its Limits

Ridolfo and Ward make no mention in their text of church/religious participation, although they do list it in their qualitative interview protocol.[14] However, the 2004 *Survey of Americans with Disabilities* conducted for the National Organization on Disability by the Harris Poll determined that people with disabilities are "less likely to attend religious services at least once a month compared to people without disabilities (49 percent versus 57% respectively), despite the fact that people with and without disabilities are

11. Ibid., 68–77.
12. Ibid., 73.
13. Carter, *Including People with Disabilities in Faith Communities*, 67–68.
14. Ridolfo and Ward, *Mobility Impairment*, 171.

equally likely to consider their religious faith important to them."[15] Persons with "slight" disabilities attend religious services more often, although the survey determined "persons with very severe disabilities are more likely to say that their religious faith is very important to them than are people with slight disabilities (63% versus 53% respectively)."[16] This dovetails Hendershot's study of data from the 1998 National Health Interview Survey, which indicates that people with disabilities are more likely to seek out pastoral care.[17]

Most congregations, start, and often end, their ministry with physically disabled and chronically ill persons by addressing architectural access. Usually, these steps entail building ramps and installing an elevator and an accessible bathroom. Making these changes focuses attention on getting the person into church to worship. Additional features such as pew cutouts and access to classrooms, meeting rooms and fellowship spaces are considered ancillary. Altar areas often remain the most inaccessible spaces in sanctuaries, implying that no person with mobility impairments would ever assume a lay or clergy role during worship services.

Stories exist documenting many congregations that either outright refuse or display strenuous resistance to building accessible features. Reasons cited include that no physically disabled persons currently come to church, that costs are prohibitive, and that needed monies could be put to better use elsewhere. Rarely do you find outright refusals based on fear and hostility toward people with physical disabilities or chronic illness. Sometimes congregations have refused to relocate a Sunday school class to an accessible area so that a person with mobility impairment can participate. This seems to be based on able-bodied inconvenience rather than on outright discrimination. Most often, congregations are willing to make architectural changes if a longtime member is unable to attend due to mobility limitations. What is also clear is that beyond the basic changes in architecture outlined above, specific changes made for one need may, in fact, create obstacles for someone who has a different need. For example, the placement of a bar in a toilet stall may work for those having enough strength, but not for one whose arms are not strong enough to lift oneself.[18]

15. National Organization on Disability and Harris Interactive, 2004, 76
16. Ibid.
17. Hendershot, "People Seeking Pastoral Care" (2002).
18. Shakespeare and Watson, "The Social Model of Disability," 9–28.

Moving beyond Accessibility

While there is much to commend accessibility as an approach to fostering greater participation of persons with physical disabilities and chronic illnesses in congregational life, its use as a framework is limited. Some authors, including Jennie Weiss Block, have sought to extend the term to make it the basis for an entire theology, which seeks to be in dialogue with people in the disability rights movement.[19] On the other hand, authors such as Richard B. Steele are inclined toward limiting the concept of accessibility to work designed to alter the physical environment. At any rate, Steele's reflection on the experience of raising a daughter with a rare and serious chronic illness leads him to focus on the need for addressing issues of attitude and welcoming.[20]

Attitudes of able-bodied people toward people with disabilities and chronic conditions range from refusal to make a contact, even eye contact, to overindulgence. In some churches, the physically disabled and chronically ill are exposed to healing services designed to take away their impairments. Some Christians have been known to remark that if an individual had enough faith the person would be healed. However, there is some indication that these views are changing, as even groups from the evangelical camp are moving away from these intrusions and focusing on changing attitudes.[21]

In general, those with disabilities and chronic illness are viewed by the able-bodied as people to be ministered to rather than as people with whom to minister. This is especially the case with respect to pastoral leadership. Persons with various impairments are often rejected for pastoral ministry, even if they have the necessary credentials. Here too, change is afoot: seminaries are addressing issues of physical and programmatic access as students with disabilities are seeking admission to pastoral training programs. Still, there is resistance at the congregational level as lay leadership frets over whether a pastor with a physical disability or chronic condition will be accepted by parishioners and community residents.

Nevertheless, physical disability and chronic illness is a good place to begin developing a sound foundation for disability ministry. Many churches are experiencing aging memberships, and many of these members have chronic illnesses and are struggling with functional limitations in contrast with their former selves. They may be uncomfortable with being labeled disabled, using phrase "I'm not disabled, just old," but they are disabled,

---

19. Block. *Copious Hosting*, 19.
20. Steele, "Accessibility or Hospitality?," 11–26.
21. See ch. 3, above.

however unwillingly. Somehow the congregation needs to communicate that being disabled is acceptable.

All humans are embodied and therefore deal with life as embodied creatures. Even spirituality, in this life, can only be mediated through our bodies. Some bodies are different than others. They differ in terms of gender, race, ethnicity, and sexual preference. However, lumping together all people with disabilities and calling them a minority group ignores a significant difference between an identity as a person with disabilities and an identity as another minority group. Many minority groups are defined by race or ethnicity, for instance. Yet anyone, at any time, may become a member of the disability community regardless of gender, race, ethnicity, or sexual preference.[22]

Our culture sorts out people by distinguishing between the normal and the disabled bodies. Most often this sorting occurs based on sight, as people distinguish between the two. But even disabilities that are at first invisible can be exposed. Once an able-bodied person obtains knowledge of someone else's previously invisible disability, the able-bodied status of the newly disabled person can be discredited, and the person might be forced to make disability visible and to accept the category of person with disability. In our culture being a person with a disability grants one an inferior status relative to the status of an able-bodied person. McRuer refers to our society as assuming the "compulsory able-body-ness" of everyone around.[23]

Nondisabled individuals may "feel fear, pity, fascination, repulsion, or merely surprise, none of which is expressible according to social protocol."[24] Therefore, the nondisabled person does not know how to react or "how or whether to offer assistance; whether to acknowledge the disability; what words, gestures, or expectations to use or avoid."[25] Some of the ambiguity in these situations can be handled by the person with the disability, who may be able to read and diffuse the situation. Regardless, such encounters clearly indicate how people with physical disabilities and chronic illness are viewed by society.[26]

In addition, parishioners bring cultural viewpoints into parish life. This observation should lead to frank discussions about how the congregation can examine cultural stereotypes and advocate for a different perspective toward people with all kinds of disabilities: this is a multidimensional

---

22. See Carter, *Including People with Disabilities in Faith Communities*, ch. 3.
23. McRuer, *Crip Theory*, 2–3.
24. Thomson, *Extraordinary Bodies*, 12.
25. Ibid.
26. Ibid.

subject that will be examined in each of the chapters on other categories of disability.

Over the years, several denominational and church-related groups have offered resources that challenge attitudes toward disability from churchgoers. One of the most well known of these is *That All May Worship*, published originally by the National Organization on Disability and now available through the American Association of People with Disabilities.[27] Major denominations have produced materials that have targeted attitude change. Elim Christian Services has produced "5 Stages: the Journey of Disability Attitudes," which addresses attitudinal change at the congregational level with individual-level terms: "ignorance, pity, care, friendship, and co-laborers." Congregations are urged to adopt the program as a way to enhance disability ministry, but its approach provides scant reference to the origins of disability attitudes in culture.[28]

Attitudes are socially constructed. That is, they are not fixed in people's minds, as if psychological tendencies are formed in the brain independent of social interaction. Attitudes are formed as the result of human interaction with other humans. As Susanne Rappmann argues, "The community precedes the individual," and while she is referring to viewing the body of Christ as a community, she is also speaking of changing the church's position with regard to disability.[29] The church has tended to merge its views with those of society where normalcy reigns and bodies are viewed as moldable and happy; bodies that do not fit (in our case bodies with physical disabilities and chronic illness) are moved to the fringes and are used for comparison.

In contrast, the *body* of Christ is held up as offering both a countercultural entity and a true reflection of the nature of the Christian church. The body of Christ is a better reflection of Christ, or a more useful notion than the image of God found in much literature, because views of the image of God tend to emphasize human intellect and prowess.[30] Instead, the body in the body of Christ is, according to Rappmann, "disabled and bruised," and the church is a "communion of struggle and justice." In fact, it is argued that such a community is "a better and more realistic way to look at social life."[31] I argue here that the body of Christ, the embodiment of Christ we aim to

---

27. Davie and Thornburgh, *That All May Worship*. Download a PDF here: http://www.aapd.com/wp-content/uploads/2016/03/That-All-May-Worship.pdf.
28. Elim Christian Services, *5 Stages* (2015).
29. Rappman, "The Disabled Body of Christ."
30. Hull, "The Broken Body in a Broken World."
31. Rappman, "The Disabled Body of Christ," 33.

become, can be a countercultural force that moves real congregations of human bodies to include people with disabilities.

But can such a stance work? William Rush was a member of First Baptist Church, Lincoln, Nebraska.[32] Upon the urging of his mother, who felt he needed a "church home" to nurture his nascent Christian faith, this writer and activist with cerebral palsy chose this congregation because he could roll from his home nearby and enter the building through accessible doors. After worshiping in the sanctuary on a Sunday, he returned the following Wednesday for a Bible study only to find out that it was held in an inaccessible space. However, the senior pastor met with him and invited him to return the following Sunday. After accepting the situation for a number of weeks, he was asked to be on the congregation's planning committee, whose task it was to ask, how can we better serve the community? Rush suggested installing an elevator. This suggestion reminded the committee's members that the membership was getting older and that the entire building should be "accessible to all."[33]

The congregation responded positively to the idea, choosing to install a full-size unit as well as bringing other features up to code. So the congregation made itself architecturally accessible and spiritually as well. William Rush was baptized by immersion, participated in two reenactments of Leonardo da Vinci's *The Last Supper*, and received rides to church from members when his wife was away and when weather did not permit travel via city sidewalks. Members also assisted him with home repairs and cooked dinners when needed. Rush also notes that church members took the time to have a conversation with him despite his slow speech and taught their children to be unafraid of him.[34] His presence in the congregation allowed other people with disabilities to join and be active. However, the board of deacons did not permit a man with intellectual disabilities to become a greeter, in part because of reports of inappropriate touching.[35] At the least, this report serves as an indication that the study of integration of people with disabilities into congregational life is potentially useful to mainstream social science.

---

32. Rush. "Harvesters with Disabilities," 65–72.
33. Ibid., 67.
34. Ibid., 69.
35. Ibid.

5

Ministry among People with Sensory Disabilities

This chapter reviews the implications that arise when people with sensory disabilities are considered to have an impact on the ministry of the church under two broad categories: deafness and blindness. To consider "deafness" is to include those who are Deaf, hard of hearing or hearing impaired, and the late deafened. To consider "blindness" is to include those who are blind, those who are visually impaired (including legally blind), and those who are both deaf and blind. While whole monographs could be written about each of these groups, only a brief discussion of each will be sufficient here, enough to consider what type of ministry each group might need to enable inclusion and belonging.

Deafness

It is with some caution that I include a discussion of deafness and Deaf ministries in a book on disability. After all, is it not the case that when we speak about the Deaf in general, and Deaf Christianity in particular, we are speaking about ministry to a distinct culture and its institutions, and not about disability ministries designed to meet a "special need"? Yet, as with all disabilities, it is not as simple as most assume. If the "late deafened" and "hard of hearing" are included, then can we speak of disability? That, too, is a simplistic conclusion. The hard of hearing and late deafened may not consider themselves to be part of Deaf culture because they have enough residual hearing to have learned how to communicate without using sign language. As with the Deaf, they have one thing in common: the inability to communicate effectively in a hearing world.[1]

---

1. Barnartt, "Hearing Impairment," 2:847.

The National Institute on Deafness and Other Communication Disorders (NIDCD) estimates that "approximately 15 percent of Americans (26 million people) between ages twenty and sixty-nine have high frequency hearing loss due to exposure to noise at work or during leisure activities."[2] Another report issued by the Office of Research Support and International Affairs at Gallaudet University indicates that about 2 to 4 of every one thosuand people in the United States are "functionally deaf," that is, "identified as either unable hear normal conversation at all, even with the use of a hearing aid."[3]

However, this does not offer sufficient clarification of the various populations living with hearing loss in order to derive contexts from which to identify and evaluate ministries. Sharon Barnartt[4] suggests a fourfold typology of hearing impairment based on the severity of hearing loss and whether it occurs prior to or after the onset of language development. The first type refers to those whose severe hearing loss occurs prior to language development. These individuals have problems with learning to speak, to read, and to write, which may lead to educational impairment and difficulty gaining employment. However, if they are afforded the opportunity to learn sign language at an early age, they are more successful and likely to consider themselves as culturally Deaf.

The second category refers to people with severe postlingual hearing loss due to a variety of factors, including illness and injury. Onset may lead to difficulties in communication with the hearing world and a subsequent decision to assimilate into Deaf culture and its language with its associated stigma and the need to negotiate family, occupational, and social networks. A third category consists of people with less severe prelingual hearing loss who may be "even more marginalized than those with more severe impairments." Children may be labeled as "hard of hearing" and taught to lip-read with varying success, leading to eventual difficulties in employment and social integration. And should they choose to enter Deaf culture, they may not be accepted as "deaf enough" or hampered by limited skills in signing. The fourth category refers to people with "less severe, postlingual hearing loss. These are most likely to have lost their hearing later in life and are the largest portion of those with hearing impairments. Isolation from family and social life may occur, especially if hearing devices are inadequate or not used."[5]

---

2. National Institute on Deafness and Other Communication Disorders, "Quick Statistics" (2015).

3. Ibid.

4. Barnartt, "Hearing Impairment," 2:848–49.

5. Ibid.

Each of these populations requires a different response from the church. Ministry to those tied to Deaf culture, who have learned sign language as their first language, have different needs from those whose late onset and contact with mainstream culture mandates a different response from the church. Ministries to the Deaf have a rich history that is largely unknown to people of faith today. As early as the seventeenth century, Roman Catholic clergy, largely from cloisters, were engaged in finding ways to communicate with the Deaf through sign language. Starting in Spain and then centered in France, these men of faith grappled with its structure, syntax and forms in order to enable the Deaf to function in society. As well, there was a religious bent in that the Deaf must learn the faith so that, after Paul and Augustine, they can inherit eternal life.[6]

Sign language was carried to the United States in the early 1800s by Thomas Hopkins Gallaudet (1787–1851), who upon graduating from seminary in 1815, was sent to Europe to learn to communicate with the Deaf. In 1817, he returned, bringing with him Laurent Clerc, and together, they worked to establish American Sign Language (ASL) as the principal way for the Deaf to communicate with each other and to gain respect in secular as well as religious circles. In fact, they are credited with organizing several congregations for the Deaf throughout New England and in the Mid-Atlantic states. They also established sign language as the main vehicle for education of Deaf students in state schools.[7]

In the middle and late 1800s, "oralism" emerged as the preferred way to train people who were deaf. This approach emphasized speech as more important than hearing in asserting one's "God-given humanity," thus reversing the view that sign language was the key to a deaf person's humanity. A young deaf child would be fitted with hearing aids, trained to lip-read and taught to speak. The use of sign language was strictly prohibited and children who were caught using it were punished (although the use of sign language survived, especially in state schools). Over a period of years, deaf instructors were gradually replaced by hearing instructors, and the medical model became dominant as doctors and audiologists held sway over a deaf child's diagnosis and treatment. Medical practitioners determined the level of impairment, the remedy to be pursued dovetailing into oralist education.[8]

While oralism has been largely curtailed, the influence of the medical model of deafness continues today with the current emphasis cochlear

---

6. Lane, *When the Mind Hears*, 58.
7. Ibid.
8. Ibid.

implants. As of December 2012, approximately 324,200 of these devices have been implanted worldwide, while in the United States 58,000 adults and children have received implants.[9] Deaf communities have strongly protested against these measures, arguing that deafness with its sign language is more than sufficient to enable Deaf children and adults to function in society. Just as oralism did not enable deaf people to fully integrate into the hearing world, so neither do cochlear implants fully reverse hearing loss. Communication and integration into society are still difficult.[10]

If Deaf culture is taken seriously, then it must be acknowledged that what we have is a group of individuals who communicate using a visual language complete with its own syntax and vocabulary. Their way of living, their culture, is good, in and of itself. Their way of living doesn't require the hearing aids, implants, lip-reading, or learning to speak. Deafness is not a disability. It does not require the remedy that the medical and educational establishments have sought to create. Instead, deafness constitutes an entry point into a culture with its own values, norms, and ways of incorporating young people through Deaf clubs, networks of Deaf schools, and more recently the Internet. Members of Deaf culture eschew the medical model, which seeks to prohibit them from using what comes naturally. Gone are the days when school-age Deaf were punished for using sign language. Instead, it is okay to be born Deaf or to acquire deafness early in life. Not surprisingly, the Deaf community seeks to offer this view as a way to combat medical dominance of the Deaf by pointing to the success of those using sign language.[11]

This is not to say that ministry to the Deaf should fall outside the purview of the church. Indeed, there is a long tradition of reaching out to the Deaf community—a tradition that acknowledges the status of being Deaf and seeks to establish ministries that provide access to liturgy and fellowship, a trend which extends back to the early 1800s. Today, Deaf congregations are found among nearly every denomination in America. Kathy Black, in a United Methodist context, discusses three "models of Deaf ministry": the Deaf Church, the Deaf congregation, and "interpreted ministries." The Deaf church refers to a "separate Deaf congregation with committees and budgets," while the Deaf congregation refers to those groups who gather for worship, nurture, and fellowship but are not stand-alone entities. Many of their services take place at times and places different from hearing/speaking

---

9. National Institute on Deafness and Other Communication Disorders, "Quick Statistics" (2015).

10. National Association of the Deaf, "Issues and Resources" (2016).

11. Ibid.

congregations. These often seek to provide social contact with others who share their beliefs and ways of doing Christianity. Interpreted ministries are conducted within hearing congregations and use sign language interpreters to make the worship service and other services of the church community accessible for its Deaf members.[12]

Many denominations conduct ministries/missions to/with the Deaf with structures beyond the congregational level. The International Catholic Deaf Association has three sections: the United States, Canada and Venezuela. National meetings are held on a regular basis, providing opportunities to study, socialize, and celebrate events such as the ordination priests and deacons who are Deaf, planning to work among the Deaf, or both. A newsletter shares these events, providing a forum for theological and spiritual reflection usually under the authorship of priests related to the movement.[13]

The same is true for many mainline and evangelical denominations. The United Methodist Church, for example, has recently begun to expand its Deaf ministries, building upon four historic congregations. In the early 1990s, the United Methodist Congress of the Deaf (UMCD) lobbied the denomination's General Conference to establish the United Methodist Committee of Deaf and Hard of Hearing Ministries with an annual budget of $200,000. Since then, the committee with the cooperation of the UMCD, has sponsored a number of events and training programs designed to strengthen both clergy and lay leadership within Deaf congregations. As well, new ministries to the Deaf have been established across the United States and in other countries around the globe where regular United Methodist missions have a presence.[14]

In 2014, the Evangelical Lutheran Deaf Association (ELDA), the Episcopal Conference of the Deaf (ECD), the United Methodist Congress of the Deaf (UMCD), and the United Methodist Committee on Deaf and Hard of Hearing Ministries (UM-DHM) held a joint meeting in Chicago, Illinois. The event's agenda included time for dialogue, worship, Bible study, and fundraising for missions in Haiti and Jamaica. The ELDA was invited the group to meet again in 2016.[15] The Episcopal Church also has a long tradition of mission among the Deaf, including laying claim to the Reverend

---

12. Black, *Signs of Solidarity*, 28–40.

13. International Catholic Deaf Association, "From ICDA-Canada Section 2012 Conference."

14. Hudspeth, "Ignore Not the Deaf" (2015).

15. United Methodist Committee on Deaf and Hard of Hearing Ministries, "Joint Statement" (2015).

Thomas H. Gallaudet, and currently has several ministries and at least eight cogregations.[16]

The level of sophistication of Deaf ministries within American mainline Protestant denominations is matched by ministries in some evangelical denominations. The Lutheran Church–Missouri Synod's Lutheran Deaf Mission Society produces "Models of Deaf Ministry," which expands the variety of forms of Deaf ministry to include such forms as "preaching stations," a "missionary-at-large," "bivocational ministry," and "lay-led Deaf Ministry."[17] In addition to affirming Christian evangelism and nurture, the document cites Public Law 94–142 (the Education of All Handicapped Children Act) as emphasizing mainstreaming, which necessitates these new forms of ministry designed to meet the needs of Deaf in the community.[18]

Predecessors to the Evangelical Lutheran Church in America (ELCA), especially in the Upper Midwestern and the Plains states, have a long tradition of service and congregational missions to the Deaf. These ministries grew out of the desire to reach Deaf people of Scandinavian heritage.[19]

Some evangelical ministries argue that the Deaf are the "largest unreached people group in North America,"[20] while another publication claims that the deaf count "for more than 29 million strong in the United States."[21] The latter is obviously in error as the figure most likely refers to the hearing-impaired population, which numbers more than 20 million—a group that is the most likely not to be interested in identifying with the Deaf community.[22]

Deaf Ministry: Make a Joyful Silence by Peggy Johnson[23] provides a glimpse into the life of a Deaf congregation and what it is like to serve as a hearing pastor of the Deaf. Her long road of socialization into their culture began with her own disability (the loss of one eye) and her fascination with sign language. This led to several experiences with ministries among the Deaf including Christian education at schools for the Deaf and a chaplaincy at Gallaudet University. In this context, she discovered a "definite sense of audiological class distinction" in which "everyone knew his or her place in

16. Ibid.

17. Lutheran Deaf Mission Society, "Models of Deaf Ministry" (2015).

18. Ibid.

19. Herzog, "History of Disability Advocacy in the Evangelical Lutheran Church in America."

20. Three Angels Deaf Ministry, "Why Deaf Ministry Is Needed?" (2015).

21. McClain, "Being Aware of the Silent Majority." n.d.

22. See National Institute on Deafness and Other Communication Disorders, "Quick Statistics" (2015).

23. Johnson, *Deaf Ministry* (2007).

the pecking order": those who were Deaf were at the top, and those were hard of hearing and voice-using with little or no ASL were at the bottom. Finally, Johnson was appointed to serve as pastor of Christ United Methodist Church for the Deaf in Baltimore, Maryland. However, there was initial resistance to her appointment from among the congregation's Deaf members, and it took some time and effort for her to gain their acceptance.

Nevertheless, her ministry in this congregation was to span twenty years! During this time, she preached, married, and buried as well as taught and counseled. At times, she advocated for persons in the larger Deaf community who were often poor, uneducated, and jobless, and who were generally different from the middle-class members of her congregation. On numerous occasions, she advocated on behalf of those needing access to services and financial support. She also became involved in numerous family disputes that concerned issues of spousal abuse, child neglect, and contact with police and parole officers. On many of these occasions, she became a reluctant interpreter as many community services offered no sign-language access despite being required by law to do so.

In 2008, to the surprise and delight of many, Johnson was nominated and elected a bishop in the United Methodist Church and assigned to serve the congregations in the Eastern Pennsylvania and Peninsula Annual Conferences.[24] Since then, she has used her status to broker the establishment of new ministries and resources for ministry among people with all types of disabilities, in addition to those who are Deaf. Included among her efforts is a new study on disabilities designed for women's groups, establishing missions among the Deaf in her Episcopal Area, opening a Deaf camp, and speaking about Deaf ministries.

Even though much has been done in the area of Deaf ministries, there is an implied need to do more. Johnson has promoted United Methodist ministries among the Deaf in the Philadelphia area and established week-long camps for the hearing impaired in addition to the Deaf. On Palm Sunday 2009, Bishop Johnson preached at Epworth United Methodist Church in Rehoboth Beach, Delaware. Word got out that she would bring an ASL interpreter with her since there was no signed service at the congregation. Several members from the Deaf community came, to the surprise of many. Since then, Johnson has continued to use her office to advance the causes of Deaf ministry and disability ministry throughout the denomination.[25]

The allusion above to the hard-of-hearing population needs further expansion. The fact that this population represents the largest segment of

24. Ibid.
25. General Board of Global Ministries, "Embracing Deaf Ministry in Peninsula-Delaware Conference" (2015).

the disabled population in the United States should cause concern when dealing with disability statistics. The reference to the disability population in the United States in excess of fifty million is greatly reduced by the subtraction of the twenty-nine million people with hearing loss. These people would normally not consider themselves as disabled as they have not been hearing impaired most of their lives. They have not learned sign language and they can still hear enough to get along in the hearing world, albeit with hearing devices, and despite having difficulty making connections when listening to others. While churches have been slow to respond to the needs of persons who are hard of hearing, many churches are beginning to offer services such as hearing loops, which afford the individual the option of seating anywhere in the sanctuary or meeting room. These can be effective if someone remembers to turn on the system as Barbara Stenross reports in her study of person who are hard of hearing.[26]

Deafness, blindness, and disabilities affecting other senses have received attention from biblical scholars in terms of "sensory criticism," which is "premised on the idea that concepts and expressions of the body and its senses are valuable features for study." This follows from the Bible's repeated references (aside from in healing narratives) to the blind being asked to see and the deaf to hear. These references are plentiful enough that a chapter titled "Introducing Sensory Criticism in Bible Studies," with a subtitle "Audiocentricity and "Visiocentricity" is included in a book of essays on disability and biblical studies.[27]

Until recently, there hasn't been a significant amount of theological (and for that matter, biblical and historical) reflection on what it means to be a Deaf Christian in today's world. Hannah Lewis has written *Deaf Liberation Theology*, which speaks of the forms and experiences in the United Kingdom, but so far such theological reflection has not been conducted on deaf experiences in the United States. Like those who embrace disability, Lewis insists that the Deaf themselves must take responsibility for their own ministry.[28] On the other hand, evangelical sources focus on ministry and pay less attention to the larger social issues surrounding the emergence of Deaf culture. Thus, while DeAnn Sampley emphasizes the importance of Deaf culture and the need for respecting the Deaf way of life, she avoids any serious discussion of the past when Deaf people were forced to conform to oralist methods, which essentially made deafness a disability.[29]

26. Stenross, *Missed Connections*.
27. Avalos, "Introducing Sensory Criticism in Biblical Studies," 47–48.
28. Lewis, *Deaf Liberation Theology* (2007).
29. Sampley, *A Guide to Deaf Ministry* (1990).

Ministry among people who are Deaf is particularly difficult, especially worship and Bible study. For one, persons equipped with ASL or BSL (British Sign Language) may have difficulty with direct translations of texts because there may be no exact equivalent words in sign language. In addition, the education of the Deaf may not provide for readily available knowledge to translate from the English text. Sermons among the Deaf are more likely to be interactive. In his study of British Deaf congregations, Wayne Morris found that Deaf participants at worship services "felt free to interrupt the leader, to ask questions and engage in whatever discussion is appropriate at any time." Morris notes these interruptions did not show disrespect but were engaging in a process of "think[ing] together" about the meaning of both the Scripture and sermon for the Deaf congregants' lives.[30]

Blindness

According to the American Federation of the Blind (AFB), almost 7.4 million people in the United States have a visual disability.[31] Beth Omansky lists three categories of blindness and visual impairment: the totally blind, the legally blind, and the partially sighted. To be legally blind one must have 20/200 visual acuity or less in the best corrected eye. Partially sighted persons have 20/70 visual acuity in the best corrected eye or can see only 20 degrees or less in the visual field. Whereas many sighted people view blindness as the inability to see, people in all three of these groups are eligible for financial and social services. Indeed, those who are legally blind may have similar needs to those who are totally blind, including the need to use Braille or alternate print sources, the need for orientation and mobility training (training in how to move in the world with a white cane), or the need for a guide dog.[32]

Often those who have trouble seeing (folks in all three categories) have difficulties in a number of areas.[33] They may have difficulty getting access to orientation and mobility training and to other aids such as computers or guide dogs simply because of red tape. Often, rehabilitation caseworker turnover slows down the process, forcing a client to acquaint a new counselor with his or her needs again. Omanski argues that "rehabilitation rests on the assumption that it knows what is best for its particular population." On the one hand, rehabilitation services emphasize making the blind or

30. Morris, *Theology without Words*, 126–27.
31. American Council of the Blind, "Religious Resources" (2015).
32. Omansky, "Blindness and Visual Impairment," 1:186.
33. Ibid.

visually impaired client as "normal" as possible, in keeping with the medical model that uses normal vision as its standard. On the other hand, rehabilitation counselors often channel clients into low-paying, dead-end jobs rather than taking into consideration client interests and abilities, which might result in the counselor seeking and supporting advanced training or education for clients.[34]

Being blind has implications for how one lives. Rod Michalko lost his sight early in life and spent a good deal of energy in his youth "passing" as sighted. Since his loss of sight was gradual, he was able to do so, but only to a point. As he grew older, he was less able to conceal his blindness. As school went on, he moved closer and closer to the blackboard and to the books he was required to read, and was less able to walk without an aid. Eventually, Michalko was forced to use a white cane and then a guide dog. (Orientaton and mobility training in the use of the white cane is often required before one can apply for a guide dog, which also requires training).[35]

This information has implications for how the church views those who have difficulty seeing. While the totally blind may need items (including worship bulletins, hymnals, and Bibles) in Braille, others may need these same items in large-print formats or as computer programs that can be customized and downloaded. The American Council on the Blind (ACB) offers a list of "Religious Resources," and a list of organizations that provide various forms of assistance, including Braille and large-print Bibles and audio recordings of the Bible. Many of the groups listed are evangelically based; these include the Assemblies of God Center for the Blind, and the Gospel Association for the Blind. The list also contains items from various Lutheran organizations, including the Lutheran Blind Mission and Lutheran Braille Evangelism Association.[36]

But the church's response needs to be deeper than providing resources. It must recognize that within the biblical tradition, problematic sayings and references create negative views of blindness. John M. Hull asserts that "the Bible was written by sighted people," which should not be news to most readers. Blind and visually impaired readers should be aware of this because their first readings might cause them to feel alienated from the Bible "without knowing why." However, "When it is recognized that the Bible was written by and for sighted people (and after all, they are the vast majority in any society), it can be understood that this is not a permanent or particularly significant aspect of the message of the Bible. It is just the way

---

34. Omansky, *Borderlands of Blindness*, 88–89.
35. Michalko, *The Difference that Disability Makes*.
36. American Council of the Blind, n.d.

MINISTRY AMONG PEOPLE WITH SENSORY DISABILITIES

that was unconsciously adopted by the sighted people who wrote it." Hull's work details biblical phrases and passages that refer to vision or sight. For instance, in Ps 69.17, "Do not hide your face from your servant, for I am in distress" refers to the "idea of hiding one's face [as] a sighted person's way of describing displeasure or shame."[37]

The Man Born Blind

Perhaps there is no better-known biblical passage that features blindness than chapter 9 in the Gospel of John: the story of the healing of the "man born blind." The entire chapter constitutes a complete story and includes the initial question of who sinned, the healing of the man by Jesus, and the ensuing encounters with the religious authorities. However, space only allows for including here the first twelve verses:

> As he walked along, he saw a man blind from birth. His disciples asked him, "Rabbi, who sinned, this man or his parents, that he was born blind?" Jesus answered, "Neither this man nor his parents sinned; he was born blind so that God's works might be revealed in him. We must work the works of him who sent me while it is day; night is coming when no one can work. As long as I am in the world, I am the light of the world." When he had said this, he spat on the ground and made mud with the saliva and spread the mud on the man's eyes, saying to him, "Go, wash in the pool of Siloam" (which means Sent). Then he went and washed and came back able to see. The neighbors and those who had seen him before as a beggar began to ask, "Is this not the man who used to sit and beg?" Some were saying, "It is he." Others were saying, "No, but it is someone like him." He kept saying, "I am the man." But they kept asking him, "Then how were your Eyes opened?" He answered, "The man called Jesus made mud, spread it on my eyes, and said to me, 'Go to Siloam and wash.' Then I went and washed and received my sight." They said to him, "Where is he?" He said, "I do not know."

This story combines a rejection of the link between the man's disability and sin and the metaphorical contrast between the physical blindness of the healed man and the spiritual blindness of the synagogue leaders. The man's experience as the marginalized other frees him from the normative perspective of the sighted community.[38] However, Colleen C. Grant focuses on the drama of the story:

37. Hull, *In the Beginning There Was Darkness*, 67.
38. Grant, "Reinterpreting the Healing Narratives," 79.

Unlike any other healing story, John 9 presents the reader with a well-developed character, a personality with whom we can identify. Indeed, despite his anonymity, the man born blind comes alive in this healing narrative in a way that few other characters do. He appears not simply as a broken figure in need of compassion and healing but as a person in his own right. We are able to get to know him as a thoughtful, brave, amusing, but above all, ordinary person.[39]

Once the healing takes place, the formerly blind man is free to become the focal point of the Pharisees' investigation of the healing, and a reluctant spokesperson establishing Jesus's authority as God-given.

Deaf-Blindness

The deaf-blind represent a small number of individuals, who can neither see nor hear as the result of genetics, diseases, illnesses, or accidents. Age of onset plays a role and not everyone who is labelled as deaf-blind is totally deaf and totally blind.[40] There are approximately ten thousand deaf-blind children in the United States, and 90 percent of children who are identified as deaf-blind have additional physical or cognitive disabilities.[41] These students require special teaching methods and accommodations to succeed in school provided trained teachers are available. Adults who are deaf-blind also need assistance in finding suitable employment—employment that uses their strengths—and enjoyable social lives. With some assistance, adults who become deaf-blind later in life may be able to function better than children who become deaf-blind because the adults likely have language skills that matured before the onset of deaf-blindness.[42]

Evidence of church programs for deaf-blind persons is limited. Peggy Johnson presided over a gathering at Towson University that included interpreted worship. The use of sign language benefited the fifty or so who gathered on this occasion, but overall strategies to include this small but significant population in the church do not appear to exist.[43]

---

39. Ibid.

40. Hoffman, "Deafblindness," 357.

41. National Institute on Deafness and Other Communication Disorders, "Quick Statistics."

42. Hoffman, "Deafblindness," 358.

43. Baltimore-Washington Conference, "Deaf-Blind Share Impulse to Soar."

6

Ministry among People with Developmental Disabilities

Developmental disabilities refer to "a diverse group of severe chronic conditions that are due to mental and/or physical impairments. People with developmental disabilities have problems with major life activities such as language, mobility, learning, self-help, and independent living. Developmental disabilities begin anytime during development up to 22 years of age and usually last throughout a person's lifetime."[1] The concept of developmental disabilities emerged in the 1960s as an umbrella term designed to focus on impairments diagnosed during pregnancy, immediately after birth, or in early childhood.[2] The Centers for Disease Control (CDC) list five specific impairments within the larger category of developmental disabilities: autism spectrum disorders, cerebral palsy, hearing loss, mental retardation or intellectual disability, and visual impairment.[3] We will limit discussion in this chapter to intellectual disability, cerebral palsy, and autism. This chapter will also include a discussion of profound mental and physical disabilities.

Intellectual Disability

Intellectual disability is the most common developmental disability. "Intellectual disability is characterized both by a significantly below-average score on a test of mental ability or intelligence and by limitations in the ability to function in areas of daily life, such as communication, self-care, and getting

---

1. Centers for Disease Control and Prevention, "Key Findings."
2. Fujiura, "Developmental Disabilities," 1:394–97.
3. Centers for Disease Control and Prevention, "Facts about Developmental Disabilities."

along in social situations and school activities."[4] In the past, intellectual disability has been referred to as cognitive disability or mental retardation. However, in 2006 the American Association on Mental Retardation (AAMR) voted to change its name to the American Association on Intellectual and Developmental Disabilities. While this has given the organization the ability to attract a new generation of members (i.e. scholars and service providers), the use of the term "intellectual disability" for the impairment, itself, is perhaps less stigmatizing and is now in wide use.[5]

Intellectual disability can be "caused by injury, disease, or a brain abnormality" before the child is born or during childhood before age eighteen.[6] In many cases the cause is unknown. However, among the most commonly known causes are

> Down syndrome, fetal alcohol syndrome, and fragile X syndrome, all of which occur before birth. Other causes that take place before a child is born include genetic conditions (such as Cri-du-chat syndrome or Prader-Willi syndrome), infections (such as congenital cytomegalovirus), or birth defects that affect the brain (such as hydrocephalus or cortical atrophy). Other causes of intellectual disability (such as asphyxia) happen while a baby is born or soon after birth. Still other causes of intellectual disability do not happen until a child is older. These may include serious head injury, stroke, or certain infections such as meningitis.[7]

In most instances, a psychologist rather than a medical doctor would confer the label of "intellectual disability." Psychologists have the training to conduct tests for intelligence and to determine social functioning. Whether referred to as intellectual disability or mental retardation or developmental disability, such labels initially may have more relevance to the clinician rather than the individual with the disability or the parents. Such labels would normally need to be explained to parents and a determination made as to when and how the label should be applied. Regardless, such a label indicates a whole range of implications for such issues as care and supervision, placement in various educational options, employment, even end-of-life care.

Given our culture's emphasis on intellectual prowess, orderliness, and general physical well-being, people with developmental disabilities have had a difficult time finding a place in American society. Until the 1960s

---

4. Ibid.
5. Gaventa, personal communication (2016).
6. Centers for Disease Control, "Intellectual Disability."
7. Ibid.

many people with intellectual disabilities (and some people with cerebral palsy and autism) were housed in institutions operated by the state. Beginning in the late 1960s and on through to the 1980s these institutions were depopulated in favor of community-based group homes, apartments, and smaller residential facilities. This coincided with the rise of county boards of mental retardation and developmental disabilities (often referred to as MRDD boards), which offered sheltered workshops, activities, and oversight of people with developmental disabilities living within its jurisdiction. These services were also provided to people with developmental disabilities living in their parents' homes, a generation of people who had never been institutionalized.

Today therefore, most people with developmental disabilities are community residents who need various supports to live more or less independently. Religious supports are part of the picture in the recognition that all people, regardless of disability, have aspects of their lives that can be referred to as "spiritual." And part of living in the community is finding (if it is desired) a church home: a place where one can worship, learn about faith, and interact with others who share beliefs. In some locations, community-based chaplains were/are available to assist individuals from group homes to select and integrate into a congregation. Chaplains would also work with congregations to create an atmosphere of welcome and to offer suggestions as to how the process could lead to a relationship of inclusion and belonging.[8] Of course most communities do not have community chaplains to assist in the process of integrating people with intellectual disabilities into congregations. However, it is likely that a member of an MRDD agency would be willing to assist in this process, and if a member does not volunteer, then that person should be prodded by the congregation, to do so.

Congregations face a number of challenges when seeking to minister to persons with intellectual disabilities. Depending on their level of intellectual functioning and the presence of other disabilities, persons with intellectual disabilities may not be able to understand the content of a traditional worship liturgy or mass, including the sermon or homily. Their inability to adapt to their surroundings may also present difficulties in participating in a regular Sunday school class or youth group, or in regular fellowship activities. Even the expectation that a child or adult with intellectual disabilities should enter a room, find a seat, and remain seated, or follow the movements of the liturgy (e.g., standing for a hymn, kneeling for a prayer, or passing the peace) may seem impossible for persons with intellectual disability to meet. Given that people with intellectual disabilities tend to

---

8. Brock, "Theologizing Inclusion" 351–76.

disrupt normal, taken-for-granted expectations of congregational life, a certain degree of distance may open between the regular membership and people with limited skill sets. This may lead to any number of congregational reactions, including assigning people with intellectual disabilities to one set of pews (worship segregation), designating a person "to take charge of them," (as if relating is a task for "experts"), or asking people with intellectual disabilities to leave (the ultimate rejection?).[9]

Sometimes this kind of response to a person with intellectual disabilities can be taken as an insult, especially when a church member is the parent of a child or of an adult identified as among those whose viability as a congregation member is in question.[10] Several years ago, I visited a congregation that offered a full range of services for people with disabilities. I asked a couple with a disabled child how the program came about. They said that they had taken their son with multiple disabilities to another congregation. After they had attended services and Sunday school with that congregation, a member of that group approached them indicating that they were welcome anytime, but they could not bring their child![11]

More stories can be told, especially with the anonymity available on Internet sites, which discuss rejection and attitudes toward people with disabilities. Ellen Stumbo's website is a place where parents of children with "special needs," especially "mothers with of children with special needs," can share their stories of dealing with their children and the church. Stumbo shares her own story of being a mother of a daughter with Down syndrome, and her attempts to elicit a response from her congregation. Then she invites her readers to share their own stories. These stories are personal, heartbreaking, and disturbing in relating of the church's dismissal, ignorance, and outright rejection of their children and others with special needs.[12]

However, more is at stake here than the immediate response to people with intellectual disabilities. In all likelihood the presence in a congregation of people with intellectual disabilities calls into question the identity of the congregation—a questioning that lies behind the uneasiness of some able-bodied members.[13] People who cannot read, who cannot understand the meaning of sermons or liturgical acts, and who have difficulty conforming to the rules governing behavior present a challenge to the identity of a congregation. To successfully integrate people with developmental disabili-

---

9. See Carter, *Including People with Disabilities in Faith Communities*.
10. Reynolds, *Vulnerable Communion*.
11. Herzog, *An Analysis of the Disability Rights Movement*.
12. Stumbo, "The Church and Disability."
13. Ammerman, "Culture and Identity in the Congregation," 78–104.

ties, the congregation must adjust its understandings of what it means to be a "people of God" to the new reality of having someone with intellectual disabilities in the congregation. If the congregation fails to adjust its own image of its identity, then any formal response to persons with intellectual disabilities who want to participate will have no permanent place in its program, and participation by people with intellectual disabilities in the church will likely dwindle over time (as people posting on Stumbo's weblog testify).

Cerebral Palsy

The second major developmental disability is cerebral palsy (CP). In general, "cerebral palsy refers to a group of disorders that affect a person's ability to move and maintain balance and posture" as the result of "a nonprogressive brain abnormality, which means that it does not get worse over time, though the exact symptoms can change over a person's lifetime." The CDC notes that approximately "10,000 babies born each year develop cerebral palsy."[14]

There are four main types of cerebral palsy—spastic, athetoid, ataxic, and mixed. People with spastic cerebral palsy have stiff muscles which result in awkward movements, and the diagnosis is usually described by the parts of the body affected as, for example, spastic quadriplegia which "affects a person's whole body (face, trunk, legs, and arms)." The CDC reports that "Seventy to eighty percent of people with cerebral palsy have spasticity."[15]

People with athetoid or dyskinetic cerebral palsy "have slow, writhing movements that they cannot control." These movements usually involve the hands, arms, feet, and legs and sometimes the ability to control movements of the face and tongue (which results in difficulty speaking) as well as muscle control that can change from day to day and even during the day. According to the CDC, "Ten to twenty percent of people with cerebral palsy have the athetoid form of the condition."[16]

People who have ataxic cerebral palsy (5 to 10 percent) "have problems with balance and depth perception. They might be unsteady when they walk. They might have a hard time with quick movements or movements that need a lot of control, like writing. They might have a hard time controlling their hands or arms when they reach for something." The fourth type of cerebral palsy is commonly referred to as "mixed." That is, "Some people

---

14. Centers for Disease Control, "Cerebral Palsy."
15. Ibid.
16. Ibid.

have more than one type of cerebral palsy. The most common pattern is spasticity plus athetoid movements."[17]

Often people with cerebral palsy are considered to be "mentally retarded" because of their difficulty in speaking and their inability to control their movements. This should not be a conclusion based on first impression. According to Shiel, "up to half of patients with cerebral palsy have cognitive disabilities."[18] People with cerebral palsy can learn and function successfully in society. What is important is that one should not assume that a person with CP is intellectually disabled. While speech may be difficult, in time one can learn to understand the speech patterns of someone with CP. Some with CP have learned to use voice systems that can produce speech, even by using their toes.

Autism

The term "autism spectrum disorders" (ASD) refers to a range of developmental disabilities that "cause substantial impairments in social interaction and communication and the presence of unusual behaviors and interests."[19] Individuals with these symptoms present unique to the usual ways of learning, especially because of the way these individuals focus their attention and react to sensations around them. According to the CDC, "The thinking and learning abilities of people with ASDs can vary—from gifted to severely challenged. An ASD begins before the age of 3 and lasts throughout a person's life." ASDs include autistic disorder, pervasive developmental disorder, not otherwise specified (PDD-NOS, including atypical autism), and Asperger syndrome. These conditions have some of the same symptoms but differ in terms of when the symptoms start, how severe they are, and the exact nature of the symptoms.[20]

While ASDs can occur in all racial, ethnic and socioeconomic groups, they are "four times more likely to occur in boys than in girls." A study released in 2007 by the CDC's Autism and Developmental Disabilities Monitoring (ADDM) Network indicated that "about 1 in 150 8-year-old children in multiple areas of the United States had an ASD."[21] The CDC notes that "More people than ever before are being diagnosed with ASD. It is unclear how much of this increase is due to a broader definition of ASD and better

17. Ibid.
18. Shiel, "Cerebral Palsy."
19. Centers for Disease Control, "Autism Spectrum Disorders Overview."
20. Ibid.
21. Ibid.

efforts in diagnosis. However, a true increase in the number of people with an ASD cannot be ruled out. The increase in ASD diagnosis is likely due to a combination of these factors."[22]

For many families, a child with autism presents a challenge. This is true for Christians as well and is documented by pastoral theologian Brian Brock, whose son, Adam, has been diagnosed with autism. Brock outlines four difficulties in loving someone with autism. The first is frustration that having a loved one with autism disrupts attitudes about space, place, and the ordering of things. The second difficulty surrounds unmet expectations that the child will be "polite, communicative, cooperative, and outgoing."[23]

Third, parents with an autistic child often experience grief that results from the child's seeming inability to understand the social aspects of living, especially those taken-for-grated behaviors such as not eating food that has been on the floor, or not darting into traffic. Grief can come about because of the absence of groups who understand the parents' dilemmas and because parents and children thus experience ostracization. The fourth difficulty in loving a child with autism surrounds parents' longing for emotional and physical closeness with their autistic child, who is normally distant because of the autism spectrum disorder. This longing can grow when, for instance, the child is ill and needs a parent to come close. Uncertainty can arise when parents don't know whether their child will accept their closeness in one instance or another. According to Brock, uncertainty "is not an emotion but is a cognitive state of confusion or lack of clarity that tends to generate the emotion of anxiety. In any case, it is the opposite of closure, of certainty and the ability to put something out of one's mind associated with it."[24]

Given these realities, persons with ASDs not only challenge ordinary, everyday, taken-for-granted interactions such as interpreting a smile but also have difficulty understanding religious concepts and stories. Swinton and Trevett point out that stories about a man dying and rising, concepts such as that God can live in one's heart or that God is real even if he cannot be seen can be especially difficult for persons with Asperger's syndrome. These and other difficulties present a challenge to how religion is experienced. In many cases, spirituality becomes an issue of importance because of its abstraction and its bewildering array of expressions. Hence, there is a real need to explore alternative forms of communicating the beliefs, rituals and other faith issues relevant to the ordinary lives of people with ASD's.[25]

22. Ibid.
23. Brock, "Autism, Care and Christian Hope," 13.
24. Ibid., 14–15.
25. Swinton and Trevett, "Editorial," 33.

Many Christian responses to people with an autism spectrum disorder are shaped by the ability of someone with an ASD to understand beliefs and to participate in the life of the church. Asperger's syndrome (AS) is challenging because it is only recently that theologians and Christian educators have focused on how to approach communicating the faith to people whose high intelligence is often expressed in scientific ideas. To date, much writing on these issues seems to be focused on faith issues rather than on how to communicate the faith. Nick Dubin and Janet Graetz approach the study spirituality and AS from a psychological point of view, emphasizing cognitive development in general and theory of mind in particular. Theory of mind relates to deficits in differentiating one's point of view from those of others, including the ability to "be able to somewhat accurately interpret other people's behavior and the intention behind the behavior."[26] Most important is that people with AS "derive meaning in a social situation in entirely different ways from typically developing individuals." This substantive article extends the discussion by adding existential features to the concept of theory of mind, emphasizing "a biologically based way that individuals perceive meaning in certain life events." The conclusion as the result of this study is that a science orientation is a prominent feature of the belief systems of persons with AS. It is suggested that "perhaps their propensity for the sciences and the need to understand 'how' things work extends to the area of spirituality as well." Nevertheless, while their path to spirituality is affirmed as being different from others, "their exploration of faith may promote their sense of connectedness with others and with the divine"[27] Based on this conclusion, Dubin and Graetz argue that "faith-based communities can assist in this endeavor. Since many communities of faith are organized and structured, they may appear welcoming to an individual seeking organization and structure in their lives." In addition,

> the structure may include religious rules (the Ten Commandments) and the familiarity of traditional spiritual services (taking communion, reading of scriptures). In addition to providing needed structure, participation in a faith-based community (churches, synagogues, mosques, for example) may contribute to self-esteem and a feeling of connectedness . . . Religious institutions are places of communal solidarity where like-minded individuals come together to celebrate or work towards a common cause. Personal interactions in religious settings may be more structured than social interactions which take place in

---

26. Dubin and Graetz, "Through a Different Lens," 33.
27. Ibid., 35–36.

casual settings. There is a clear purpose for interacting with others as they worship together or work towards a common goal.[28]

However, other authors are not convinced that people with autism are able to function within religious settings, in general, especially in congregational life. In addition, there is the obvious fact that those with Asperger's syndrome are on the high end of the autism spectrum, which raises the question of whether the traditional aspects of Christian worship—participation in congregational life and personal acts of piety such as prayer—are both possible and meaningful. Much of the research on autism and Christianity focuses on the latter issue. For example, Paul Dearey raises the question: "Do the Autistic Have a Prayer?,"[29] while James Gordon asks, "Is a Sense of Self Essential to Spirituality?"[30] These articles find the issue of self-awareness problematic. Evidence shows that many on the autism spectrum cannot differentiate between the self and any other personal entity—whether between the self and another person or between the self and a personal God.

While much emphasis continues to be placed on the spirituality of persons with autism (especially those with Asperger's), there has been relatively little attention paid to how persons along the autism spectrum have been treated by the church. However, the end of a two-issue collection of articles on autism in the *Journal of Religion, Disability & Health* features the "Faith and Autism Resource Collection," which was compiled by the Elizabeth M. Boggs Center.[31] This collection lists several items under different categories, including "first person inspirational stories about individual families, congregations and organizations," "practical resources" on religious education and congregational inclusion, resource contacts, and books covering a wide range of topics related to autism and religious involvement. At the time of this writing, there hasn't been a comprehensive analysis of what is currently being done by denominational agencies with respect to autism. Perhaps the resource *Autism and Your Church: Nurturing the Spiritual Growth of People with Autism Spectrum Disorders* from Friendship Ministries serves as a model for developing more denominational or congregational responses to autism.

---

28. Ibid., 36.
29. Dearey, "Do the Autistic Have a Prayer?," 40–50.
30. Gordon, "Is a Sense of Self Essential to Spirituality?," 51–63.
31. Elizabeth M. Boggs Center, "Faith and Autism Resource Collection," 154–62.

L'Arche Ministries and Severe Disabilities

L'Arche (French for "the Arc") is a worldwide movement of communities designed primarily as places where people with severe intellectual and physical disabilities receive care and nurture through interaction with a caregiver. L'Arche was founded by Jean Vanier, a lay Roman Catholic theologian who had visited an institution for the severely disabled where a friend, Father Thomas Philippi, was chaplain. In 1964, they decided to bring two young men into their home where they formed a community of mutual support and caring. This action developed into a network of homes around the globe, including in the United States and Canada. Today there are 136 L'Arche communities in thirty-six countries. In the United States, there are sixteen communities."[32]

A community is usually a group of three to five homes, each with five to nine members.[33] Disabled residents of L'Arche are referred to as "core members": they live in community with their caregivers who are referred to as "assistants."[34] Vanier looks at the L'Arche communities as places where people come to serve and end up being served by the very people they come to help. At the time of the first L'Arche house, Vanier "was searching—not quite knowing what [he] was searching for."[35] His work with the two men and Philippi convinced him that he had learned as much about himself as about those he was serving. His description of his work and the numerous writings he has produced over the last forty-plus years seem to hover around a few streams of thought. The people with disabilities who came to live in the homes (i.e., the core members) were viewed as having deep needs, including lack of self-esteem, wounded hearts from a lifetime of rejection, and psychological and physical difficulties. They exhibited self-destructive behaviors and feared growth. Given that many of the core members are nonverbal and often severely disabled, physically as well as developmentally, that Vanier could know that the core members feared growth is difficult to understand. Nevertheless, Vanier argues that when Eric (a young man who was blind, deaf, and unable to walk) was welcomed into one of the homes in Trosly, France, after spending several years in an institution, assistants were able to bring about change by bathing him in warm water each morning.

---

32. L'Arche USA Fact Sheet.
33. McDonald and Keys, "L'Arche," 3–28.
34. Reinders, "Human Vulnerability," 5–18.
35. Venier, "What Have People with Learning Disabilities Taught Me?" 19.

Over the ensuing months, Eric became more relaxed and the assistants became able to interpret his body language.[36]

Materials from various writers and from Venier himself make readily apparent that the L'Arche movement says much about both the core members and their assistants. Venier sets the tone for drawing the following conclusions. He argues that "each person, whatever his or her abilities or disabilities, needs to be nurtured in love," and that "the desire to be loved as a person, as someone unique, is at the source of the person's development and at the source of all self-esteem."[37] Second, "the fear in couples of giving birth to a child with a disability is imprinted in the culture of every society." People with disabilities are viewed as "subhuman, and they are rejected—or put aside in some way." "Throughout the world, hundreds and hundreds of institutions exist where people with learning disabilities live in subhuman conditions."[38] Third, "the values many modern societies hold are independence, individualism, and success for every citizen." "In richer societies," he argues, "the weak are seen as an economic and human liability. And so people with learning disabilities are pushed to the margins of society."[39] Finally, he argues:

> Many people with learning disabilities need help from professionals in order to overcome physical and psychological difficulties, to grow to greater autonomy and to develop their capacities in various fields. But, above all, they are yearning for meaningful, authentic, respectful, and committed relationships. Their cry for love also flows from their deep loneliness and their lack of self-esteem. They have called me to listen and to respond to their cry with competence, to welcome their vulnerability with tenderness, and then to be in communion with them.[40]

This detailed perspective in Venier's own words enables the raising of crucial questions with regard to how people with severe developmental disabilities should be considered by the church. How is it that Venier or the numerous homes and assistants associated with L'Arche know that their nonverbal, intellectually disabled core members have the kind of interactions that nonintellectually disabled assume? What seems to occur in these settings is the imputing of certain thoughts and feelings that assistants have but that core members can rarely articulate. These issues have been raised in

36. Ibid., 21–22.
37. Ibid., 20.
38. Ibid., 20–21.
39. Ibid., 21.
40. Ibid.

a review of Michael Hyrniuk's book *Theology, Disability, and Spiritual Transformation: Learning from the Communities of L'Arche* by Kevin S. Reimer.[41] Remer asks in relation to L'Arch's core members: "Whose spirituality are we talking about? Which transformation is operative?" These questions point to the fact that numerous accounts of the interaction between core members and assistants derive from the latter's reports since many core members are nonverbal. Reimer's more extensive treatment of this topic from a seminar in Trosly puts these questions in a more positive light through a challenge to Kohlberg's rationally conceived moral socialization. Any moral development as the result of encounters between assistants and core members would depend upon "action and experience" rather than on intellectual ascent:

> Core members offer moral instruction that is deeply embedded in action and experience, much of which eschews deliberative reasoning or calculation. Core members may love others deeply, demonstrate great patience, or regularly extend forgiveness. Yet, when they are called upon to answer the question as to why this is true, they often struggle to provide rational explanation. The challenge is to consider caregiver experience of moral transformation influenced by unexpected sources (e.g., core members) and directed toward earthy outcomes in character.[42]

Such moral transformations may in fact cause a reconsideration of the basis of theological reflection as we move away from a rational approach to thinking about disability. The L'Arche approach to ministering among people with developmental disabilities offers a critical reflection on how care is normally provided. In most cases, people with severe developmental disabilities are not given the same level of attention that is afforded core residents at L'Arche. Direct care attendants at residential facilities operated under government auspices do not receive the pay equal to the importance of their tasks and often are not expected to provide services to residents beyond the basic necessities. This is also the case even among church-sponsored facilities. Part of the difference may be the adherence to the medical model of disability, which often places people with disabilities in certain and often rigid categories and subsequently refers to a set of treatment protocols that conform to medical judgments.

Nevertheless, the L'Arche movement certainly raises questions regarding the normal way people with severe disabilities are viewed and treated. Vanier's approach to ministry flies in the face of individual power and

---

41. Reimer, "Review of *Theology, Disability, and Spiritual Transformation*," 332–33.
42. Reimer, "Moral Transformation in L'Arche," 64–65.

autonomy so prevalent in society. The notion of friendship is referred to often in discussions about L'Arche, and with the realization that people with disabilities are often located at the bottom of social hierarchies.

Also, the L'Arche is "Roman Catholic in root and ecumenical in modern form."[43] The communities it has formed and sponsored have a certain life-style and rhythm clearly reminiscent of monastic life including sharing of meals, celebration of the Eucharist and shared decision making. While the mission statement of L'Arche USA does not refer to its Roman Catholic roots, and refers to the fact that communities have been formed "in many cultures and religious traditions throughout the world," still L'Arche has close ties to the Church. In 1997, Pope John Paul II granted Venier the International Paul VI Award and recognized the L'Arche the "seed of the civilization of love." Vanier and L'Arche have been recognized by the Roman Catholic Church in the United States as well as abroad.[44]

---

43. L'Arche USA Fact Sheet.
44. McDonald and Keys, "L'Arche," 7.

7

Ministry among People with Mental Illness and Dementia

Mental illness and dementia (considered separately in this chapter) are important topics in a society, with an aging population, that has emphasized better mental health care. Every pastor, lay leader, and seminary student needs some skill in dealing with mental health issues as they relate to the ministry of the church. This chapter provides a preliminary frame for asking what are the right questions, and suitable paths for the church to respond effectively and to use its resources both theologically and practically.

Mental Illness

According to the National Alliance on Mental Illness (NAMI), during any given year, approximately 61.5 million Americans experience some form of mental illness, and 13.6 million suffer from a severe mental illness. Approximately one in five youths ages thirteen to eighteen experience a severe mental illness in a given year; for young people ages eight to thirteen the estimate is 13 percent of the U.S. population. NAMI also reports that approximately 1.1 percent of American adults—about 2.4 million people—live with schizophrenia; approximately 2.4 percent of American adults—4.1 million people—live with bipolar disorder; approximately 6.7 percent of American adults—about 14.8 million people—live with major depression; and approximately 18.1 percent of American adults—about 42 million people—live with anxiety disorders."[1]

From a closer point of view, these statistics refer to mental illness as a condition (or as conditions) that impacts "a person's thinking, feeling or

1. National Alliance on Mental Illness (NAMI), "Mental Illness Facts and Numbers."

mood and may affect his or her ability to relate to others and function on a daily basis."[2] Serious Mental Illness or SMI refers to "a mental, behavioral, or emotional" illness that is "diagnosable currently or within the past year," is "of sufficient duration to meet diagnostic criteria specified within the 4th edition of the *Diagnostic and Statistical Manual of Mental Disorders* (DSM-IV)," and results in serious functional impairment, that substantially interferes with or limits one or more major life activities.[3]

However, mental illness is a highly social phenomenon. People who are labeled as having a mental health problem endure not only the illness itself but its social ramifications. People with mental illness face a "daily struggle . . . to carve out an accepted space within a society that is often fundamentally opposed to their presence."[4] Persons with mental health problems have psychological difficulties that are frequently "destructive, incapacitating, and soul-destroying."[5] Just as other disabilities do, so too mental illness and dementia raise serious challenges to society's "taken-for-granted" notions of what it means to be human. As a result people with mental illness or dementia are often marginalized. Just as other disabilities do, so too mental illness and dementia raise serious challenges to society's "taken-for-granted" notions of what it means to be human. As a result people with mental illness or dementia are often marginalized. They are impoverished, and not only economically—for as John Swinton points out, poverty "has to do with personhood, fulfillment, and enabling individuals truly to reflect the image of God as free beings, able to love, to make choices, and to develop to their potential."[6]

In the broader social arena there still exists widespread ignorance and fear that continues to play a major role in perpetuating the stigma associated with having mental illness, even in the face of increasing knowledge of the brain's role as a causal factor. Such an atmosphere makes it difficult to advocate for proper treatment services, insurance coverage, and provision of housing and employment. Media portrayals of people with mental illness are often "stereotypical, negative or flat-out wrong—meaning many people gain an unfavorable or inaccurate view of those with psychological disorders simply by skimming a few sentences or picking up a remote control."[7]

---

2. NAMI, "Mental Health Conditions."
3. NAMI, "Serious Mental Illness."
4. Swinton, *Resurrecting the Person*, 9.
5. Ibid., 10.
6. Ibid., 18.
7. Fawcett, "How Mental Illness Is Misrepresented in the Media."

For many years people with severe mental illnesses were cared for in private or public institutions. Sometimes mental health patients were institutionalized for many years with no set time for release, but since deinstitutionalization emphasis has been placed on community care with institutionalization being the last resort, and usually for only brief periods of time. Community services can range from medical care to counseling, job training and placement to group homes and other residential alternatives. However, the "community" in community care is called into question, not only with respect to the existence or nonexistence of services, but in terms of the notion of community. Patients may be discharged into settings where no real sense of community exists. In such instances, community care services may offer no more life enhancement than the institutions provided.[8] People living with mental illness still become alienated and marginalized by society's labeling and fear. Stigma is associated with having a mental illness, and oftentimes family members and friends of the mentally ill are stigmatized as well. The stigma around mental illness affects whether adequate coverage is available for mental health treatment. Stigma also breeds fear and mistrust of those identified as mentally ill, and the stigma of mental illness may pressure family members or friends to turn their backs on their relatives or friends with mental illness. Finally, stigma around mental illness results in outright prejudice and discrimination against those living with mental illness.[9]

In some communities programs have emerged run entirely by mental health consumers for their peers. Underlying these programs is the idea that "rehabilitation is not enough," and that the needs of people with mental illness are not being addressed. Reasons for drawing this conclusion include the following: (1) the need exists to address "a broad range of life crises, medical conditions, and disabilities"; (2) the struggle exists for the mentally ill to "re-enter community life after deinstitutionalization," and to participate in "psychosocial rehabilitation programs to address the need for life-skill training and socialization"; and the possibility for those living with mental illness to explore "mental patients' rights movements," antipsychiatry and "consumer/survivor alternatives to traditional mental health treatments."[10]

These programs offer a combination of "emancipatory" and caring functions. Emancipatory functions, Campbell notes, are "now called empowerment, the struggle for rights and advocacy services at the individual, interpersonal, organizational, and societal level of society." Caring functions

8. Swinton, *Resurrecting the Person*, 58–59.
9. NAMI, "Facts about Stigma and Mental Illness in Diverse Communities."
10. Clay, "About Us," 5.

turn "away from the psychiatric systems and mutual support groups" to emphasize "personal contact, communication, and concern."[11] These programs are based on a number of assumptions, including (1)" Peer support programs cultivate an atmosphere that is entirely different from that of professionally provided services"; (2) the problems facing mental health consumers/survivors are often purely practical ones—where to live, how to get a job, or how to obtain welfare; and (3) the diagnosis of mental illness permeates all aspects of a mental health consumer's life and so constricts material, and emotional resources that give people meaning in life and allow them to act as historical subjects of their own lives.[12]

Where Is the Church?

The question is, where is the church positioned with respect to people with mental illness? A recent survey conducted Matthew S. Stanford of Baylor University indicates that Christian congregations are not consistently hospitable to people with mental illness.[13] The study involved 293 participants ("mentally ill Christians") who were asked what they encountered when they sought counsel from the church. The results indicated that "while a majority of the mentally ill participants were accepted by the church, approximately 30% reported a negative interaction." Negative interactions that were reported (via an anonymous online survey) included "abandonment by the church, equating mental illness with the work of demons, and suggesting that the mental disorder was the result of personal sin." The study also found that "women were significantly more likely than men to have their mental illness dismissed by the church and to be told not to take psychiatric medications."[14]

On the other hand, church practices can be helpful if resources such as *The Gentle Bible* can be used.[15] Chaplain Craig Rennebohm and colleagues offer biblical passages that provide people "wounded" by mental illness comfort, love and forgiveness. Another possibility, especially among Roman Catholics, is to modify liturgies used in worship services. Such liturgies acknowledge that not all people have the same experiences with the

---

11. Campbell, "Historical and Philosophical Development of Peer-Run Support Programs," 19.

12. Ibid., 20–24.

13. Stanford, "Demon or Disorder."

14. Ibid.

15. *The Gentle Bible* was originally accessed at www.mentalhealthchaplain.org/. It appears to be no longer available.

Bible, prayers, and other aspects of faith. In fact, even the experiences of those who previously lived in institutions are not same as those who have experienced their illness entirely in the community.[16]

Of interest here is that NAMI has recognized the work of Pathways to Promise and other ministries as playing an important role in persuading the church to effectively respond to people with mental illness. NAMI cites numerous resources produced by such ministries as helping to train clergy, pastoral care staff, and interested laity about mental illness and its impact on the whole family. NAMI's *FaithNet* provides slide presentations, scripts and tools in support of congregational ministries to persons and families who have been impacted by mental illness.[17]

In some denominations, the presence of mental illness has provoked reflection on the relation of mental illness and Christian faith. The National Catholic Partnership on Disability (NCPD) has issued a paper called "The Word of God Affirms the Dignity of all People," which affirms that "interpretation of Scripture should be consistent with the current understanding of mental illness.[18] This conviction is based upon the realization that "for many Catholics experiencing mental illness and their families, the church can be both a place of welcome [and] alienation. Just as society has struggled with how to deal with those with mental illness, U.S. parishes and dioceses have found the area equally challenging." Oftentimes the way the Catholic faith is presented can result in guilt, anxiety, and fear. One Catholic psychologist noted, "It was a sin if you thought of anything negative. You got the wrath of the church, and that produced a lot of guilt, especially with people who were a little fragile emotionally."[19]

Also of significance is that mental illness has received the increased attention of the church, although not to the same degree as physical disability. NAMI took the initiative by recognizing that faith communities can be places where awareness, welcome, inclusion, support and spiritual care are available for individuals and families facing mental illness.[20] The Catholic Church subsequently established the Council on Mental Illness through the NCPD. Janice Benton, its director, notes that they had "always advocated for all people with disabilities, but we hadn't done enough for people with

---

16. Dell, "Healing."
17. NAMI, *FaithNet*.
18. National Catholic Partnership on Disability (NCPD), "Mission Statement."
19. Ibid.
20. NAMI, "Facts on Stigma."

mental illness." It was her desire to "have an informal network of people around the country who are doing outreach to people with mental illness."[21]

Other mainline denominations have also developed extensive statements on mental illness that contain not only policies in the traditional form of a resolutions but also tools for congregational study and guidelines for congregational ministries for and with persons with serious mental illness. In 2008, the Presbyterian Church (U.S.A.) issued *Comfort My People: A Policy Statement on Serious Mental Illness with Study Guide*.[22] Its eighty-four pages contain a policy statement, numerous stories of people with mental illness, an appendix with listings of Presbyterian and other resources on mental illness ministry, and an outline of a four-session study for use in local church settings. Throughout the document, emphasis is placed on the mentally ill as marginalized, giving a biblical context through the use of the term "exile." Also emphasized is the need for hospitality, education and support from the congregation and suggestions of possible ways to overcome the common experiences of exile and exclusion. Curiously, the policy makes a distinction between "mental illness" and "serious mental illness." The former is defined with the definition provided at the beginning of this chapter whereas the latter is defined based on the various forms of mental illness; the definition stresses the long-term nature of serious mental illness.[23]

The Evangelical Lutheran Church in America (ELCA) has also developed an extensive statement concerning mental illness in a format that is designed to be used as a study guide. The document, "A Social Message on the Body of Christ and Mental Illness," was adopted by the denomination in November 2011.[24] Its opening paragraph acknowledges that people who live with mental illness "seek solace in Scripture, they often turn to the Psalms. The anguish and isolation expressed in such scriptures are all too familiar to anyone who has experienced depression, anxiety disorders, bipolar disorder, or cared for someone with mental illness." But the document also recognizes the terror and anguish described in the gospels, when, for instance, Jesus encounters the Gerasene demoniac, or when Jesus experiences his own anguish in the garden of Gethsemane.[25]

The statement acknowledges the impact of mental illness on society as well as in the ELCA. A study by the denomination found "16 percent of

---

21. Executive director of the National Catholic Partnership on Disability Janice Benton is quoted in Weaver, "Through a Glass Darkly."
22. Presbyterian Church (U.S.A.), *Comfort My People*.
23. Ibid.
24. Evangelical Lutheran Church in America (ELCA), "A Social Message."
25. Ibid., 1.

male clergy and 24 percent of female clergy to be suffering from depression." It also recognized that

> The need for understanding and treatment of mental illness is a crisis affecting the entire Nation. For example, 10 years of extended overseas military campaigns have resulted in a large population of combat victims who are experiencing mental health issues and are prone to suicide. At the same time, the veterans' health system is widely deemed inadequate to address the massive mental health needs among our troops.[26]

The pages of the ELCA statement are filled with numerous references to mental illness as a problem for the individual, for the church, and for society. The document also points to the importance of considering mental health treatment in timely discussions about public health provision, health insurance, and health care costs.[27]

However, under the heading, "Hope for the Message," "the social message hopes to proclaim the gospel's powerful news and offer up the body of Christ as a sign of healing and hope." It also intends to "raise awareness in the church that mental illness, which is so often hidden away, is present in congregations and communities, and is a major public health issue." The message is "a call for ELCA members to acknowledge those living with mental illness and for the church to claim the responsibility it has as the body of Christ." From its point of view, "the body of Christ is incomplete if people experiencing mental illness are not integrated as a visible part of the whole."[28]

This message also recognizes that the church has played a significant role in perpetuating the stigma surrounding mental illness. However, in "confessing" its negative role it also affirms the church's role in overcoming the alienation that mental illness entails. It specifically addresses "the question of sin" as the cause of mental illness, choosing to reemphasize the biological basis of mental illness while shifting the church's focus to promoting health and maintaining interaction with those with mental illness. In affirming "the call to companionship," the ElCA "Social Message on the Body of Christ and Mental Illness" asserts that "no one can weather mental illness alone, whether that be the person diagnosed, the family member, or the practitioner. The church is called to challenge outdated views of mental illness and to foster loving practices within our communities.[29]

26. Ibid., 2.
27. Ibid.
28. Ibid.
29. Ibid.

Evangelical Responses to Mental Illness

When it comes to work on mental illness from an evangelical point of view there are a variety of responses, including those from groups who do not normally respond formally to any disability issues, let alone to mental illness. In June 2013, leaders from the Southern Baptist Convention were forced to deal with the suicide of Matthew Warren, the son of Pastor Rick Warren of Saddleback Church in Lake Forest, California. Also, the suicide of Melissa Page, daughter of Pastor Frank Page, president of Southern Baptist Convention's Executive Committee, presented a major challenge. Page has written a book titled *Melissa: A Father's Lesson from a Daughter's Suicide*, which addresses openly the issues of mental illness.[30]

After these experiences the Southern Baptist Convention (SBC) approved the resolution called "Mental Health Concerns and the Heart of God."[31] Working from the premise that mental illness arises from the fall of Adam and Eve, the statement affirms that "humanity is subjected to many kinds of mental health problems including autism spectrum disorders; intellectual disability; mental health conditions like schizophrenia, clinical depression, anxiety disorders, bipolar disorders, and eating disorders; and diseases of the aged such as dementia and Alzheimer's disease." It also recognizes struggle, isolation, stigma, and rejection often associated with mental illness. Suicide is acknowledged as "a tragedy, leaving heartache, pain, and unanswered questions in its wake." In keeping with its evangelical stance, the Southern Baptist Convention supports "research and treatment of mental health concerns when undertaken in a manner consistent with a biblical worldview," but affirms that "families who have lost a member to suicide deserve great care, concern and compassion from Christians and their churches, including the assurance that those in Christ cannot be separated from the eternal love of God that is in Christ Jesus."[32]

While this is a giant step for a denomination that previously had no emphasis on mental health (or on any disability-related issues for that matter), it remains to be determined the extent to which this statement will impact local SBC churches. Even as the resolution addresses issues surrounding suicide and mental illness (including the attitudes of the people in the pews), its including autism spectrum disorders, intellectual disabilities and Alzheimer's disease under the mental health umbrella will likely create confusion, as these conditions are normally considered separate from

---

30. Page, *Melissa*.
31. Southern Baptist Convention, "Mental Health Concerns and the Heart of God."
32. Ibid.

mental health problems (although some people with these disabilities do have mental health problems).[33]

Another evangelical voice expressing concern is that of Amy Simpson, whose articles on mental illness have appeared in *Christianity Today* and in book form as *Troubled Minds: Mental Illness and the Church's Mission*.[34] Simpson's entrée into the sphere of mental illness and mental illness ministry is through her mother's mental illness and subsequent suffering and numerous contacts with others who have dealt with mental illness in various ways. Also included in her book are results from a survey of five hundred churches conducted in partnership with *Leadership Journal*; the survey found, among other things, that an overwhelming majority (98.4 percent!) of churches had people in their congregation with some form of mental illness.[35]

Simpson spends about half the book exploring various facts about mental illness, including its pervasiveness, its impact on the family and the suffering connected to both the disease itself and to society's response, including the church. At one point Simpson describes the "persistent stigma" associated with mental illness, and the lengths to which family members go to hide the fact that someone in the family is mental ill. Simpson discusses how her mother left the church to embrace the occult only to return to Christ after her mental illness was under control. Emphasis is placed on the need for patience, allowing the person to find their way back and on the need for church to be supportive during the long trajectories of disease onset, treatment, and recovery. Such supports include not only pastoral care and counseling, but support groups and supportive relationships, the latter involving relationships requiring little or no formal training.[36]

Toward the end of the book, Simpson provides a list of what congregations can do in response to mental illness. She suggests a return to embracing "the least of these," which represent the "very people Jesus said represent him as objects of our ministry." She calls the church to "draw itself out of the shadow of the world around us and dare to treat people affected by mental illness with the same compassion and generosity that Jesus showed the lepers and other outcasts he encountered in his time on earth." Most clearly, she calls the church and Christians to be open, accepting, and a "lighthouse in the darkness." She desires "that the church will be synonymous with hope in the minds of people who can find hope nowhere else." She advocates for

---

33. Ibid.
34. Simpson, *Mental Illness and the Church's Mission*.
35. Shelley, foreword, 10.
36. Simpson, *Troubled Minds*, 197–98.

the church to witness against a "self-centered, self-sufficient, self-promoting society of the rugged individualist."[37]

However, John Swinton goes further to suggest "friendship" as the primary mode through which the church, at the congregational level, reaches out to people with a history of mental illness. He argues that "Christian friendships based on the friendships of Jesus can be a powerful force for the reclamation of the centrality of the *person* in the process of mental health care." The priority for these friendships is on the person rather than the illness. Such friendships aim at "resurrection" of the person's humanity from the often dehumanizing process that occurs when psychological diagnoses, drug therapy, and various systems of care rob the affected person of normal social functioning.[38]

In the chapter titled "Creating a Context for Care," Swinton[39] outlines a program whereby laity from congregations "befriend" of people with mental illness. A community chaplain becomes the facilitator of these one-on-one relationships. He/she enlists the congregation and provides an overview of the mental health system and the need for volunteers, facilitates one-on-one relationships; the chaplain also troubleshoots and evaluates the program. Community mental health chaplain programs are found scattered throughout the United States, although I am not aware of any study that documents their number and how they operate. There is a program in the Seattle area headed by the Reverend Craig Rennebohm that has been established for some years and has served as a model and base for other programs across Washington and in other states. However, such programs would hinge on trained chaplains and the necessary funding.[40]

Mental health ministry as such has received some attention from empirical researchers. Stetz et al. studied eleven congregations in the Pacific Northwest that were involved in mental health ministries, including through fellowship groups, prayer and Bible study groups, support groups and transitional housing. In addition, some of these congregations were involved in providing lay counseling along with overnight housing. The researchers found that even among these congregations the stigma of mental illness was prevalent. The existence of these programs of ministry to people with mental illness is encouraging, especially in light of earlier findings indicating dismissal of its symptoms altogether.[41]

37. Ibid.
38. Swinton, *Resurrecting the Person*, 36–37 (italics original).
39. Ibid., 164–92.
40. United Church of Christ, "Mental Health Chaplain" (2014).
41. Stetz et al., "Mental Health Ministry."

A new partnership between the Interfaith Disability Advocacy Coalition (IDAC) of the American Association of People with Disabilities (AAPD) and the American Psychiatric Association has emerged. (The AAPD replaced the Religion and Disability Program of the National Organization on Disability.) Together they have produced a Mental Health and Faith Community Partnership, which seeks to "reduce stigma and provide help and healing"—the first manifestation of which is a full issue of the *Christian Citizen* titled "Communities of Care: The Church & Mental Illness."[42] Its contents range from editorials to descriptions about how congregations can respond to mental illness, to personal stories of pastors and lay members who have responded to their own diagnoses, and issues of biblical interpretation and theological reflection. At the time of this writing it is unclear as to whether this format will be used by other church publications. (The *Christian Citizen* is a publication of the American Baptist Home Mission Societies.) In addition, it is unknown whether such a publication will impact the local church in terms of its active response to people with mental illness within its membership or within the communities served by these congregations. If tradition holds, other denominations will use these articles in their own publications.[43]

Will the church, especially at the congregational level, come to realize the importance of mental health care and the need to befriend people with various mental illnesses? American Christianity does not have a good track record when it comes to effective responses to people with mental illness. Nevertheless, the church has provided care for those in need. Now, it seems that the real project is to address the stigma that Christians have toward people with mental disabilities.[44] Time will tell, and there will be a need to evaluate the programs reviewed above, and in the near future.

Dementia

Dementia refers to a broad range of symptoms associated with "a decline in memory or other thinking skills severe enough to reduce a person's ability to perform everyday activities."[45] While Alzheimer's is commonly assumed to be identical with dementia, in fact there are a number of conditions falling under its umbrella including corticobasal degeneration and frontotemporal

---

42. Ramsey-Lucas, ed., "Communities of Care."
43. Ibid.
44. Vacek, *Madness*.
45. Alzheimer's Association, "Dementia."

disorders.[46] The number of persons with dementia in the United States is in the millions and grows each year. According to the Alzheimer's Association, "An estimated 5.3 million Americans of all ages had Alzheimer's disease in 2015." They also report that: "One in nine people age 65 and older (11 percent) has Alzheimer's disease," while "Eighty-one percent of people who have Alzheimer's disease are age 75 or older.[47]

Persons familiar with dementia normally associate these conditions with memory loss, difficulty in knowing love ones, disorientation with respect to surroundings, lack of self-care, and overall decline in the ability to reason and make judgments. However, such assumptions are often based on medical definitions, which tend to emphasize a straight-line decline toward dependency and death. Some people with dementia, including Alzheimer's, may experience loss of memory early on and then very little loss of memory thereafter. Some may need a great amount of assistance in managing their dementia and the problems of living while some may need a moderate amount of support, and still others may need very little help. The point is that even medically there may not be cause for drastic changes once a firm diagnosis of dementia is made.[48]

The important point, as far as ministry is concerned, is that a person with dementia is still a person. Depending on any number of neurological and nonneurological (i.e., social) factors, different people respond differently to dementia. Dementia does not destroy the person as behaviors such as "aggression, depression, withdrawal, and anxiety and deterioration in emotional control, social behavior, or motivation may not be in fact be caused by failing neurological processes alone." The diagnosis entails the neurological condition as well as how the society, the family, and the individual respond to the presence of the neurological condition. This refers to the neurological condition as well as how the society, the family, and the individual respond to the diagnosis. According to Swinton, dementia provokes others to respond in particular ways, and these responses adhere to the diagnosis itself. The diagnosis and the social accretions shape the way the patient and those around the patient make sense of the new reality.[49]

Anthropologist Athena McLean studied two separate Alzheimer's units of a nursing home located in the eastern United States. One unit presumed that its residents were on a downward slope to total dysfunction

---

46. National Institute of Neurological Disorders and Stroke, "Dementia: Hope through Research."

47. Alzheimer's Association, *2015 Alzheimer's Disease* (2016).

48 Swinton, *Dementia*.

49. Ibid., 108.

and eventual death. Behavioral disturbances such as yelling out in middle of night, stripping naked in front of others, or throwing food were considered symptoms of the disease to be dealt with by medication, restraints, and other forms of discipline. Patients were fed, bathed, and dressed on a strict schedule based upon the nursing staff's need to accomplish a set of tasks during a particular time.[50]

By contrast, the other unit was more interested in observing patients' behavioral functioning and then finding ways to resolve behavioral disturbances. The patients were treated as persons whose needs were identified and responded to with great flexibility. Patients were allowed to get out of bed when they were ready; breakfast food could always be reheated. Attention was given to each patient's comfort in taking a bath or getting dressed. Nursing assistants were expected to pay attention to their patients and not force them to adhere to a schedule mandated by the management. As a result, patients were more content, easier to work with, and less likely to act out.[51]

This of course raises questions about care and caregiving. "In 2014, Americans provided nearly 18 billion hours of unpaid care to people with Alzheimer's disease or other dementias." Persons affected by dementia, more often than not, relinquish their independence to a caregiver who is usually a spouse, child, or relative. Also, approximately two-thirds of all caregivers are women, 35 percent being over the age of sixty-five. Many work at paying jobs in addition to their caregiving, and many earn less than fifty thousand dollars per year. Often caregivers have their own families to care for, many with small children.[52]

Caregiving within the home raises questions for theologian M. J. Iozzio, who constructs an interdependent/Trinitarian model of existence that centers on her "mom's faithful care of dad" with Alzheimer's disease (AD). Her basic argument is that in care of her dad, her mother performed numerous tasks (including taking charge of her husband's bathing and dressing, and of other actions that her husband would normally have taken himself) and developed virtues such as "flexibility, stamina, humor, fidelity, and self-care" that enriched her caregiving.[53] With the knowledge gained from her observations, Iozzio offers a critique of the U.S. health care system, which "inadequately finds justice for persons marginalized either by

---

50. McLean, *The Person in Dementia*, 201–5.
51. Ibid.
52. Ibid.
53. Iozzzio, "The Writing on the Wall," 49.

their unwelcome dementia or isolating care-giving."[54] All of this is based on analogy to the Trinity in which its three separate persons (God, Son, and Holy Spirit) is interdependently related so that no one person stands alone. Likewise, humans are made to be interdependent so that in the case of Iozzo's dad (and, for that matter, in the case of anyone with a disability) responsibility for caring is shared, even if the person with disability cannot respond by normal means. The caregiver is a "moral agent" who emphasizes the importance of the spouse, children, and other relations and deemphasizes care of people who do not know the person. In Iozzio's view, "The daily work of AD patient care locates our ethics in being with and doing for the other in need—those qualitatively important interactions between persons."[55]

Caregiving and the treatment of people with Alzheimer's and other forms of dementia are issues for the congregation as well as the nursing home and the significant other providing home care. The question is raised, is your church dementia friendly? According to Mind and Soul:

> Disability friendly churches are churches that welcome and include people with dementia. People with dementia have difficulty remembering what has happened and working things out. They often find themselves excluded from the roles and relationships they had with other people and the local community. Churches are an important group in many local communities, and can promote the inclusion of people within the church and the local community.[56]

From this position, a number of "tips" are provided that serve as guidelines for interaction between able-bodied people and people with dementia. The tips suggest how to provide welcome, how to visit people with dementia, and how to help people with dementia move about church facilities. John Swinton argues that "the key, then, is to create places of belonging where people with dementia and those who offer care and support to them can find a place that is truly theirs and within which the full experience of dementia—its pain, its affliction, and its lament as well as its joys and its possibilities."[57] Can congregations become such places?

---

54. Ibid.
55. Ibid.
56. Mind and Soul, "10 Tips for Creating Dementia Friendly Churches."
57. Swinton, *Dementia*, 278.

8

Disability and the Christian Biblical Heritage

The Bible is a foundational document of the church, especially for Protestants, and increasingly so for Roman Catholics and Orthodox.[1] Therefore, it plays a central role in the church's efforts to interpret the Christian message to new and old adherents, in any given era and social location. However, the Bible, and the way it is interpreted, has been singled out as a major problem for people with disabilities. Its stories involving direct injury, prohibitions against priests with blemishes, care of disabled people, issues of suffering, as well as the use of blindness, deafness, and healing stories all make the Bible problematic for those who are working for inclusion of people with disabilities. As I indicated earlier, in order for the church to move beyond programmatic acceptance of people with disabilities, the major sources of faith, including the Bible, must be interrogated.

This has not been lost on those who have advocated within the church. Harold Wilke states that "Within the biblical tradition itself, not just interpretation, there is a tremendous negative response to physical disability, and we need to see this quite clearly."[2] Stewart Govig describes four terms in which disability is represented as brokenness: "crippled, marked, pitied, and avoided." He points to passages in the gospels that refer to people with "unclean spirits," and "demoniacs" as the basis for why Christians avoid people with mental illness.[3] Kathy Black takes on the healing narratives of the gospels in order to clarify their implications for how the church responds to people with disabilities, especially in what is rendered in the pulpit.[4]

---

1. Bransfield, "Bible at Core of Catholic Beliefs."
2. Wilke, *Creating the Caring Congregation*, 22.
3. Govig, *Strong at the Broken Places*, 53.
4. Black, *A Healing Homiletic*.

More recent contributions to a "theology of disability" have also cited the Bible as "problematic." Jennie Weiss Block argues "that the way the disability passages [in the Bible] are often interpreted contributes to the oppression and marginalization of people with disabilities,[5] and concludes,

> Therefore, scriptural exegesis of disability passages begins with a "hermeneutic of suspicion," asking a question not unlike the question posed by many feminist theologians when they inquire if Scripture, with its decidedly patriarchal bias, can be relevant and meaningful to women. Likewise, disability advocates must ask difficult questions such as: Do the Scriptures have an "ableist" bias that ultimately oppresses people with disabilities? Does the focus on "curing and healing" in the disability Scripture stories encourage the thinking that there is something wrong with being disabled?[6]

Among disability studies scholars, the role of the biblical tradition is blamed as the partial origin of negative or ambivalent attitudes toward persons with disabilities. For instance, Barnes, Mercer, and Shakespeare argue that "ancient Judaism regarded many impairments and diseases as signs of wrongdoing, and a justification for separating people because of their supposed uncleanness and ungodliness."[7] They specifically refer to Lev 21:16–20, which "catalogues those human impairments which precluded the possessor from participating in religious rituals—crooked nose, sores, missing limbs, leprosy and skin diseases, and crushed testicles." With regard to Christian Scriptures, they maintain that it "exhibited a similarly ambivalent response, viewing some of those with impairments as warranting healing and general support, while also interpreting impairment as punishment for sin."[8]

Avi Rose argues that "the root of the apparent alienation of individuals with disabilities by religion may lie in the ancient belief systems of the Judeo-Christian theology which views disability in a highly negative manner."[9] Rose also argues that "the views of Western religious institutions have helped to create the social construct of disability as a political state of oppression and have been instrumental in maintaining its power and pervasive nature." She groups these attitudes under four general theological views toward disability: "disability as sign of punishment or evil incarnation; disability as

---

5. Block, *Copious Hosting*, 101–2.
6. Ibid.
7. Barnes et al., *Exploring Disability*, 17.
8. Ibid.
9. Rose, "'Who Causes the Blind to See,'" 395.

challenge to divine perfection; disability as object of pity or charity; and disability as incompetence and exemption from religious practice."[10]

The Bible and Disability Studies

That certain Bible passages refer to people with disabilities in negative as well as positive ways has not been lost in the recent work of scholars engaged in biblical disability studies. In 1995, the American Academy of Religion and the Society of Biblical Literature held the first session of the "Religion and Disability Studies Consultation." The theme of the session was "People with Disabilities and Religious Constructions of Theodicy and Tragedy."[11] Nine years later, "the debut session" of the "Biblical Scholarship and Disabilities Consultation" was held with the theme "The Blind, the Deaf, and the Lame: Biblical Representations of Disability." Over the following years, this consultation has provided a venue for scholars and students to discuss and develop research on matters of disability within biblical literature.[12]

Out of these consultations, a series of articles emerged that were subsequently included in the volume *This Abled Body: Rethinking Disabilities in Biblical Studies*, edited by Hector Avalos, Sarah J. Melcher, and Jeremy Schipper.[13] The editors sketch out three identifiable approaches that scholars employ to deal with a specific disability text: (1) redemptionist, (2) rejectionist, and (3) historicist. A redemptionist approach "seeks to redeem the biblical text, despite any negative stance on disabilities, by recontextualizing for modern application" much like approaches that have sought to rescue biblical texts for other marginalized minorities and women. The rejectionist approach seeks to do the opposite by arguing that the Bible "has negative approaches to disability that should be rejected by modern society," and so this approach seeks to repudiate the text rather than to recontextualize it. Finally, historicist biblical scholars undertake examinations of disability by exploring the dynamic relationship between writers, texts and the cultures to which they belong.[14]

Regardless which approach is taken, the common goal is to challenge "normate" approaches to biblical texts. Originating in the work of Rosemarie Garland Thomson, the term "normate" "designates the social figure through which people can represent themselves as human beings." It is "the

10. Ibid., 397.
11. Avalos et al., "Introduction," 1–9.
12. Ibid., 2.
13. Ibid., 3.
14. Ibid., 4–5.

constructed identity of those who, by way of the bodily configurations and cultural capital they assume, can step into a position of authority and wield the power it grants them."[15] In terms of the biblical texts discussed in this chapter, "normate" refers to the normal way a biblical text is interpreted or what an "able-bodied white Protestant heterosexual" would preach on any given Sunday morning.[16]

In the following review of Old and New Testament texts referring to disability, I employ an outline based in part on the work of Sharon L. Snyder and David T. Mitchell, who focus on cultural representations of disability in Scripture.[17] I have also examined an outline implied by the articles from *This Abled Body* and the work of Amos Yong, whose focus is on redeeming those texts that have had the most (and often negative) impact on the treatment of people with disabilities.[18] I also include extensive excerpts from the Bible (using the New Revised Standard Version), although not every passage can be included due to lack of space.[19]

The Old Testament

Jacob's Limp

Genesis 32:23-32 tells of the origin of Jacob's limp:

> He took them and sent them across the stream, and likewise everything that he had. Jacob was left alone; and a man wrestled with him until daybreak. When the man saw that he did not prevail against Jacob, he struck him on the hip socket; and Jacob's hip was put out of joint as he wrestled with him. Then he said, "Let me go, for the day is breaking." But Jacob said, "I will not let you go, unless you bless me." So he said to him, "What is your name?" And he said, "Jacob." Then the man said, "You shall no longer be called Jacob, but Israel, for you have striven with God and with humans, and have prevailed." Then Jacob asked him, "Please tell me your name?" But he said, "Why is it that you ask me my name?" And there he blessed him. So Jacob called the place Peniel, saying: "For I have seen God face to face, and yet my life is preserved." The sun rose upon him as he passed Peniel, limping because of his hip. Therefore to this day the Israelites

---

15. Thomson, *Extraordinary Bodies*, 8.
16. Wynn, "'The Normate Hermeneutic,'" 92.
17. Snyder and Mitchell, *A History of Disability*.
18. Yong, *Theology and Down Syndrome*, x-xi.
19. Bruce and Murphy, eds., *The New Oxford Annotated Bible*.

> do not eat the thigh muscle that is on the hip socket, because he struck Jacob on the hip socket at the thigh muscle.

Jacob is given a new name and limp, as signs of not only God's blessing, "but the renewal of the patriarchal covenant with the ancestors of the nation Israel." His dream in which he wrestles with God results in permanent disability. Later generations of Israel will participate in Jacob's disability by not eating the meat of the thigh muscle.[20] Again, modern "normate" assumptions are called into question by biblical texts that treat "impairment as metaphor," especially those interpretations that affirm marginalization by assuming that disabled people are rightfully perceived as being "weird and odd misfit[s]" who are "never going to be beautiful people."[21] Instead, Jacob's disability is "neither the cause nor the result of the blessing/name." The disabling touch occurs before his request for a blessing. "The blessing," concludes Kerry Wynn, "was not a result of disability, nor was the disability a result of the blessing. It is something he took away as a lifelong reminder of what happened there—lifelong for Jacob but, for all of Israel, a sign for all time."[22] However, contrary to a common assumption about Jacob, it also suggests that he is no less a patriarch because of his disability. Jacob's disability is a sign of strength rather than weakness.[23]

Levitical Laws

A second set of passages is found in the book of Leviticus, chapters 13–14 and 21. The passage that sets the tone for the entire set of laws is found in Lev 21:17–23:

> Speak to Aaron and say: None of your offspring throughout their generations who has a blemish may approach to offer the food of his God. For no one who has a blemish shall draw near, one who is blind or lame, or one who has a mutilated face or a limb too long, or one who has a broken foot or a broken hand, or a hunchback, or a dwarf, or a man with a blemish in his eyes or an itching disease or scabs or crushed testicles. No descendant of Aaron the priest who has a blemish shall come near to offer the LORD's offerings by fire, since he has a blemish, he shall not come near to offer the food of his God. He may eat the food of his God, of the most holy as well as of the holy. But he shall not

---

20. Snyder and Mitchell, *A History of Disability*, 5:84–85.
21. Wynn, "The Normate Hermeneutic," 97.
22. Ibid., 100.
23. Yong, *Theology and Down Syndrome*, 31.

come near the curtain or approach the altar, because he has a blemish, that he may not profane my sanctuaries, for I am the Lord, I sanctify them.

Across the centuries, this passage has been used to deny people with disabilities entrance into the priesthood in the Roman Catholic Church, the Orthodox churches and many Protestant denominations.[24] Its focus is specifically related to the theme of holiness and is directed at the people of Israel in general, with parts addressed specifically to the priestly class (i.e., chapter 21). Israel's laws are intended to produce a "holy people, a holy nation, who collectively will be [a] royal priesthood, a rich treasure belonging to God."[25] These passages, along with the entire book of Leviticus, are attempting to delineate Israel as a people separate from surrounding nations. Hence, the codes are designed to reinforce this distinction, and in particular Lev 21:16–24 lists visible "physical impediments to the ministry of the office of the priesthood."[26] Their original intent was "concern for one's total wholeness and complete separation to God with purity," and while persons of the priestly class with deformities were permitted a portion of the sacrifice, "nevertheless, the standard of wholeness is vividly illustrated by excluding from priestly service persons who evidenced any of these twelve maladies."[27]

In *A History of Disability*, Henri-Jacques Stiker raises the basic question "which representation and which *social* situations of disability are offered by these texts?"[28] He notes that in the Bible, "disability is an everyday reality. But, as the text of Lev 21:16–24 reveals, it was also a sacred reality. Legal uncleanness was attached to the disabled, who could, of course, participate in cultic observances, but never as priests who made sacrifices."[29] In this instance, disability serves not only to differentiate between the sacred and the profane, but to protect the community.[30]

However, these prohibitions do not always carry into social life. Insisting "on the consistency of Jewish thought," Stiker maintains that while sin and defect deny the disabled a religious role, nevertheless an "ethical and social imperative" was introduced. The person who is suffering (e.g., Job) does so on the human level as God is "the Other," and is not to blame. Thus the Hebrew Bible "permits the double practice of religious prohibition and

24. Wilke, *Creating the Caring Congregation*, 32–33.
25. Kaiser, *The Book of Leviticus*, 1:993–97.
26. Ibid., 1:1147.
27. Ibid., 1:1149.
28. Stiker, *A History of Disability*, 23 (italics original).
29. Ibid., 24.
30. Ibid., 26–27.

ethical obligation," which carries over into "the denunciation of violence done to the unfortunate and disfigured."[31]

The Story of Mephibosheth

The story of Mephibosheth in 2 Samuel presents another case where disability studies can be applied. It is part of the Deuteronomic history (DH), dating from the seventh and sixth centuries BCE, which tells about King David's "covenant to Jonathan, Mephibosheth's father, and by promise to Saul to show loyalty to Mephibosheth, so he cannot raise a hand against Mephibosheth."[32]

> Saul's son Jonathan had a son who was crippled in his feet. He was five years old when the news about Saul and Jonathan came from Jezreel. His nurse picked him up and fled, and, in her haste to flee, it happened that he fell and became lame. His name was Mephibosheth. (2 Sam 4:4)

> David asked, "Is there still anyone left of the house of Saul to whom I may show kindness for Jonathan's sake?" Now there was a servant of the house of Saul whose name was Ziba, and he was summoned to David. The king said to him, "Are you Ziba?" And he said, "At your service!" The king said, "Is there anyone remaining of the house of Saul to whom I may show the kindness of God?" Ziba said to the king, "There remains a son of Jonathan; he is crippled in his feet." The king said to him, "Where is he?" Ziba said to the king, "He is in the house of Machir son of Ammirel, at Lo-debar," Then King David sent and brought him from the house of Machir son of Ammiel, at Lo-debar. Mephibosheth son of Jonathan son of Saul came to David, and fell on his face and did obeisance. David said, "Mephibosheth!" He answered, "I am your servant." David said to him, "Do not be afraid, for I will show you kindness for the sake of your father Jonathan: I will restore to you all the land of your grandfather Saul, and you yourself shall eat at my table always." He did obeisance and said, "What is your servant, that you should look upon a dead dog such as I am?" (2 Sam 9:1–8)

Mephibosheth's disability is not specified but was the result of a childhood accident. David's act of kindness toward him is due to control and not charity for Mephibosheth's neutral stance during Absalom's revolt and his claim

---

31. Ibid., 24.
32. Albrecht et al., eds., Snyder and Mitchell, *A History of Disability*, 5:91.

to Israel's throne. Nevertheless, Mephibosheth "has no qualms about using his disability—and poor attendant care—as an excuse for his action."[33]

On the subject of Mephibosheth an extended discussion is both possible and potentially productive. Jeremy Schipper has written a major scholarly monograph titled *Disability Studies and the Hebrew Bible: Figuring Mephibosheth in the David Story*.[34] Such an endeavor is justified, in Schipper's view, for a number of reasons. First, while scholars have recently authored a great number of articles and anthologies on Michal, the wife of David, because she is a woman who represents a "larger social group (women) which is subjugated by patriarchal ideology," there has been little attention paid to Mephibosheth. "Scholars," Schipper asserts, "do not often read Mephibosheth's story as a representation of an oppressed social group by a dominant ideology." More important, scholars "seem to locate Mephibosheth's characterization as disabled solely in the individual isolated from any larger social ideologies."[35]

This leads to the contention that Mephibosheth's story can be told using the social model of disability identified and examined within disability studies. Here Schipper offers the general thesis that

> If, like Michal, one sees Mephibosheth as a member of an oppressed social group, then the reader may understand his story as an occasion to investigate the social and political ideologies encoded in biblical representations of a particular social group. As with Michal and other "minor" female biblical characters, Mephibosheth's story provides the opportunity for a counter-reading that interrogates larger ideological currents with the David story.[36]

While acknowledging several studies that have focused on "biblical laws regarding disability, such as those restricting the cultic activities of Israelite priests with disabilities in Lev. 21:16-23," Schipper maintains that "the field still needs a close study of a figure with a disability as a sustained character trait." In addition, Schipper argues that "disability never occurs in the abstract but is always embodied in a particular person at a particular time and place." Thus," he concludes, "a study of Mephibosheth's character can draw attention to the gap between the actual experience of people with disabilities and what literary depictions of characters with a disability often suggest."[37]

33. Ibid.
34. Schipper, *Disability Studies in the Hebrew Bible*.
35. Ibid., 6.
36. Ibid., 7.
37. Ibid., 8-9.

Schipper's study proceeds in a manner subject to the norms of contemporary biblical scholarship including detailed notes and references that are often longer than his actual text! His conclusion after working through Mephibosheth's role in the DH, is that the "character and motifs that surround him have an impact on the use of kingship and Zion as metonyms for Israel."[38] Mephibosheth's character cannot be reduced to his disability in part because his role is deeply intertwined with the story of David's reign. The disability imagery surrounding his character "participates in a larger rhetorical technique that heightens the irony of David and his dynasty's changing fortunes while also embodying Israel's possibilities and limitations."[39] In conclusion, "disability research in the DH is not just an exercise in identity politics for the sake of identity politics. Rather, as seen in this study, it offers a substantive contribution to scholarly efforts to map the ideological and theological landscape in the DH." Mephibosheth's story "alters the rhetoric on kingship and national identity in the DH. His presence in the story helps to construct the characters around him. He both affirms and interrogates the logic of certain ideological positions encoded in the story.[40]

Infertility as Disability

In 2 Sam 6:23, Michal confronts her husband, David, for "uncovering himself" before his female servants as he brought the ark to Jerusalem. David's response is that Michal's infertility has led him to seek someone to honor him with a child, presumably a male child. This highlights the fact that in Israelite culture and in ancient societies in general, being infertile was a serious impediment; viewing infertility as a disability uncovers an important but often overlooked aspect of ancient Israelite religion. Even if the fact of Michal's infertility is subject to debate based on the text, the cultural context of ancient Israel affirms it, as well as a link between infertility and physical and cognitive disabilities. The disability resulting from infertility is connected to God's approval of David's reign and dynasty, which can be continued if David has an infant son.[41]

More recently, the topic of infertility has attracted scholars who approach the Bible from a disability studies perspective. Whether it is the barrenness in the Hebrew Bible, the role of "the eunuch who does not beget," or sexual disabilities in the Hebrew Bible in general, these scholars explore the

---

38. Ibid., 126.
39. Ibid., 128.
40. Ibid.
41. Baden, "The Nature of Barrenness in the Hebrew Bible," 14.

notion that in biblical times infertility constituted disability. Baden asks, "If disability is defined as a deviation from a culturally defined normative state, as a social construction rather than any objective reality, then to classify infertility as disability requires that its opposite, fertility, be understood as normal."[42] Indeed, the social stigma of barrenness was woven so deeply into Israelite society that even women who had given birth to children prayed to become fertile again! Biblical passages that focus on barrenness highlight God's power over a common human condition, a condition central to a drama in which God's will triumphs. Nevertheless barrenness is linked with blindness and lameness in that the barren, the blind, and the lame are prohibited from worshiping in the temple.[43]

We may ask, what if anything can be derived from looking at biblical instances of infertility for understanding how disability is represented? The most obvious conclusion would be the extension of the list of those who could not enter the temple to worship. The study of barrenness in a disability studies framework gives greater depth to the context in which disability passages are situated, and also gives current scholarship credit for expanding the lists of social exclusion, especially from worship in the temple and at other sites. Such studies provide more nuanced analysis of the various texts related to disability—examination that extends well beyond the simplistic analysis of biblical texts.

The Hebrew Prophets

The last two Old Testament passages are from Isaiah chapters 29 and 35:

> [Shall] the fruitful field be regarded as a forest?
> On that day the deaf shall hear
> the words of a scroll,
> and out of their gloom and darkness
> the eyes of the blind shall see.
> The meek shall obtain fresh joy in the LORD,
> and the neediest people shall exalt in the Holy One of Israel.
> For the tyrant shall be no more,
> and the scoffer shall cease to be;
> all those alert to do evil shall be cut off—
> those who cause a person to lose a lawsuit,
> who set a trap for the arbiter in the gate,
> and without grounds deny justice to the one in the right. (Isa 29:17–21)

---

42. Ibid., 11.
43. Ibid., 15.

> Then the eyes of the blind shall be opened,
> and the ears of the deaf unstopped;
> then the lame shall leap like a deer,
> and the tongue of the speechless sing for joy.
> For waters shall break forth in the wilderness,
> and streams in the desert;
> the burning sand shall become a pool,
> and the thirsty ground spring of water;
> the haunt of the jackals shall become a swamp,
> the grass shall become reeds and rushes. (Isa 35:5–7)

In both passages, the prophet employs apocalyptic imagery to describe a restoration of God's people, of Israel and its promised land. Here the deaf are promised hearing, the blind seeing, the lame leaping, and the mute singing as part of a series of radical reversals to happen in the immediate future. Metaphor in the hands of the prophets become a "tool for social commentary," but more than that metaphors communicate meaning. Metaphor clusters (including references to healing the blind, deaf, and the lame) enhance the prophetic goal of "the restoration of the divine-human relationship."[44]

However, in reference to Isa 45:9–12, Melcher identifies a text that can serve as a resource for constructing a "disability liberation ethic":[45]

> Woe to you who strive with your maker,
> Earthen vessels with the potter!
> Does the clay say to the one who fashions it, "What are you doing"?
> or "Your work has no handles"?
> Woe to anyone who says to a father, "What are you begetting?"
> or to a woman, "With what are you in labor?"
> Thus says the LORD,
> the Holy One of Israel, and its Maker:
> Will you question me about my children,
> or command me concerning the work of my hands?
> I made the earth,
> and created human kind upon it;
> It was my hands that stretched out in the heavens,
> and I command all their host.

The text, itself contains no reference to disabilities (a jar without handles) but instead affirms God's sovereignty over his creation with specific references to his hands as shaping all of human life. God's questions apply to all, including those with a physical disability. Melcher concludes that

---

44. Melcher, "With Whom the Disabled Associate?," 118.
45. Ibid., 127.

The passage suggests that all persons are created through the will of God, in ways that reflect God's sovereign choice. In addition, these verses argue that God continues to work with creation, to bring God's purpose to fruition through unexpected means. For persons with physical and cognitive impairment, the passage suggests that the divine purpose can be fulfilled through a great variety of people, from all walks of life.[46]

Recent research on Jeremiah from a disabilities perspective has also sought to show how disability imagery is employed to demonstrate Israel's plight. A "female whore" and "crippled male" are identified as indicative of the state of Israel that must end. The prophecy would seek the restoration of the "sexually monogamous woman" and the "abled-bodied male," an indication that Israel is once again seeking its god and the way of life to which the nation is called.[47] In the case of Jeremiah, "stock disability tropes—impairment of vision, hearing and mobility—appear frequently and are almost invariably attributed to male figures." Among these, hearing is of a different order in that "it provides the explanation of how the implied audience came to be in a condition of (abled) or (disabled) disobedience."[48]

Olyan pursues a more deliberate disability studies orientation by exploring generic ideas that have been suggested by various writings. He also targets Israelite religion's contribution to both the classification and stigmatization of persons with disability. These contributions include constructing beauty and ugliness, classifying certain physical disabilities as defects or not as defects, defining mental disability, laying out a prophetic utopian vision, and determining nonsomatic parallels to wholeness and defect.[49] From these studies, Olyan draws a number of conclusions about disability in the Hebrew Bible: (1) biblical representations of disability resemble those found in other west Asian materials and are used in biblical texts to "stigmatize" and "assign marginal social positions to persons with disabilities"; (2) biblical texts often imply "a hierarchy of stigmatization" in which some disabilities "are subjected to a larger number of stigmatizing strategies than are others"; (3) biblical texts offer various classifications that place disabilities in groups about which various assumptions are made: these assumptions include that disabilities carry with them character defects such as ignorance, and the ability to be manipulated or a threat to holiness; (4) disabilities can be of "divine origin" or from accidental or natural causes; and (5) that God is "an

---

46. Ibid., 127–28.
47. Raphael, "Whoring after Cripples," 104.
48. Ibid., 107.
49. Olyan, *Disability in the Hebrew Bible*, 119–21.

advocate for disabled persons, just as he is for other categories of persons represented as weak or marginal."[50]

The New Testament

If Old Testament texts communicate mixed views of disability, it is not surprising that New Testament texts do as well. For persons with disabilities living in the twenty-first century, its gospels, letters, and other materials present challenges to a theology of disability that embraces persons with disabilities and enables them to belong and serve in the Christian community. This is especially the case with respect to the healing miracles in the gospels and references to healing in the book of Acts. When today's Christians force or imply that persons with disabilities need to be healed or are possessed by demons that need to be exorcized, people with disabilities are placed in awkward position. Nancy L. Eiesland refers to this as "religious abuse," as when someone with a disability is imposed upon to attend a "healing service" or is approached by a faith healer; the religious abuse can also take less overt forms, such as when church leaders make casual allusions to someone's healing, or when preachers make careless references made to healing miracles in the Bible.[51] Yet looking at religious healing across history in general, and viewing the New Testament miracles in particular, is important for any analysis of Christianity and disability. Healing cannot be ignored. It is there in the New Testament. It is reported throughout the church's history, and it is still an issue for Christianity today.[52]

Zechariah

In the first reference is to the birth story of John the Baptist in Luke 1:5–25, Zechariah's muteness becomes a "sign" at the annunciation of John's birth. Also noteworthy is Luke 1:62 where the "vocally normative characters make the assumption that because Zechariah is mute he must also be deaf."[53]

---

50. Ibid., 123–28.
51. Eiesland, "Barriers and Bridges," 219–21.
52. Porterfield, *Healing in the History of Christianity*, ch. 1.
53. Albrecht et al., eds., Snyder and Mitchell, *A History of Disability*, 5:95.

The Centurion's Faith

Matt 8:5–17 contains the story of the centurion's faith and the suffering servant:

> When [Jesus] entered Capernaum, a centurion came to him, appealing to him and saying, "Lord, my servant is lying at home paralyzed, in terrible distress." And he said to him, "I will come and cure him." The centurion answered, "Lord, I am not worthy to have you come under my roof; but only speak the word, and my servant will be healed. For I also am a man under authority, with soldiers under me; and I say to one, 'Go,' and he goes, and to another, 'Come,' and he comes, and to my slave, 'Do this,' and the slave does it." When Jesus heard him, he was amazed and said to those who followed him, "Truly I tell you, in no one in Israel have I found such faith. I tell you, many will come from east and west and will eat with Abraham and Isaac and Jacob in the kingdom of heaven, while the heirs of the kingdom will be thrown into the outer darkness, where there will be weeping and gnashing of teeth." And to the centurion Jesus said, "Go; let it be done for you according to your faith." And the servant was healed in that hour.

Here, the man who was a leper (not quoted) and the servant with paralysis are healed by Jesus. While leprosy and paralysis are still found in our society today, they were seen and treated differently in ancient Israel. While paralysis was a physical disability, leprosy was a physical impurity that required cleansing more than healing. Thus we have impaired purity, physical disability, and physical illness addressed in such passages.[54] However, Snyder and Mitchell maintain that

> The faith of the centurion is not a condition for healing but is motivation for healing. His faith's primary function is to prefigure the inclusion of Gentiles as followers of Christ. The primary purpose of these healings as stated in Matthew 8:17 is not to exhibit Jesus' power, but to identify him as the suffering servant of God fulfilling Isaiah 53:4, who does not erase disability but takes it upon himself."[55]

---

54. Ibid., 5:96.
55. Ibid.

Demoniacs

In Matt 9:32–33, Matt 12:22–32, and Luke 11:14–15 demon possession is viewed as "the cause of muteness and deafness"; Jesus is pitted "against both demonic forces and the religious opponents who claim he works his healings by demonic power," while setting the stage for viewing the casting out of demons as indications of the kingdom of God.[56]

The story of the Gerasene demoniac, found in Mark 5:1–20, is quoted here at length:

> They came to the other side of the sea, to the country of the Gerasenes. And when he had stepped out of the boat, immediately a man out of the tombs with an unclean spirit met him. He lived among the tombs; and no one could restrain him any more, even with a chain; for he had often been restrained with shackles and chains, but the chains he wrenched apart, and the shackles he broke in pieces; and no one had the strength to subdue him. Night and day among the tombs and on the mountains he was always howling and bruising himself with stones. When he saw Jesus from a distance, he ran and bowed down before him; and he shouted at the top of his voice, "What have you to do with me, Jesus, Son of the Most High God? I adjure you by God, do not torment me." For he had said to him, "Come out of the man, you unclean spirit!" Then Jesus asked him, "What is your name?" He replied, "My name is Legion; for we are many." He begged him earnestly not to send them out of the country. Now there on the hillside a great herd of swine was feeding; and the unclean spirits begged him, "Send us into the swine; let us enter them." So he gave them permission. And the unclean spirits came out and entered the swine; and the herd, numbering about two thousand, rushed down the steep bank into the sea, and were drowned in the sea.
>
> The swineherds ran off and told it in the city and in the country. Then people came to see what it was that had happened. They came to Jesus and saw the demoniac sitting there, clothed and in his right mind, the very man who had had the legion; and they were afraid. Those who had seen what had happened to the demoniac and to the swine reported it. Then they began to beg Jesus to leave their neighborhood. As he was getting into the boat, the man who had been possessed by demons begged him that he might be with him. But Jesus refused, and said to him,

---

56. Ibid., 5:98.

"Go home to your friends, and tell them how much the Lord has done for you, and what mercy he has shown you." And he went away and began to proclaim in the Decapolis how much Jesus had done for him; and everyone was amazed.

Its description of the demoniac living among the tombs and the reported failure of his community to restrain him fits well with contemporary understandings of mental illness, where various treatment protocols (both in institutions and in the community) meet with limited success. Viewing this story from the standpoint of the social model of disability reveals the fact that society often views people living with disability (including mental illness) as "damaged goods." Just as in Mark's Gospel the demon once inside can take control "to such a degree that he was unrecognizable as a human being," those who experience severe mental illness today "often describe, too, that something descends into their bodies and takes control of them, often resulting in uncharacteristic human speech and behavior."[57] At the end of her article on this story, Toensing provides a challenge:

> The story of the Gerasene demoniac offers numerous and more richly complex possibilities for addressing the alienation surrounding severe mental illness than what, at first glance, seems possible from a simple miraculous healing story. Through narrative, readers are invited to (1) honor the enormity of the battle of mental illness; (2) create communities, strong networks of care that foster mental health; (3) tell and listen to the stories of struggle and victory with mental illness; (4) be compassionate; and (5) to find and name the numerous commonalities between people regardless of mental status.[58]

Healing Miracles

In the accounts of Jesus's healing of the man with a "shriveled" hand found in Matt 12:9–14, Mark 3:1–6, and Luke 6:6–11, Jesus is again pitted against the Pharisees in a controversy about observing the law. Jesus employs "rabbinic augmentation to justify healing on the Sabbath." And while there is some variation between these texts, they all clearly demonstrate "that the healing of the man's disability is a great enough 'good' to justify the 'work' of healing" on the day set aside for worship and reflection."[59]

---

57. Toensing, "Living among the Tombs," 136.
58. Ibid., 143.
59. Snyder and Mitchell, *A History of Disability*, 5:98.

Matt 20:29-34 relates the healing of two blind men who cry out "Lord, Son of David, have mercy on us!" This story "portrays Jesus as greater than David since, unlike David, Jesus embraces the blind and the lame, the very ones whom David barred from his house."[60]

Another significant passage is the "Invitation to a Wedding Feast" found in Luke 14:13-24. Jesus refers to "the crippled, the lame, and the blind" as being in the same situation as the poor in that the "socially acceptable elite refuse to come to the feast but the poor and those with disabilities will be invited and thus will be those who enter the Kingdom of God."[61] However, the context of this passage in light of Luke's writing shows that such a statement is designed to counter other responses to the poor and the disabled. In the Qumran community (producer of the Dead Sea Scrolls) in particular such people were "barred from entry" into the "Assembly of God" and declared "unfit to occupy a place in the midst of the congregation."[62] In addition,

> The contrast between such restrictions and the spirit of Jesus' teaching could hardly be more striking. Jesus does not merely prohibit inviting those in a position to benefit us if our reason for inviting them is to curry favor. He advises not to invite the powerful or well-to-do because they *might* return the invitation. Instead, we should invite those who have never had such a meal, who could never return the favor, who could never be our superiors.[63]

Mark 2:1-12 and its parallels in Matt 9:1-8 and Luke 5:17-26 tell the story of Jesus healing a paralytic. The story unfolds in a house in Jesus's hometown where the crowd inside had become so dense that the paralytic's friends hauled him onto the roof and lowered him down through a hole that they made in order to set him at Jesus's feet. Angered by Jesus's authority, the "teachers of the law" who were present accused him of "blaspheming" and usurping God's prerogative to forgive sins. Subsequently, Jesus not only repeats that the paralytic's sins are forgiven but orders him to pick up his mat and go home. According to Snyder and Mitchell, Mark's version of this story is not only the earliest account, but in it "a clear distinction is made between sin and disability."[64] And while the story does not tell readers why the man's

---

60. Ibid., 5:99.
61. Ibid., 5:101.
62. Culpepper, *The Gospel of Luke*, 9:287.
63. Ibid.
64. Albrecht et al., eds., Snyder and Mitchell, *A History of Disability*, 5:101.

friends brought him to Jesus, Jesus does have compassion for him, and offers forgiveness without any request on the part of the man or his friends.

Mark 10:46–52 (and also Luke 18:35–43), tells how Jesus cured Bartimaeus, whom Snyder and Mitchell characterize as "a blind beggar."[65] Interestingly, they note that Jesus "rejects the attempt to socially marginalize the person with a disability, yet does not presume that the disability is the source of the man's concern. Jesus asks what the man desires before he heals him." Both texts record the miracle as an event immediately before Jesus entered Jerusalem. Mark's version is particularly significant because after the miracle, the man follows Jesus, as opposed to the rich man in the same chapter, who would not (v. 22). Bartimaeus's spontaneous enthusiasm provides a counterpoint to the fear, silence, and hesitation of the twelve disciples.[66] In Luke's version, the healing of the blind man fulfills part of Jesus's ministry, in which the Messiah is "sent to proclaim release to the captives and recovery of sight to the blind, to let the oppressed go free."[67]

The Man Born Blind

Chapter 9 in the Gospel of John contains the well-known story of the healing of the "man born blind," which was discussed above, in chapter 5. Here, in the context of biblical disability studies, it is important to remind readers that this story combines a rejection of the linkage between the man's disability and sin and the metaphorical contrast between the former physical blindness of the healed man and the persistent spiritual blindness of the synagogue leaders. The man's experience as the marginalized 'other' frees him from the normative perspective of the visually able community.[68]

Once the healing takes place, the formerly blind man is free to become the focal point of the Pharisees' investigation of the healing, and a reluctant spokesperson for establishing Jesus's authority as God-given.[69]

Other Healing Stories

John 5:1–15 relates an account of "the healing at the pool of Bethesda" where many disabled people lie—the blind, lame, and paralyzed—for long

---

65. Ibid., 5:104.
66. Grant, "Reinterpreting the Healing Narratives," 79.
67. Ibid.
68. Albrecht et al., eds., Snyder and Mitchell, *A History of Disability*, 5:105.
69. Ibid.

periods of time, and where, occasionally, "an angel of the Lord would come down and stir up the waters." John 5:4 indicates that "the first one into the pool after each such disturbance would be cured of whatever disease they had." In this instance, Jesus asks if one of the men lying near the pool actually wants to be healed, and he responds with an excuse. However, Jesus bypasses the excuse by healing the man directly.[70]

In Matt 11:2–6 and Luke 7:18–23, a question from the imprisoned John the Baptist is asked of Jesus: "Are you the one who was to come, or should we expect someone else?" Jesus replies by directing the messengers to go back and tell John the Baptist that "the blind receive sight, the lame walk, those who have leprosy are cured, the deaf hear, the dead are raised, and the good news is preached to the poor." Here again, however, "the stress is not on Jesus' compassion on those perceived as less fortunate but on the sign of apocalyptic reversal."[71]

Another approach to the healing narratives in the gospels is to speculate on "the representation and experience of disability within the disparities of power that constituted the Roman imperial world from which the Gospel emerged." In John's Gospel disabilities "are signs and sites of the assertion and negotiation of imperial power."[72] They are more than representations that often seek to mask the disparities between the colonizer and the colonized (i.e. between Rome and Israel).[73] Disabilities in John's Gospel "are signs, at least in part, of the destructive system of power that was the empire's food supply privileging elites and depriving non-elites of access to nutritionally adequate food."[74] The context of this story involves all the ramifications of a colonized world with its violence, disease, and nutritional limitations. The paralyzed and blind in John's Gospel belong to such a context, while Jesus's healings enact "life of the age" that points to a divinely constituted world of renewed bodies, wholeness, and fertility.[75]

Healing in the Book of Acts

The book of Acts has additional references to healing miracles, this time by Jesus's apostles. Acts 3:1–10 tells the story of a "mobility-impaired" beggar who is healed by Peter and John, on their way to the temple:

70. Ibid., 107.
71. Ibid., 5:108.
72. Carter, "'The Blind, Lame and Paralyzed,'" 129.
73. Ibid., 137.
74. Ibid., 141.
75. Ibid.

> One day Peter and John were going up to the temple at the hour of prayer, at three o'clock in the afternoon. And a man lame from birth was being carried in. People would lay him daily at the gate of the temple called the Beautiful Gate so that he could ask for alms from those entering the temple. When he saw Peter and John about to go into the temple, he asked them for alms. Peter looked intently at him, as did John, and said, "Look at us." And he fixed his attention on them, expecting to receive something from them. But Peter said, "I have no silver or gold, but what I have I give you; in the name of Jesus Christ of Nazareth, stand up and walk." And he took him by the right hand and raised him up; and immediately his feet and ankles were made strong. Jumping up, he stood and began to walk, and he entered the temple with them, walking and leaping and praising God. All the people saw him walking and praising God, and they recognized him as the one who used to sit and ask for alms at the Beautiful Gate of the temple; and they were filled with wonder and amazement at what had happened to him.

In response to the beggar's attention in the hope of "expecting to get something from them," Peter offers "no silver or gold," but on his command "in the name of Jesus Christ of Nazareth, stand up and walk" (v. 6), the man jumps up and goes with them "into the temple courts, walking and jumping, and praising God" (v. 8). However, the significance of this passage is not only that Jesus's disciples have authority to heal, or that they can provide charity, but that Peter "provides for his reintegration into the community—[as] seen in his entry into the temple—by means of healing."[76]

The second set of references to healing (in Acts 8:56–58 and Acts 14:8–18), are intentionally designed to show that "the power Jesus is manifested in his follower [i.e. Phillip] as he proclaims him as Messiah or Christ." In the second passage, the power employed by Paul and Barnabas is mistaken as the power of Hermes and Zeus; this mistake "provides the opportunity to clarify that this divine power does not originate with the followers but originates with God." Also the point is made that the phrase "he had faith to be healed" in Acts 14:9 would probably be better translated "he had faith to be saved."[77]

---

76. Albrecht et al., eds., Snyder and Mitchell, *A History of Disability*, 5:108.
77. Ibid., 5:109.

Paul

While the New Testament usually tells of God's power as revealed through healing miracles, some passages manifest divine power through "blindness." In Acts 9:1–19, Saul (i.e., Paul) is blinded when he encounters Jesus on the road to Damascus. Paul is questioned because he has been actively persecuting followers of Jesus referred to as "people of the Way." In response to his encounter with Jesus, Paul is blinded and must be escorted to Damascus where a follower of Jesus, Ananias is dispatched (reluctantly because of Paul's actions against Christians) to proclaim Paul's receiving of the Holy Spirit. In Acts 22:4–16, this story is retold by Paul in an effort to vindicate his change from a persecutor to a fully credentialed advocate for the Way.[78]

There is also a passage in Acts (Acts 13:6–12) that tells of Paul's blinding of the "Jewish sorcerer and false prophet named Bar-Jesus. Its purpose appears to be another demonstration of the power of the Holy Spirit." However, as Snyder and Mitchell indicate, "while Paul tells Bar-Jesus that he will be 'blind for a while,' Paul's own blindness seems to have been a permanent disability that required the healing intervention of Ananias, who proclaimed healing and the filling of the Holy Spirit in one sentence. In this instance, it is reported that 'something like scales fell from his eyes, and his sight was restored.'"[79]

Martin Albl asks and seeks to answer a question that Snyder and Mitchell do not address: "What is Paul's own contribution to a Christian understanding of disability?"[80] He argues that examining the heart of Paul's "authentically written" epistles yields evidence of his personal experience with a disability as a factor in the shaping of his theological approach. Albl asserts that the closest term for disability in Paul's vocabulary is "weak" or "weakness," which is characteristic of all human bodies. Following this logic, Jesus is the "disabled" Christ in that he was crucified in weakness (referring to 2 Cor 13:4), "but also the glorified, powerful Christ—the Christ beyond all disabilities and limitations, including the limitation of death itself (e.g., Rom 6:9)."[81] Albl then continues: "It is the paradoxical connection between the two that is the center of Paul's message."[82] From this point of view, followers of Jesus participate in both his "disability" and "ability," so that "it is sharing in the disability of Christ, including his atoning death, that the fol-

---

78. Ibid.
79. Ibid.
80. Albl, "'For Whenever I Am Weak, Then I Am Strong.'"
81. Ibid., 146.
82. Ibid., 147.

lowers of Christ will be able, ultimately, to overcome all disability by sharing Christ's resurrection and glorification."[83]

Another account of Paul's theology examines the function of his "thorn in the flesh." Candida Moss argues that Paul "utilizes the ambiguous meaning of the 'thorn' in conjunction with ancient medical theories of the body and notions of possession." Paul also "uses the physiology of the weakened body [to] claim a direct connection to Christ and to trump the claims of his hypermasculine 'strong' opponents." His employment of these claims operates to argue that supposed weakness is in reality, strength.[84]

Conclusion

This chapter's discussion of biblical texts related to disability is an effort to understand the relationship between disability and Christianity and to present a positive response to the impact of disability studies on the part of biblical scholars. It will be interesting to see what kind of scholarly output will materialize as the field grows toward maturity. Indeed, as this book goes to press, there are indications that the study of biblical texts with respect to disability is growing deeper, as Sarah Melcher's article "Blemish and Perfection of the Body in the Priestly Literature and Deuteronomy" indicates.[85]

One curious aspect of this research does not become apparent from reading this chapter. Many of the scholars referenced have had a personal experience with disability. Jeremy Schipper, whose work on Mephibosheth was discussed extensively, has cerebral palsy. After completing his study of Mephibosheth, Schipper joined the faculty of the Department of Religion at Temple University and has published three additional books: *Disability and Isaiah's Suffering Servant*, *Disability Studies and Biblical Literature* (coeditor), and *Parables and Conflict in the Hebrew Bible*.[86] I am sure that many of the other scholars referenced have been impacted by some form of disability as well.

Finally it is appropriate to ask if any of the materials presented in this chapter will have an impact on how the scriptural interpretations offered are received by the people in the pews. While many Christians claim to have some biblical knowledge, they may not be ready to take on a study of the Bible without some preparation. Nevertheless, one book attempts to assist

---

83. Ibid., 149.

84. Moss, "Christly Possession and Weakened Bodies," 319.

85. Melcher, "Blemish and Perfection of the Body," 1–13.

86. See Schipper, *Disability and Isaiah's Suffering Servant*; and Schipper, *Parables and Conflict*.

laypeople in coming to terms with the issues that disability raises for biblical interpretation: Amos Yong's *The Bible, Disability, and the Church: A New Vision of the People of God* which was published in 2011.[87] In contrast to his *Theology and Down Syndrome* (which is a much larger work, designed for students of academic theology, that will be discussed in chapter 10), *The Bible, Disability, and the Church* intends "to expose the normate prejudice and to urge its displacement by a more inclusive and hospitable set of attitudes and commitments." In place of what Wynn calls the "normate hermeneutic," Yong argues for a "disability hermeneutic, an approach to the Bible that is informed by the experiences of disability."[88]

To understand how this "disability hermeneutic" works, an example from Yong's chapter on "One Body, Many Members" can be examined. Yong's example refers to Paul's First Letter to the Church at Corinth, in which members are reminded that all people have an essential place in the church regardless of their place in the larger society. Yong argues not only that the disabled are to be part of the church but that their presence is "given greater honor and granted greater respect." Thus, "no gift—and no individual believer—is to be suppressed, dismissed, or minimized, and there is no hierarchy of gifts." Thus, from a disability perspective, "people with disabilities are by definition embraced as central to fully healthy and functioning congregations in particular, and to the ecclesial body in general."[89]

Of course, the disability hermeneutic is more difficult to apply in some Bible passages that are difficult to apply in general. This is especially true when disabilities are related to sin as in many passages in both testaments, including from Deuteronomy and Job. In these cases, more effort is required to sort out the differences between a normate interpretation (e.g., disabilities are the result of sin) and a disability hermeneutic (which would strip away layers of text to arrive at an interpretation that places disability in a more positive light). One wonders how information about the normate hermeneutic and the disability hermeneutic can be shared: in a Bible study, or in a seminary classroom? It seems easier to establish a social process of creating a scholarly community around the study of the Bible and disability than to share the material across the church, especially at congregational level.

---

87. Yong, *The Bible, Disability, and the Church*.

88. See Wynn, "The Normate Hermeneutic"; Yong, *The Bible, Disability, and the Church*, 13.

89. Yong, *The Bible, Disability, and the Church*, 95.

9

The Church and Disability through the Ages

Whereas Christians depend on the Bible in various ways to resource their faith, such resources are mediated through two thousand years of tradition. As well, various minority groups, including people with disabilities, find it necessary to trace their histories over the centuries in an effort to better understand the ways they have been represented and treated by the church today. This has been made possible by the emergence of recent scholarship that has uncovered a great deal of information about the lives of people with disabilities. Historians have explored, among other issues, the response of the church to the presence of people with various impairments, the care the church has provided, and the social location of people with disabilities with respect the life of faith, the sacraments, and the degree to which they have been perceived as ministers in their own right.

Just as scholars in the field of biblical studies have, so "disability historians reject the reigning medical paradigm of 'disability' and substitute a minority-group or social model." They view disability as an "elastic category" that is "highly mutable," with different meanings and interactions depending on the historical period.[1] However, additional issues need to be addressed: the tradition of the Christian church must be "interrogated," especially if the intention is to build a picture of people with disabilities across the church's tradition. There is also the need to focus on the effects of treatment on the social lives of people with disabilities, and the attitudes and stereotypes of those who are not disabled toward people with disabilities. Important also is to pinpoint the theologies that undergird various forms of treatment, attitudes, and stereotypes. All these must be situated in their particular historical period so that false applications of the past are not pursued. Also, it cannot be assumed for any era that the church's response

---

1. Longmore, "New Paradigm, New Approaches," 4.

to disability was uniform, as the diversity of the materials covered in this chapter will show. Each age has its own contradictions in which care of people with disabilities existed alongside theological speculation, miracle/healing activities (e.g., healing at saints' shrines), and various forms of care under church sponsorship.[2] However, it does not appear that historians who specialize in church history have chosen to embrace the need to interrogate its body of knowledge to the same degree as have general historians. For example, in his *The Changing Shape of Church History*, Justo Gonzalez makes no mention of disability but does refer to issues of gender and race as important areas of inquiry as the field looks to the future.[3]

Many of the concerns and conflicts raised by biblical texts continued to be debated in the church in each era up to and including the present. For example, the early church fathers debated whether to expose deformed infants to the elements, whether God's creation was good and what that meant, and whether bodies in the afterlife would retain their deformities.[4] Also debated were the merits of various healing forms such as exorcism and miracle cures, and outreach to the sick and poor; these debates about healing forms and outreach led in some cases to the establishment of "a holistic system of religiously based health care, in which churches and monastic communities provided nursing care and medical services as well as religious rituals."[5]

While the study of disability in different eras of the church has emerged only recently, it is possible to provide a more nuanced presentation of disability across the history of the church than previously.[6] For most of the material covered in this chapter, secondary sources will be used because a great amount of work yet has to be done before a chapter such as this can be written using exclusively primary sources. While my discussion is not aimed at providing a thorough rendering of history of disability in the Christian church, this chapter intends to provide a foundation sufficient to understand where the church has been "located" with respect to disability in the past. Thus, it is possible to provide only an outline of what has transpired over the centuries with respect to the topic of disability in the church. Where current scholarship has enabled more detail than anticipated, I will bring these contributions into the discussion.

2. Metzler, *Disability in Medieval Europe*, 126–85.
3. Gonzalez, *The Changing Shape of Church History*.
4. Kelley, "The Deformed Child."
5. Porterfield, *Healing in the History of Christianity*, 45.
6. Metzler, *Disability in Medieval Europe*, 28.

Ancient/Early Christianity

In the New Testament, people with disabilities, who previously had been viewed as outcasts, such as the blind and the lame, were now to be welcomed into the most holy of places.[7] Stiker observes that

> the texts of the Gospels put the integration of the unfortunate back into the hands of ethical and spiritual conscience. The interdiction excluded in well-defined terms, but it also protected the impaired. Now there is no longer exclusion, but the impaired are even more exposed. The legal violence done to the poor is denounced, but society is even more returned to its violence, of which it can be quit only through love. With the Gospels a completely different system begins for the disabled.[8]

However, evidence does not appear to indicate that this two-pronged approach of stigmatizing and ministering was automatically curtailed in favor of full integration and participation of people with disabilities in the church. Included in the repertoire of the post–New Testament church was the continuation of healing in terms of wholeness as well as miracles. As early as Paul's letters there was a this-worldly emphasis on "the body, the need for healing, and the importance of pure and righteous behavior." Whether this investment in human bodies and behavior resulted in a new alternative to the more extreme spiritualizing tendencies that interpreted the new creation in disembodied terms is difficult to determine.[9]

Indeed, "baptism represented full admission into a covenant relationship with God. It also involved identification with Christ, receipt of his healing and death-defying power, and membership in a community identified with his living, resurrected body."[10] However, "if baptism was the ultimate healing rite of early Christianity, the performance of exorcism of demons was an act of discipleship that displayed the power of Christ in a dramatic way." This spiritual power harked back to Jesus, who confronted and expelled demons, and was used by leading figures of the church well into its fourth century.[11]

The early church expressed some interest in the deformed children as to their fate and their location within Christianity. Nicole Kelley has sought to raise such questions as, "What, if anything, do we know about deformed

---

7. Stiker, *A History of Disability*, 35.
8. Ibid.
9. Porterfield, *Healing in the History of Christianity*, 59.
10. Ibid., 62.
11. Ibid., 63.

children in ancient Christianity? How were deformed and disabled children treated by Christian parents, *and* did they fare differently than deformed children born into non-Christian families? What were Christians' attitudes toward deformed children, and did those attitudes differ from those of their non-Christian contemporaries?" And, "what theological and social significance was assigned to childhood deformity by Christian authors?"[12]

In answering these questions, some conclusions can be derived from examining (1) Christian arguments against the exposure of infants (*expositio*), and (2) Christian appeals to the inherent goodness and perfection of God's creations.[13] While references to the exposure of infants do not directly refer to the condition of babies, "early Christian authors consistently prohibit the exposure of infants, virtually without qualification."[14] However, the rhetorical denunciation of the exposure of infants in early Christian writings does not provide evidence of actual practices among ordinary Christians. Nevertheless, widespread evidence shows Christian denunciation of the general practice of exposing of deformed infants to the elements, which at least suggests that ancient Christians may have been less likely to kill or expose deformed children than were their pagan counterparts.[15]

Considerable space can be given to theological and ethical issues of deformity, particularly with respect to what *caused* physical abnormalities. Such questions as "Were physical deformities tangible evidence of individual sin? Were they accidents of fate? Were they signs of divine punishment?" were pressing "since many Christians were reluctant to say that deformed infants had committed sin in utero or that congenital deformity could be punishment for ancestral sin."[16] Here the record of ancient Christianity is not as consistent. While the previous chapter noted that John 9:1–41 contains explicit testimony that no sin had caused the man's blindness, some later writings seem at least to entertain the possibility that sin may lead to deformity. While Irenaeus affirms the message of John 9, "on at least two other occasions," he "concluded from Gospel healing narratives that deformity and disability could be the result of sin." On the other hand, materials from the "Pseudo-Clementine *Homilies*" clearly favor the view that deformed children were not deformed because of sin, following the John 9 text.[17]

12. Kelley, "The Deformed Child," 199.
13. Ibid.
14. Ibid., 204.
15. Ibid., 205–6.
16. Ibid., 208–9.
17. Ibid., 209.

In the conclusion of her article, Kelley affirms that "childhood deformity sat at the center of a complex, and elusive, web of considerations." However, while she cautions that it is difficult to know how ordinary Christians regarded deformed children, "many Christian authors condemned the exposure of infants, and did not seem to have made exceptions in the case of deformed newborns as their pagan counterparts routinely did." And while many ancient Christian writers were consistent on this point, still "more often than not Christian texts mentioned deformity—including congenital and childhood deformity—as a tool for theological thinking."[18] None of the passages suggests that their authors were familiar with the day-to-day realities of deformed children's lives. The deformed child was for these authors less a historical reality than an abstraction with religious significance. Christian discussions of deformed children are a small subset of conversations within a much larger conversation about the physical body and its significance for Christian belief and practice.[19]

At the end of the patristic era, Christian ideas and treatment patterns toward people with disabilities were beginning to emerge. The Cappadocian fathers—Basil the Great (330-79), Gregory of Nazianzus (c. 330-389), and Gregory of Nyssa (c. 335-94)—played a prominent role in formalizing them. Their activities and writings established Christian philanthropy as decidedly different from Greek and Roman views, in which "a human being was considered to be of value in view of his or her potential to contribute both materially, and through acquired virtue, to the good of the family and of society."[20] Accordingly, "the advent of Christianity marked a turning point in late antiquity in its appreciation of human life as having intrinsic value."[21] This sentiment was made more concrete in the writings and actions of Gregory of Nyssa, who admonishes his readers that in fleeing from sickness, they are abandoning their own nature.[22] In this vein, he urges those who are capable not to "fail to do good for the needy with the gifts which your soul is blessed, for God made you rich in this way, too."[23]

In terms of providing care for persons with disabilities in ancient Christianity, the cloistering of disabled persons can be viewed as a natural outgrowth of the monastic impulse, and, in these times, proved advantageous, as it protected them from the dangers confronting them in the

18. Ibid., 225.
19. Ibid.
20. Caspary, "The Patristic Era," 29.
21. Ibid., 25.
22. Ibid.
23. Ibid., 51 (excerpt from Gregory of Nyssa).

general society.[24] Indeed, by the third and fourth centuries, Christians had enacted the monastic impulse in a variety settings and locations. In coenobitic monasticism—a highly organized community living in a compound—health care was delivered through two main outlets, inpatient care in an infirmary and outpatient care provided in individual cells.[25]

Many monastic writers devoted a great deal of thought to issues of sickness and health. These writers struggled with the question, what role could the sick, disabled, and elderly play within monasticism? The records of ancient Christian monasteries indicate that over time, a set of behavioral expectations was established for the sick in the form of written and oral rules that consisted of benefits and privileges for the sick balanced with behavioral obligations. In contrast to the surrounding Greco-Roman society, the Jewish and Christian traditions established a system of care where "the sick man, the cripple, the weakling" were not viewed as less than worthwhile. Those who entered monastic life were most likely to encounter "the Christian ideals of charity" as part of their socialization.[26] Warnings were issued to healthy and non-disabled monastic residents not to stigmatize those who were ill, infirm, or disabled. Andrew Crislip argues that "the innovative social structure of coenobitic monasticism allowed for the provision of charity on a whole new scale, such as dormitories for visitors; hostels for the crippled, the elderly, the terminally ill; education for orphans; [and] refectories for the poor."[27]

A hospice for the blind was opened in the fourth century at Caesarea in Cappadocia. Soon hospices offering forms of care (to other groups as well as the blind) began to spread throughout Europe. Yet most of the evidence of early care of the church has been found in the Middle East and northern Africa. Basil, bishop of Caesarea in 370, gathered all types of disabled people into the monastic institutions under his control. Each disability group had its separate quarters but was engaged in common work and worship."[28] In effect, what the Cappadocian fathers were about was establishing a pattern of philanthropy linking the fate of the disabled to their nondisabled caregivers. Philanthropy was in existence long before their activities, but it received new force "through the connection 'between an active, socially radical concern for humanity and all serious religious observance.'"[29]

24. Ibid., 64 (excerpt from Gregory of Nazianzus).
25. Crislip, *From Monastery to Hospital*, 3.
26. Ibid., 9.
27. Ibid., 8.
28. Ibid., 69–70.
29. Caspary, "The Patristic Era," 29.

An indication of Christian views toward deformed children in late antiquity can be found also in Augustine's *City of God*. Writing in the early fifth century, Augustine (354–430), according to Kelley, "argues that physically deformed individuals contribute to the diversity, and hence the beauty, of God's creation." As in the previous discussion, physically deformed infants are mentioned only in passing, but such references had implications for how Christians may have viewed such children.[30] Augustine's views are contained within his extended discourse on monstrous individuals and races, which Kelley analyses (in some detail), leading to the conclusion that

> By arguing that even seemingly imperfect bodies reveal their Creator's benevolence and infallibility, Augustine invites his Christian readers to view deformed individuals, including deformed children, as intentional and valuable parts of God's creation. Augustine's revaluation of the deformed body in light of creation, then, would seem to encourage Christians to regard physically abnormal children as a part of a larger, perfect, and beneficent divine plan. Likewise, he discourages the devaluation of such persons on the grounds that doing so is tantamount to challenging God's wisdom. Those who would question the value of deformed bodies are thereby marginalized as individuals who "cannot view the whole"—that is, as persons with an imperfect and incomplete view of creation in the divine plan.[31]

Another indication of Augustine's significance for Christian thought regarding disability may lie in his acceptance of the notion that "man is a rational animal" situated "between angels and beasts," with the "soul, mind, or reason" as the "superior part."[32] And while his view is documented as having a very broad understanding of humanity as including the monstrous, "Augustine's concern was not out of sympathy for the 'monsters' but the desire to preserve the rationality of the divinity and the intrinsic morality of God's design."[33] In addition, Augustine's emphasis on the reality and impact of God's grace on the daily lives of people leads to fulfillment of righteousness "by subjugation of the body, prayer and almsgiving." The conclusion reached by Stainton is that with Augustine's "combination of Platonic ideals with Christian doctrine, the stage is set for a harsh paternalism legitimated

---

30. Kelley, "The Deformed Child," 206–8.
31. Ibid., 208.
32. Stainton, "Reason, Grace, and Charity," 485–90.
33. Ibid.

by the association of reason with value, virtue and responsibility, reinforced by the separation of the earthly and divine worlds."[34]

Augustine is also mentioned in reference to the deaf in that "the church could only comfort people who were deaf, as they had no means to learn about God and acquire faith," stemming from the apostle Paul's teaching that "Faith cometh by hearing."[35] Under the assumption that the faith could be communicated only orally, people who were deaf "were lost souls." Thus, according Saint Augustine, "faith was not possible for people who were deaf because they could not learn faith without spoken language." Later, medieval citizens would argue that what separated humans from animals was the ability to speak, and the inability to speak was commonly associated with deafness (e.g., in the phrase "the deaf and dumb") Some evidence suggests that Augustine endured "a mysterious, painful chest condition in his 32nd year," which impaired his teaching, cutting short his rapid rise in the Roman academies. He was "plagued by recurrences of this condition and by many disabilities of aging" for the remaining years of his life. These experiences (as well as his conversion to Christianity) "notably affected his faith and his writings." Walton Schalick argues that in Augustine's works "we find numerous connections with disability," including his expanded articulation of "the code of the evolving ecclesiastical percept of Christian charity," and also his "insights into the Christian supremacy of the soul and yet the author's profound dependence on experiences of the body to interpret the soul."[36]

The Middle Ages

The history of disability in the medieval west (making up the thousand years between 500 and 1500 CE) can be characterized in many ways. It can be characterized as a time when many disabilities, including intellectual disability, mental illness, deafness, and epilepsy, were thought to have supernatural or demonological causes. Hence, "attempts to cure people with disabilities from early medieval times reflect supernatural beliefs in the abilities of magic and religious elements."[37] People with physical disabilities were not given care during this time because their conditions were "regarded as the embodiment of God's punishment for sin. [And] "they had

---

34. Ibid.
35. Covey, *Social Perceptions*, 47.
36. Ibid.
37. Schalick, "History of Disability," 2:869.

to wander around the streets hoping to receive alms from those who were charitable."[38]

However, historians using models derived from disability studies seek to uncover a more complex view challenging simplistic notions. Schalick notes that while disability history during this period is still "highly fractured," significant strides have been made in the most recent years. Historians of disability studying this period have determined that conditions such as tuberculosis, plague, and leprosy (as well as other diseases) resulted in lifelong disabilities. In addition, miracle records from the shrines of saints suggest a range of symptomatic/diagnostic conditions, including blindness, deafness, mutism, a variety of paralyses, and leprosy.[39] The world around the medieval person was potentially disabling at all times, due to "the vagaries of nature, accident, happenstance, and bad fortune."[40] Orme reports that births with "disfigurements, with missing limbs, or as twins joined together" were common enough to be studied and reported beginning as early as 1249.[41]

Several figures of the time were reported to have various disabling conditions, including Henry the Minstrel (who was referred to as "Blind Henry") and Herman von Reichenau or "Herman the Lame," who was born into nobility and held positions of great intellectual productivity after being educated in an abbey. Also included on this list of notable medievals with disabilities are Teresa de Cartagena, who became deaf as a child and wrote *Grove of the Infirm*, and later became a nun; and Hildegard of Bingen, who was said to have severe migraine headaches but was nevertheless able to function as mystic, theologian, and composer.[42] The church during these centuries was involved with disability on several fronts. Just as it had been in antiquity, so in the Middle Ages monastic-inspired hospices for persons with blindness and other impairments continued to expand as places of refuge and care. Toward end of the Middle Ages, larger-scale projects developed such as the Priory of St. Mary's of Bethlehem founded in London in 1247. Braddock and Parish describe the evolution of this institution:

> Although the order may have begun supporting physically ill persons as a hospital as early as 1330, it did not begin to care for mentally disabled persons, except perhaps incidentally and temporarily, until 1403. After this date, mentally disabled persons

38. Braddock and Parish, "An Institutional History," 19.
39. Ibid.
40. Ibid., 20.
41. Orme, *Medieval Children*, 96.
42. Metzler, *Disability in Medieval Europe*, 128.

gradually displaced the physically sick as the primary focus of the facility, but "it was nearly a hundred years later before there is evidence that London's magistrates thought that *only* the mad should be admitted" (Andrews et al.,1997:90). Today, Bethlehem Hospital is the longest continually operating mental hospital in Europe.[43]

Similar trends were followed in Spain, Germany, and elsewhere. Many of these institutions (including *leprosariums*) were founded and operated by religious orders as part of their charitable work. Those with leprosy were the most likely to be housed in institutional facilities that served as models for institutions that fostered segregation and confinement of other disabled populations. However, leprosy had virtually disappeared from Europe by the sixteenth century, and many converted leprosariums became madhouses for people with mental illness, and, in some cases, for persons with intellectual disabilities.[44]

During this time and extending down to the present, the church developed a system of patron saints, many of which related to disability. According to the *Catholic Encyclopedia*, "A patron is one who has been assigned by a venerable tradition, or chosen by election, as a special intercessor with God and the proper advocate of a particular locality, and is honored by clergy and people with a special form of religious observance."[45] For our focus here, however, consideration is given to saints who have significance related to various impairments and their related miracle healings, or what are referred to as "medical saints."[46] Based on the foundation of sainthood in the church, many persons with impairments would travel to a saint's shrine seeking help, and upon receiving some type of cure, returned home to share their experience. These outcomes would eventually be documented; many of these documents survive to the present—a phenomenon that has resulted in numerous scholarly studies. By the late Middle Ages a long list of specific saints had become patrons of specific ailments and disabilities, including, for example, Giles, the patron saint of "cripples, lepers, and nursing mothers."[47]

By focusing on impairments in their cultural and religious context, miracles performed by saints were modeled after the healing miracles of Christ and the apostles. However, the miracles occurring at medieval shrines did not represent the full range of diseases, illnesses, and impairments that

---

43. Braddock and Parish, "An Institutional History," 19.
44. Ibid.
45. *New Advent* (website), "Patron Saints"; see also McGrane, *Saints to Lean On*.
46. Metzler, *Disability in Medieval Europe*, 128.
47. Ibid., 129.

medieval people might have suffered from, but "only those conditions found to be difficult to treat or cure at all by normal medical means." According to Metzler, "earthly medicine . . . and divine medicine interplayed and complemented each other." Whereas many miracles involved cures of conditions that had resulted from transgressions, many miraculous cures emphasized "that the cause of a person's impairment was purely accidental."[48]

During these centuries, attitudes toward people with disabilities were still shaped within the context of Christian morality. Painters of the period often used persons with physical disabilities as subjects. Hieronymus Cock (1520–1570) painted thirty-one sixteenth-century beggars, including some who engineered creative solutions to mobility problems. Despite their creativity, persons with physical disabilities nevertheless resorted to begging as "the only occupation available to [them] in Cock's time." This reinforced the belief that nondisabled people "could gain God's favor through charitable acts to those in need, including those with disabilities." Hence, "the giving of alms and charity were common to the medieval landscape."[49] This insight is also confirmed by Stiker, whose discussion of Saint Francis of Assisi culminates with the assertion that "the poor individual was no longer one to whom you gave alms but one in whom you recognized God, one who became like a living sacrament, like the sacred itself."[50]

Even though concepts relevant to disability and people with disabilities are modern, theologians of the Middle Ages struggled with questions and concepts relating to people with disabilities. Recent studies by Miguel J. Romero indicate that while Thomas Aquinas (1225–1274) did not develop a "theology of disability" as such, "the systematic character of what he says about corporeal infirmity implicates the whole of his thought and, in this way, alludes to a consistent and versatile 'theology of bodily weakness.'" Aquinas recognized several types of infirmities including those that occur when intelligence, mental cognition or dementia prohibit normal social functioning—conditions summarized by the term *amentia*. However, Aquinas insisted that disabled people were by no means subhumans and that when brought into the church through baptism would be given the full membership in Christ's kingdom even though their human lives were difficult.[51]

Nevertheless, access to the sacrament of Holy Communion was less accessible to people with disabilities: the culture assumed that communicants

48. Ibid., 183–84.
49. Covey, *Social Perceptions*, 58.
50. Stiker, *History of Disability*, 81.
51. Romero, "Aquinas on the *corporis infirmitas*," 102.

with disabilities were required to have "an interior act of directed attention toward God, which is exhibited in an 'exterior humbling of the body' called adoration." Thus, the priest "ha[d] open cause to withhold the Eucharist from a baptized Christian if her body [did] not exhibit signs of interior humbling before the sacramental body of Christ." Just as in earlier periods, so in the Middle Ages the experience and treatment of various disabilities is far from the simple categorizing of the church's response as either negative or positive.[52]

In addition, practical realities called forth other aspects of the Christian faith. England's bout with the plague during the 1370s brought about concern for the well-being of anyone who came close to a victim. In this context, which also featured peasant revolts and challenges to the church's authority, Julian of Norwich (1342—c.1416) dared to suggest that approaching the marginalized would amount to an embrace of Christ. Amy Laura Hall suggests that Julian was advocating that "the work of the faithful is not to climb our way up toward freedom, rung by rung, away from suffering and sin, but to free-fall. We are to embody kinship with even those most marked by disability, through bodily knowledge that God has conquered the fiend."[53]

Renaissance, Reformation, and Early Modern Period

As the Middle Ages came to a close and the early modern period (1500–1800) began, the Renaissance and Reformation resulted in new challenges to be faced with respect to the relationship between Christianity and disability. A substantial increase in scientific knowledge of the human body in general, and of disability in particular, challenged theological explanations of the origin of disease and disability.[54] Hudson also notes that among the many disabling conditions recognized during the era were "chronic illness, maims, deafness, blindness, mental problems (illness and intellectual impairment), and infirmity brought on by age or service."[55]

These were times when two systems of explanation for mental illness (and for other disabilities as well) were in competition. Supernatural explanations for mental illness and insanity included divine retribution, magic, destiny, witchcraft, demonic possession, sin, lack of faith, and God's will.

---

52. Ibid., 111.
53. Hall, "A Ravishing," 162.
54. Ibid.
55. Braddock and Parish, "An Institutional History," 21.

Natural explanations included diet, genetics, biology, trauma, nurturing, health, physiology, and other natural causes."[56]

Witchcraft is one phenomenon that emerged toward the end of the Middle Ages and was prominent during the Renaissance and Reformation, and through the seventeenth century. A partial explanation for its emergence can be found in the length of time needed for Christianity to fully convert Europe to its theology and lifestyle. The roots of witchcraft lie "partly in Graeco-Roman and Hebrew thought and in the sorcery, folklore and religion in northern Europe"[57] and can be attributed to changing social patterns that lie beyond religious life. Nevertheless, religious sentiments played a prominent role in promoting hostilities "toward those who were different, odd, or powerful"—sentiments that involved "fantasies of diabolical possession, and broke out in witch-hunts claiming the lives of thousands of innocent victims, mostly women."[58]

In 1487, Heinrich Kramer (Russell refers to Heinrich Istitoris[59]) and Jacob Sprenger wrote *Malleus Maleficarum*, which became an influential guide to witch-hunting and prosecution.[60] It became so popular that by 1520 it had been reprinted fourteen times! Among its many assertions is that those engaged in witchcraft had (1) renounced the Catholic faith, (2) were devoted "body and soul to the service of evil," (3) offered up "unbaptized children to the devil," and (4) engaged in "orgies that included intercourse with the devil."[61]

However, the pursuit of witches was not only a Roman Catholic phenomenon. The Protestant Reformation fueled witch-hunting activities among the Protestants, who approached the issue with vigor equal to that of Catholics. Key Protestant leaders, including Calvin and Luther, voiced the opinion that people who were insane were possessed by Satan. In the American colonies witch-hunting was an issue as early as the first settlement. Laws based on a 1604 English Statute "made 'being a witch' punishable by death." Many women so punished practiced midwifery or had a sudden unexplained illness, bodily pains, or some other disability.[62] Mitchell concludes that

56. Hudson, "History of Disability," 2:855.
57. Covey, *Social Perceptions*, 68.
58. Russell, *A History of Witchcraft*, 42.
59. Ibid.
60. King, *Western Civilization*, 412.
61. Russell, *A History of Witchcraft*, 79.
62. Mitchell, "Witchcraft" 4:1939–40.

Witch-hunting brought together a powerful social alchemy of physical and spiritual realms. While disability status proved central to nearly every witching episode, disability itself did not automatically result in condemnation. While all witches presumably had "marks" that exposed their allegiance to the devils, many of the accusers used their own experiences of bodily vulnerability as the impetus for charges against another. Such instances help to describe the degree to which communities will pursue extravagant explanations for the existence of bodily, sensory, and cognitive variations.[63]

Another "enduring explanation" for the existence of infants born with developmental disabilities or deformities was that they were changelings. Changelings were abnormal children thought to be conceived not by their parents but rather by evil spirits such as fairies, demons, or elves. Evil spirits made these exchanges during the night when the family was sleeping.[64] Children considered changelings were described as having a peculiar appearance, with the wrong proportions; as having an ugly or wrinkled face; as having a "thick throat"; as having the ability neither to stand nor walk; and as not speaking but instead "scream[ing] and shout[ing] interminably." The changeling phenomenon continued well into the eighteenth century when it was connected to the notion of "those with changeable wills," and also to those with intellectual disabilities.[65]

A significant comment from Martin Luther (1483–1545) runs as follows: "Idiots are men in whom devils have established themselves, and all the physicians who heal these infirmities as though they proceed from natural causes are ignorant blockheads, who know nothing about the power of the demon."[66] However, this view of Luther's understanding of disability is called into question by M. Miles, who labels such statements as merely "fleeting" and "derogatory glimpses" into what Luther said and did about disability. He maintains that "to pretend to assess Luther's views on the basis of a few much-edited scraps of hearsay would be ludicrous, given that a vast [number of] annotated editions exist of his written exegetical, pastoral and political works in German and Latin, much of it also translated and published in English."[67]

---

63. Ibid., 4:1640.
64. Covey, *Social Perceptions*, 238.
65. Stainton, "Changeling," 1:35.
66. Miles, "Martin Luther and Childhood Disability," 6–7.
67. Ibid., 9.

What then were Luther's views of disability? The answer is that Luther was not prone to write systematic theological works that sought clarity. Rather, he would address issues as they emerged as when the plague struck Europe. He presumed, on the one hand, that it was spread by evil spirits, and on the other, that Christians "should care for their sick neighbor not only to please God, but also for the pleasure of spitting in the devils eye!" At one point in Luther's writing, according to Miles, he praised God for "showing more mercy than wrath, since one can see 'a hundred thousand healthy people for every ailing, blind, deaf, paralytic, or leprous person.'"[68]

Toward the end of his article, Miles summarizes Luther's views on disability. The first conclusion he offers is that Luther lived in a time when a wide range of disabilities were present and "a familiar sight in public." In addition, "ordinary people could not invest in health insurance, pension schemes or advanced medical technology. They tried home remedies, local healers, saints' bones, and put their faith in God, at least when they were in trouble and could see no other help."[69] While Luther's views toward persons with disability are not accepted now, there is evidence that he showed concern for their welfare. Over "his career as religious and social reformer, Luther repeatedly made written and spoken comments in which children and adults with disabilities were understood to have full human value and were considered worthy members of the Church." This is the case despite the fact that Luther had some beliefs and some doubts in the area of devilry, changelings and witchcraft.[70]

While the Reformation resulted in significant changes in church life, politically as well as theologically, changes also occurred in the way people with disabilities received care. Protestant regions saw a shift toward more private forms of religious expression, with diminished religious support for public health care. Eventually Protestant support for many hospitals was withdrawn where service to the sick was intertwined with veneration of healing saints, and when care of the sick and dying was celebrated as meritorious work conducive to salvation.[71] Porterfield notes that "as part of a general trend among Lutherans toward highly individualized piety, Luther's emphasis on service to others came to be defined more in terms of interpersonal compassion than commitment to public welfare."[72]

---

68. Ibid., 11 (quoting from Martin Luther).
69. Ibid., 32.
70. Ibid., 34.
71. Porterfield, *Healing in the History of Christianity*, 109–10.
72. Ibid., 110–11.

John Calvin (1509–1564) also contributed to the debates relevant to disability during the Reformation. He "condemned petitions to the saints for healing miracles as misguided and sinful and laid out a framework for Christian living that focused on the worship of a transcendent God."[73] Significantly, he viewed the healing miracles of Jesus and his earliest disciples to "reflect the momentous events of his actual appearance on earth, not ongoing practices of Christian life. Claims to make them so were false and harmful to the Christian religion."[74] As with Luther, this led to the tendency to focus health-related issues on the individual who should "discern their therapeutic purpose."[75]

Simple arguments do not do justice to the complexity of Calvin's struggle with disability. "While one can see how his argument that a person's destiny is predetermined by God might lead to," how Calvin is interpreted can lead to "personally distressing and politically dangerous conclusions."[76] Calvin tended to discuss issues of impairment in ways that either relate to all people or exemplify a condition that any of us might experience (e.g., the profound suffering experienced by Job).[77] His rugged individuality was part of an overall trend that would have increasing significance and coincide with a shift from allowing people with disabilities (except lepers) to be free and to beg to providing housing for disabled people beginning in the sixteenth century to finally, in the early seventeenth century, having begging criminalized.[78]

In the shift from church-sponsored medical care and ministries focused on pilgrimages to saints' shrines, miracle healing, and other pastoral administrations, the disabled were pushed aside as mediators of God's healing powers. Row-Heyveld argues that

> Disability in the Middle Ages was characterized by its important role in a system of spiritual exchange in which the non-standard body served as conduit for God; this exchange granted people with non-normative bodies a level of subjectivity and spiritual agency that their early modern counterparts did not experience. In part due to the example of Francis of Assisi and the rise of the Franciscans in the thirteenth century, disabled people regularly engaged in a mutually beneficial exchange with the normative

---

73. Ibid., 95.
74. Ibid.
75. Ibid., 100.
76. Creamer, "John Calvin and Disability," 216.
77. Ibid., 219.
78. Ibid., 225–26.

population. Able-bodied Christians gave them alms (sometimes small, individual sums of money, sometimes shelter, medical treatment, or large endowments continuing in annuity) and, in return, experienced an encounter with the divine facilitated by the disabled person.[79]

The English Reformation with its destruction of monasteries and shrines also brought about the elimination of that spiritual exchange, and with it, a considerable loss of agency for disabled persons.[80] Among Catholics, long-standing support for hospitals operated by religious orders was continued, and "pious laypeople, especially women, continued to engage hospital work as a means of enacting devotion to Christ."[81] In seventeenth-century France, for instance, the Catholic Church reformed its charitable institutions, creating the Hospital General in Paris that housed and detained thousands of disabled people. Soon, other hospitals were funded and nursing orders such as the Daughters of Charity (1633) provided practical nursing skills and hospital labor.[82]

Another contribution to the Christian response to persons with disabilities during later part of the early modern period came in the training of the deaf and blind. In Spain, a Benedictine monk, Pedro Ponce de Leon (1520–1584), taught deaf aristocratic sons to read and speak. These efforts were undertaken in succeeding generations by individuals (both religious and secular) in several countries in Europe.[83] In part, these ongoing efforts by representatives of the Roman Catholic Church reflect the fact that the Church essentially continued the forms of ministry of previous centuries, unscathed by the challenges of the Reformation.[84]

Into Modernity

There is a general conviction that by the middle of the eighteenth century efforts at understanding the human body in respect to disability, as well as efforts to educate persons with disabilities, reduced the role of the church.[85] Indeed, the church's role becomes difficult to trace as many of the current

79. Row-Heyveld, "'The Lying'st Knave in Christendom,'" 5.
80. Porterfield, *Healing in the History of Christianity*, 110.
81. Hudson, "History of Disability," 2:856–57.
82. Ibid.
83. Ibid.
84. Porterfield, *Healing in the History of Christianity*, 110.
85. See Turner, *Medical Power and Social Knowledge*.

histories available shift focus at this point to secular trends. Nevertheless, while pioneers in the education of the blind, deaf, and those with intellectual disabilities were heavily influenced by the Enlightenment, which allowed "liberation from superstition," many of those involved were inspired by religious sentiments, if they were not lay and clergy themselves.[86]

In colonial Virginia petitions were secured for the guardianship of a person with an intellectual disability as well as financial support for care. In Puritan New England, disabilities were still viewed as indications of God's displeasure. Covey reports that "Increase Mather (1684) provided several examples of children with disabilities that were the result of God's divine retribution (displeasure). Later, son Cotton Mather echoed this belief in his sermons and writings." In some cases persons with disabilities who were considered in need of "public charge" were "warned out" of town.[87]

Nevertheless, early attempts were made in the American colonies to provide public support. In 1662, an almshouse was constructed in Boston. Later, in 1676, a court in Delaware County, Pennsylvania, ordered a small levy to pay for the care of "madmen." This was followed by the establishment of a hospital for the care of persons with mental illness in Philadelphia, where Thomas Bond and Benjamin Franklin took the lead, apparently without recourse to theological explanations. The first mental asylum was established in Virginia in 1773.[88]

It is difficult to establish which developments were directly under the leadership of the church, church people, or both. For instance, the establishment of residential schools for the deaf in United States was undertaken by the Reverend Thomas Gallaudet (1787–1851), whose theological motivation, while covered over by later secular developments, was obvious.[89] The Reverend Gallaudet was trained at Yale and at Andover Theological Seminary (today Andover-Newton Theological School) and became interested in deaf education through a neighbor lady with whom he made early and uneducated attempts at communication and teaching. In 1814, he traveled to England and France, and returned the following year after a brief exposure to French sign language and with Laurent Clerc, a deaf-mute who been trained in use of the sign-language technique for communication and education. The story of these two men and their training was essentially Christian. Thomas Gallaudet went to seminary with the expressed goal of

---

86. Winzer, *The History of Special Education*, 40.
87. Braddock and Parish, "An Institutional History," 25–26.
88. Ibid., 26.
89. See Braddock and Parish, "An Institutional History"; as well as Schalick, "History of Disability."

exposing the deaf to belief in Christ and his offer to forgive their sins. Clerc was trained in an abbey for the deaf by a priest-monk named Sicard, whom Gallaudet persuaded to allow Clerc to come to America to start a school. Sicard gave his blessing only after he received assurances that Clerc would be able to practice his Catholicism in what was (at the time) Protestant New England![90]

Establishing religiously based schools for the deaf was a strategy used by groups who came to America from the early 1800s on. In 1837, two sisters of St. Joseph of Carondelet came from Lyon, France, to join six sisters who emigrated the previous year at the request of Bishop Joseph Rosati of St. Louis to open a school in his diocese for deaf students.[91] Around the turn of the 1900s, the Norwegian Lutheran Church began a ministry to the deaf and blind in Fairbault, Minnesota, where a state institution had been started. This effort led to the establishment of several congregations for the deaf in several Midwestern states.[92]

The Episcopal Church claims that it began work among the disabled through Thomas Gallaudet (the eldest son of the Thomas Gallaudet discussed above). The younger Gallaudet was ordained to the priesthood in 1852. He founded St. Anne's Church for the Deaf in New York City, which is believed to be "the first congregation in any denomination established for deaf people." This Gallaudet was a strong advocate for sign language and played a significant role in the debate between the use of sign language and the widely promoted oral approach. His emphasis on ministry with the deaf led to the ordination of Henry Winter Syles, the first deaf person ordained in any denomination. He and Gallaudet share a feast day, August 27, on the Episcopal calendar of saints.[93]

If Methodism is indicative of religious response to disability prior to World War II, then its combination of thought and action is instructive. As early as 1901, the *Methodist Review* carried an article by Raymond Dodge (1871–1942) dealing with the relationship between Christianity and mental illness titled "Christianity and Sanity."[94] Goodwill Industries was founded in 1902 by the Reverend Edgar Helms (1863–1942) as the outgrowth of an institutional church serving inner-city residents who had immigrated to America only to face discrimination and poverty in crowded slums. Its program of training and employment was gradually extended to persons with

---

90. Lane, *When the Mind Hears*.
91. Baum and Benton, "The Evolution and Current Focus of Ministry," 40.
92. Herzog, "Disability Advocacy in American Mainline Protestantism," 76.
93. Barbara Ramnairamie, personal communication.
94. Herzog, "From Service to Rights," 27–39.

disabilities. For many years, Goodwill Industries was viewed as a movement within the Methodist tradition, with its leaders and directors coming from the ranks of its clergy as appointed by their respective bishops. Gradually this sponsorship eroded as its local units sought wider community support.[95]

Conclusion

There is no doubt much more information that can be uncovered about Christianity and disability in the period before 1950, but this work needs more time to emerge and take its place in helping to understand its influence on our current ministries. The material reviewed in this chapter is a start toward achieving this goal.

---

95. Ibid.

10

Theology and Disability

This chapter examines the contributions coming from a number of different theologians who have chosen to reflect on disability, and to offer these contributions for the benefit of the entire church, especially to the mainstream theological community. Disability activists in churches and other parachurch organizations have repeatedly called for theological reflection as they have tried to formulate positions more inclusive of people with disabilities. These have not resulted in a wholesale response from people in the pews, but for the activists, they strike at the heart of their cause to make churches more open and accessible. It is not enough for churches to be architecturally accessible; churches need to theologically accessible as well.

Recently, some theologians have affirmed theological access as absolutely essential for real progress in the effort to integrate people with disabilities into the life of the church and also for theological reflection in general. In 2007, Amos Yong published *Theology and Down Syndrome: Reimaging Disability in Late Modernity* specifically directed to "the Christian theological academy, seminarians and graduate students in theology and religion."[1] This is also the purpose of other works around the same time, including: Thomas E. Reynolds's *Vulnerable Communion: A Theology of Disability and Hospitality*,[2] Sharon V. Betcher's *Spirit and the Politics of Disablement*,[3] and Deborah Beth Creamer's *Disability and Christian Theology: Embodied Limits and Constructive Possibilities*.[4] In addition, new articles have appeared in periodicals including the *Journal of Disability, Religion & Health*, and such

---

1. Yong, *Theology and Down Syndrome*, ix.
2. Reynolds, *Vulnerable Communion*.
3. Betcher, *Spirit and the Politics of Disablement*.
4. Creamer, *Disability and Christian Theology*.

new volumes as Amos Yong's *The Bible, Disability, and the Church*, aimed at lay audiences.[5]

These and similar works provide for a lively discussion of the role of Christian thinking about disability and the church. The way to this emerging work has been paved by numerous books and materials that appeared over the years since the late 1970s, which coincide with the beginning of the modern disability rights movement within the Christian churches. In the next section I provide an overview of these earlier works. After this I will discuss the materials listed in the preceding paragraph. The conclusion of this chapter will interrogate the challenge all these materials provide for theological education. Conducting this interrogation, as I will make clear, is no easy task, as seminaries struggle to train pastors and other church workers in areas such as biblical studies, church history, ethics, theology, and practical fields in the space of three to four years.

Theology in the Early Disability Rights Era (1980-2000)

One of the first in the early disability rights era to write about disability issues from a Christian perspective was the late Reverend Harold H. Wilke (1914-2003). Born without arms and trained in pastoral care, he worked as a pastor, chaplain, and disability advocate. His approach in *Creating the Caring Congregation* (1980) is decidedly psychological in that he examines attitudes toward the disabled as being situated in the individual: "Barriers of attitudes stand in the way of understanding and acceptance. They stand between person to person." In his view, "the barrier of attitude begins inside the individual, it is in me. It is not something out there. It is not a thing, such as a building with steps. Since it is within myself, it may not even be based in regard to the other person, but it clearly is a fact within itself."[6]

Yet, despite his focus on the individual model of disability, as the preceding paragraph suggests, and without the aid of recent biblical and theological scholarship, Wilke was willing to entertain the notion that the church needed to interrogate its Scriptures and traditions. Among the many ideas he entertained was "the imputation of wholeness and salvation," which corresponds to the imputation of righteousness, "which has long been a bedrock theme of biblical theology, lifted to high visibility by Reformation theology."[7] Coupled with the wholeness concept is the notion that someone who is disabled is not whole in the sight of God but can be made whole by

---

5. Yong, *The Bible, Disability, and the Church*.
6. Wilke, *Creating the Caring Congregation*, 15.
7. Ibid., 21.

exercising more faith. Wilke selects the New Testament story from John 9 to affirm that "throughout the New Testament, Jesus' response to disability and other handicapping conditions is any of these: to heal that condition, to consider it irrelevant, and to seek justice, as in the attempt to change the ritual law on healing." However, Wilke's work shifts to more practical issues involved in creating a "caring congregation" and dwells on resolutions developed by denominations and ecumenical organizations.[8]

Stewart D. Govig (1927–2005), a Lutheran pastor and religious scholar, also wrote during this period. In his book *Strong at the Broken Places* (1989), Govig reflects experientially, biblically, and theologically on his own disability and experience as a father of a son with a severe mental illness. Much of this book is concerned with how the church needs to respond to such conditions, but in its final chapter, Govig addresses biblical and theological issues raised by disabilities. He begins by noting that disability is basically a human phenomenon that is to be addressed with justice "beyond the injustices and cruelties of this world."[9] However, "until then we can strive (1) to put pain in its place; (2) to manifest the power of weakness; and (3) to anticipate the redemption of our bodies."[10] Putting pain in its place involves the recognition that human disability is part of the created order to which the Bible is witness, an emphasis more clearly seen in the letters of Paul. Readers are not encouraged to explore the topic of theodicy in depth, as the Bible does not seek to justify the existence of pain. "Thus," he notes, "submission and resignation in the face of pain and disease are the best response to suffering; that is to say, disability is neither good nor bad. It just is."[11] Govig urges readers not to acquiesce to pain, to seek medical assistance, and to realize that "Jesus Christ has joined our pain."[12]

In entertaining the "strength in weakness" idea, Govig asserts that weakness has "nothing to do with physical ability; [and] the word instead refers to actions of faith and the author's [i.e. Paul's] 'word power' strategy."[13] In passages across several letters—passages based on his own "thorn in the flesh"—Paul maintains that pain is increasingly realized as part of the human condition, which all groups, young and old, disabled and nondisabled, experience. Govig's theological claim is that those living with severe disabilities "have an opportunity to claim a prophetic witness to the idolatry

---

8. Ibid., 27.
9. Govig, *Strong at the Broken Places*, 11.
10. Ibid.
11. Ibid., 112.
12. Ibid., 113.
13. Ibid., 114–15.

of health, fitness, and wellness which saturates our culture." In addition, Christians can witness to the claim that the church is "one body" and that "all qualify in baptism (developmentally disabled as well as the 'normal'), and all are recipients of the Spirit's gifts (no status requirements)."[14] Govig concludes with the affirmation that brokenness will one day be transformed by God, but until then we must wait (Barth) "for the full experience of adoption as God's children."[15]

In addition, two authors wrote from their experience working with persons with intellectual disabilities: Robert Perske (1928–2016) and Wolf Wolfensberger (1934–2011). Perske spent a good amount of his career as chaplain at a residential facility for persons with intellectual disabilities and was best known for his writings and presentations on disability from a Christian pastoral perspective. His words and the drawings of his artist-wife, Martha, helped all to see people with cognitive and other developmental disabilities as having beauty and dignity.[16] He wrote extensively on the plight of people with cognitive and other developmental disabilities who encounter the criminal justice system.[17]

Arguing that "our theological views are dependent on how we deal with the disturbance of mental retardation as it is found in our pastorates,"[18] he asserts that a pastor's theological views arise from attempts either to "*void and deny*, or his [sic] attempts to *understand and deal with* the problems of his relationships at four different points." Using the generic he to refer to the pastor, Perske asserts that this view arises from (1) "how he sees his relationship with his Creator, (2) how he sees and gets along with himself, (3) how he relates to people around him, and (4) how he is able to live in the physical environment of this world." Perske asserts, "The parents of the mentally retarded in our pastorates are the ones who may provide many of the seeds for an adequate theological view." Using good listening skills and "being there" with parents, such questions may arise as "Why did God let this happen?" "What is God's hidden plan in all this?" "What does God want me to do now?" and "What does Bill need to know about God?" At the same time, a pastor should be aware that among parents of disabled children there is a "remarkable propensity for growth," which, Perske argues, "is a God-given thing, and a clue for finding theological views." This is also the

---

14. Ibid., 118.
15. Ibid., 119.
16. Gaventa, "Introduction."
17. Perske, *Unequal Justice*.
18. Perske, "An Attempt to Find," 37–39.

case as these parents gradually move from feeling guilt in these situations, to learning to live with the situation as it is.[19]

In the same article, Perske surveys theological views (past and present) of those with cognitive disabilities. Characterizations that they are "demon-controlled" and calls to "get rid of them," are found in colonial America, whereas views that those with cognitive disabilities have "bad blood," or that the "sins of the fathers" are punished through children with intellectual disabilities emerge later. Also reviewed are such labels "God's special children," and "special theology."[20] Perske emphasizes the importance of integrating people with cognitive disabilities into mainstream congregational life enlarging *the existing general theological views so that they include the mentally retarded.*"[21]

There is much more to Perske's pastoral theology of cognitive and intellectual disability, more than can be reviewed here. His writings deserve much more attention even though they originally date from the 1960s. Again, he is arguing from the inductive position where parents of children with cognitive disabilities provide points of departure for theological insights into disability. These include insights not only about theodicy but also about human finitude, a theology of worship, death and resurrection, and support for deinstitutionalization and community responsibility for persons who previously had been residents of large state facilities.[22]

Another source for theological insight was the person and pen of Wolf Wolfensberger (1934–2011). Trained as a psychologist with a specialty in mental retardation, Wolfensberger was well known for his writings and advocacy for normalization and deinstitutionalization. However, as a Catholic layperson, he gradually came to focus on work about religion and spirituality so that he moved away from his psychological work to a period emphasizing social change and policy.[23] Wolfensberger was ever the iconoclast, and he viewed the presence of people with cognitive and intellectual disabilities as a "prophetic voice and presence," with specific reference to L'Arche as a special place where this presence is known and almost taken for granted.[24] Under the heading "Retarded People Speaking in Tongues," he discusses an alternate form of "tongues," as when:

---

19. Ibid., 40–41 (italics original).
20. Ibid., 42–45.
21. Ibid., 45 (italics original).
22. Ibid., 50–51.
23. Bersani, "Wolf Wolfensberger," 7.
24. Wolfensberger, "The Prophetic Voice," 24.

(a) a person who cannot speak, or ordinarily does not speak, suddenly speaks or otherwise reveals important truths; (b) when a person who ordinarily speaks confusedly or unimportantly suddenly speaks clearly and "with authority" about religious and moral matters; (c) when a person with a speech impediment speaks clearly about the above matters; or (d) when religious truths, sentiments, or manifestations are being communicated or even mediated by persons who extensively or even exclusively use non-verbal, and possibly unorthodox, symbols and expressions and/or universal symbolisms.[25]

In this same presentation (which appeared in several places and at different times), Wolfensberger reflects on the importance of valuing persons with disability in light of such endeavors as sending astronauts to the moon and making it possible to cross the Atlantic in three hours. How can the general public support making possible these possibilities but not have the willingness to say that disabled individuals who cannot think or reason, that people who have trouble making good judgments, are not of value?[26] Yet Wolfensburger saves his scathing remarks to criticize an overemphasis on religious education as "religious colonization" as contrasted to worship participation, including shared prayer. He concludes that "there must be genuine contributive roles for retarded people in integrated worship and religious life, and not just in our own segregated human service settings."[27]

Nancy Eiesland (1964-2009) and the Disabled God

In 1994, Abingdon Press published Nancy Eiesland's *The Disabled God: Toward a Liberatory Theology of Disability*, a revision of her Master of Divinity thesis.[28] The book created quite a stir in the disability community, especially among disability activists in mainline churches. Practitioners as well as theologians quoted her extensively, and until her untimely death in 2009, Eiesland was seen and heard at meetings and seminars across the United States and abroad. She received her PhD in sociology from Emory University and was hired by its Candler School of Theology where she taught courses in social and cultural studies of religion, gender, disabilities, urban studies, religious organization, and research methods (in Emory's graduate division of religion as well as in the School of Theology).

25. Ibid., 25.
26. Ibid., 32-33.
27. Ibid., 34.
28. Eiesland, *The Disabled God*.

Within its pages, *The Disabled God* covers many issues about the relationship between disability and the church. In Eiesland's view, the church has not come to terms with the emancipation of people with disabilities that resulted from the passage of the ADA. Among her striking declarations are the following: "The history of the church's interaction with the disabled is at best an ambiguous one," and "For many disabled persons the church has been a 'city on a hill'—physically inaccessible and socially inhospitable."[29] Her goal is to find a place in the church where people with disabilities can claim for themselves dignity and respect. For Eiesland, "a liberatory theology of disability is a theology of coalition and struggle in which we identify our unique experience while also struggling for recognition, inclusion, and acceptance from one another and from the able-bodied society and church."[30]

In the first place, Eiesland claims that people with disabilities are embodied, and that by claiming their "specific stories" they take steps toward constructing a theology of disability.[31] Referring to disabled bodies as "bodies of knowledge" and employing the biographies of two women disability advocates (Diane DeVries and Nancy Mairs), Eiesland identifies how having a disability leads to both ordinary and different lives. In its ordinary sense, disabled lives acknowledge that life is vulnerable but that grief over having a disability does not always lead to tragedy and powerlessness in the face of impairment. Disability life narratives "highlight an alternative understanding of embodiment, recognizing it as an intricate interweaving of physical sensations and emotional attachments, irrespective of socially constructed notions of 'normal' bodies or 'appropriate' relations."[32] Her analysis is also informed by feminism in that both women and people with disabilities "resist" socially constructed barriers and become active participants in society by engaging in meaningful work and efforts to promote social justice.[33]

However, one cannot construct identities by focusing solely on an individual's experience with a disability. The body, according to Eiesland, is "the center of political struggle," a site that society can define any number of ways, including "as flawed, dangerous, and dependent." Yet, she notes, people with disabilities are beginning to challenge these very notions, refusing to be "warehoused in institutions, restricted from public buildings, and discriminated against in employment."[34] What Eiesland is relating here are two

29. Ibid., 20.
30. Ibid., 29.
31. Ibid., 31.
32. Ibid., 47.
33. Ibid., 48.
34. Ibid., 49.

important but interrelated ideas. The first is the social model of disability, whose roots are (in part) found in Erving Goffman's study *Stigma* and the emergence of the disability rights movement based on the minority-group model. Society is the arena where disability advocates focus their attention, taking its institutions and power structures to task.

The second idea is that Eiesland anchors personal experiences of disability (including treating people with disabilities in a condescending manner and ignoring their desire to be part of the human community) in social life and not in purely personal terms. The secular challenge to existing social order with respect to disability is acknowledged, but as Eiesland notes, the disability rights movement "has been largely ignored by the Christian Church." Of particular concern is that when the ADA was in the legislative process, churches lobbied for a "blanket exemption" from the provisions of the act. Eiesland concludes that "many religious bodies have continued to think of and act as if access for people with disabilities is a matter of benevolence and goodwill, rather than a prerequisite for equality and the foundation on which the church as a model of justice must rest."[35]

However, the most significant contribution that Eiesland makes to the theology of disability is to suggest the reconceptualization of the symbol of Jesus Christ as "the disabled God."[36] Eiesland is calling for nothing less than the "resymbolization" as the "radical symbol sedition," which results in reclaiming a part of the "hidden history" of people with disabilities in the church. Reconceptualizing the symbol of Jesus Christ comes from exploring the meaning behind Jesus's appearance to the disciples after his resurrection as recorded in Luke 24:36–43. The passage describes Jesus as appearing to his followers and showing them the wounds from his crucifixion. Eiesland argues that "in presenting his impaired hands and feet to his startled friends, the resurrected Jesus is revealed as the disabled God." She points out that "Jesus as the resurrected savior, calls for his frightened companions to recognize in the marks of his impairment their own connection with God, their own salvation. In doing so, the disabled God is also the revealer of a new humanity. The disabled God is not only the One from heaven but the revelation of true personhood, underscoring the reality that full personhood is fully compatible with the experience of disability."[37]

The naming and labeling of Jesus as the disabled God has several implications, especially with respect to marginalization. First, the disabled God "does not engage in a battle for dominance or create a new normative power,

---

35. Ibid., 67.
36. Ibid., 98.
37. Ibid., 100.

God is in the present social-symbolic order at the margins with people with disabilities and instigates transformation from this de-centered position." Second, accepting the disabled God may enable the reconciliation of disabled bodies to the church because their bodies are fully accepted by Christ. This is because "disability not only does not contradict the human-divine integrity, it becomes a new model of wholeness and a symbol of solidarity." Third, "to posit a Jesus Christ who needs care and mutuality as essential to human-divine survival does not symbolize either humanity or divinity as powerless. Instead it debunks the myth of individualism and hierarchical orders, in which transcendence means breaking free of encumbrances and needing nobody and constitutes the divine as someone in relation to other bodies."[38] Finally, hope for Eiesland is constituted as the disabled God as "the recollection and projection that even our nonconventional bodies, which oftentimes dissatisfy and fail us, are worth the living. It is knowing that the so-called curses sometimes feel like blessings."[39]

Eiesland's stance on disability resonated well with many sectors of the disability community. It is pure speculation where her work would have taken her had she lived beyond 2009. Disability studies as an academic discipline had already expanded prior to that time, but the nondisability demands of her position as a sociologist of religion required that she spend more time in that field. Because *The Disabled God* sold well, Abingdon Press had contacted her about a revised edition, but she was reluctant to proceed due to time restraints, and contemplated whether a shift in topic would be more appropriate than a simple revision.

Toward a Theology of Disability

What has emerged since 1994 is a field that I refer to as "the theology of disability." This area of study attempts to wrestle with the serious theological and ethical questions raised by disability and to bring these questions into the arena of theology as it is taught in theological seminaries and graduate schools of religion in the United States and elsewhere. Major books and papers have been published specifically for theologians—books that are challenging to read because they dig deeper into theological topics relevant to the theological enterprise itself and do not address disability merely as a special concern. They cover a wide range of topics including liberation, the body, inclusion, and hospitality—topics on which disability makes a

38. Ibid.
39. Ibid.

contribution to the larger arena of reflection. Once these have been discussed, the implications for systematic theology can be explored.

Liberation

Whereas Nancy Eiesland sought to offer and apply the theme of liberation to persons with physical disabilities, John Swinton has done this in *Resurrecting the Person: Friendship and the Care of People with Mental Health Problems*.[40] In advocating for radical friendship between persons with acute mental health problems and persons without such problems, Swinton has issued a "call to the church to rediscover its prophetic roots in the life, death, and resurrection of Jesus Christ and to reclaim its identity as the friend and protector of the poor, the outcast, and the stranger."[41] His emphasis, therefore, falls upon a "theology of practice" that involves "*critical reflection on the practice of the church in the world.*"[42] His work goes on to assert liberation theology's "centrality of the poor," in that "people with mental health problems are the subject of numerous unjust practices, negative personal and social attitudes, and other forms of oppression and impoverishment. Reflection on their life experience leaves one in no doubt that they fall firmly within the category of the poor."[43] Swinton also calls for the church to form radical friendships with those with mental health problems and to abandon its "overconcentration on specifically therapeutic relationships such as counseling and psychotherapy, and regain a vision for those who require different forms of pastoral relationship."[44] His call is also targeted at the idea of "consciousness raising," which deals with the poverty that people with mental health problems face and the need for the church to respond by developing radical friendships. Such friendships would see people with mental health problems as people who are entitled to "live lives appropriate to their status as human beings, made in the image of a relational God."[45]

Swinton maintains that the friendships offered by the church are "unlike specialist/professional relationships." They are based on "human affection that is potentially available to and from the *whole* of the Christian community and from the whole of society."[46] Swinton's approach is to focus

---

40. Swinton, *Resurrecting the Person*.
41. Ibid., 9.
42. Ibid., 11 (italics original).
43. Ibid., 19.
44. Ibid., 23.
45. Ibid., 31.
46. Ibid., 38 (italics original).

on friendship. It opens up the possibility that the care of people with severe mental health problems is a communal, lay-oriented enterprise rather than an exclusively individualized specialist task, and suggests that the church community may have a specific responsibility. Such a focus on friendship "enables the church to offer a *distinctive* contribution to the process of care."[47]

Jürgen Moltmann also deploys the liberation framework to argue that Christians should begin by liberating themselves and "accepting one another." He argues that "there are fundamentally no 'persons with disabilities,' but rather only 'people' with this or that difficulty on the basis of which the society of the strong and capable declares them to be 'disabled' and consequently more or less excludes them from public life."[48] Moltmann then adds that Christians who seek to love the other (presumably including people with disabilities) must value themselves first. In Moltmann's words, "before we talk about the integration of persons with disabilities into society and communal life, we want to go in search of own concealed self-worth." From this position he raises the question, "Is there such a thing as a liberation of persons with disabilities?"[49] His answer is that liberation involves a number of facets including "becoming free from excessive restraints," and becoming "free for necessary protest." It also involves a faith that encourages breaking away from accepted practices, including service that demeans the person with disabilities and moves away from merely providing care to offering friendship.[50]

Moltmann argues that "disability always has two sides, on the one side is the person who is disabled, on the other, the one who disables." The one who disables loses humanity in the process of singling out the person with a disability. Liberation involves overcoming fear in the sense that "persons without disabilities must be liberated from their assumption that they are healthy and from their fear of persons with disabilities."[51]

> In order to conquer this fear, nothing less than a completely new approach to life is necessary. So long as fear encourages us to strive for the ideals of health, potency, achievement, and beauty, we will continue to develop defense mechanisms around people who are weak, sick, ugly, and have disabilities. Persons who equate being human with being healthy cannot abide seeing a

47. Ibid. (italics original).
48. Moltmann, "Liberate Yourselves."
49. Ibid., 105.
50. Ibid., 107.
51. Ibid., 107–11.

sick person. Persons who identify being human with power to achieve will despise weak persons. Those who seek out beauty in persons will regard every disability as ugly.[52]

Jürgen Moltmann's article dwells so much on personal liberation in the face of the liberatory theology of Eiesland. Yet, the second half of his article talks extensively about the person as the image of God. It affirms "sickness" as part of what it means to be human as well as the reality of suffering. He tackles healing by arguing that "Jesus' power to heal lies in his power to suffer," and that "he heals, not by casting aside and getting rid of sicknesses, but by taking them on himself. People are not healed [he suggests] by Jesus' supernatural powers, but rather by his wounds."[53] He goes so far as to entertain the question, "Is every disability also a gift?" This is merely to suggest that people with disabilities can make positive contributions to the human community, especially when they are not segregated from the mainstream. The church is a "healing community" where "friendship links affection with respect."[54] It is a place where "persons with and without disabilities learn to live together, the old roles of the helper and the needy one disintegrate. It is then that both parties learn mutual giving and taking, each with her own gifts, each with her own boundaries."[55]

A more recent contribution to a liberation theology of disability is Scot Danforth's article "Liberation Theology of Disability and the Option for the Poor."[56] Danforth offers a critique of Nancy Eiesland's work from the point of view of liberation theologies of Latin America. Emphasis is placed on God's deep interest in the poor as expressed in the concern for justice that stems from "practical reading of both the Bible and the lived social context of the moment, interpreting the Scriptures and the historical situation of each in light of the other."[57] Danforth maintains that Eiesland's work does not address the implications of an emancipatory Christianity for the multiple prejudices and oppressive circumstances faced by disabled persons in the broader society. Her focus appears to be on the middle class, thus ignoring the *"preferential option for the poor."*[58] Danforth argues for a broader interpretation of the poor to include people with disabilities. In both affluent and poor countries, issues of employment, underemployment, and poverty

52. Ibid., 112–13.
53. Ibid., 115.
54. Ibid., 119.
55. Ibid., 121–22.
56. Danforth, "Liberation Theology of Disability."
57. Ibid., 5.
58. Ibid., 4–5 (italics original).

loom large. He calls for a "transformational analysis" that critiques a wide range of social institutions especially devised by nondisabled researchers "without significant involvement of disabled persons."[59]

Over the years, a number of articles and books have appeared which have referred to themes from liberation theology in discussing the practical issues of disability ministries. For instance, in 2002 Jennie Weiss Block's *Copious Hosting* used themes from liberation theology to develop a "theology of access for people with disabilities." One of her conclusions from reviewing these materials is that people with disabilities must be free to "tell their own stories, recover their own histories, and claim their own voice and language."[60]

The Body

Other theologians have expanded the role of the disabled body in doing theology. There are many reasons for using the body as a starting point for developing a theology of disability. Using the body as a starting point is viewed as more useful than starting with the image of God. The image of God as "portrayed in the Bible is that of a being whose perfect knowledge is attained through the perfection of the divine senses."[61] The problem, according to Hull, "lies in the fact that the divine perfection is imaged upon or is a projection of the ideals of a perfect human being or a perfect human life." The body, therefore, "is a suitable starting point for a Christian anthropology and especially for a theology of disability not only because disability sits, as it were, in the body, but also because the body is the source of our knowledge not only of ourselves, but of the world and everything in it."[62] In addition, approaching a theology of disability in this way helps to communicate that even the term "disability" represents a multitude of life experiences. The world of someone who is blind is decidedly different from the world of someone with multiple sclerosis, for example.[63]

What then, does the body have to with a theology of disability? Commenting on the body theology of Sallie McFague, Deborah Beth Creamer notes that "embodiment theologies begin by noting that, because we have mistrusted, feared and discounted our bodies, we have not taken our bodies seriously in doing theology." Therefore "we must remember that we *are*

---

59. Ibid., 9–10.
60. Block, *Copious Hosting*, 97.
61. Hull, "The Broken Body in a Broken World," 6.
62. Ibid., 8.
63. Ibid., 9.

bodies, and that when we reflect theologically, we inevitably do it as embodied selves."[64] Also, "body theology begins with the real, concrete, everyday experiences and particularities of the human bodied experience."[65] However, McFague doesn't employ the disabled body in her scheme, choosing instead to refer to disability as part of the "randomness of life," and to affirm that "God is with us in those experiences" and "God suffers with us."[66]

In response to this insight, Creamer offers "a new perspective," which she refers to as "limitness."[67] Limitness is basic in that "all bodies experience some degree of limitation," and by setting aside the definitions and statistics about disability, she points to wearing glasses, spraining or breaking an ankle, and even having a cold as examples of limitations all human bodies face. Creamer argues that

> An awareness of limitness encourages us to think about what we mean when we talk about human embodiment, recognizing that it is not one simple or typical thing but rather encompasses a wide range of expected experiences. Rather than automatically expecting that "body" means "normal body," it problematizes our notion of normal while also encouraging us to think about the particularity of bodies and how these particularities might affect theological reflection.[68]

Thus, Creamer makes the claim that using the term "limitness" serves to extend McFague's argument by providing the theological community with access to "previously overlooked and under-appreciated perspectives and experiences, attention to which, according to McFague's model, will act to increase our resources for knowledge of God."[69]

In the conclusion to her book, Creamer specifies that use of the term "limitness" has a number of consequences for developing a theology of disability. First, it is "valuable for contemporary theologians and religious thinkers to consider and reflect upon bodies in diverse manifestations of embodiment, and that existing models can be challenged to include awareness of and attention to disability." Under "the limits model," another option is added to the medical and minority group models. Second, the limits model adds "necessary complexity to our theological and anthropological reflections." Creamer argues that "the presence of limits is, in fact, more

---

64. Creamer, *Disability and Christian Theology*, 56 (italics original).
65. Ibid., 57.
66. Ibid., 62.
67. Ibid., 63.
68. Ibid., 64.
69. Ibid., 69.

'normal' than their absence," and that "the claim of the limits [model] is not that we should refuse to overcome or adapt to limits, nor that we should give up on medical advances or adaptive technology." And finally, the limits model makes theology of disability interesting because no one individual or community of faith experiences or interprets disability in the same way as any other. This diversity makes "a valuable contribution to theological reflection," in that "existing models need to be evaluated based on how well they can attend to experiences of disability."[70]

Inclusion and Hospitality

Over the years, many practicing Christians have reflected (theologically and practically) on the hospitality and inclusion of the church at all levels.[71] In the beginning of his book *Unexpected Guests at God's Banquet*, Brett Webb-Mitchell reflects on how people with disabilities have been treated by congregations: "They have either not been invited to come in, or even worse, have been disinvited."[72] A more recent observation from theologian Thomas Reynolds reflects on his congregation's treatment of his own son with multiple disabilities after Reynolds was asked not to bring his son back to Sunday school:

> What were we to do? Where could we go? Over the years, we had been through behavioral programs, family counseling, and psychiatric care. At this point, we were just beginning to coming to terms with our own son's recent diagnosis: Tourette's syndrome. Later, he would be diagnosed with Asperger's syndrome, bipolar disorder, and obsessive-compulsive disorder. But at this point he was about seven years old, and we knew only of the Tourette's. We stopped attending this church. In fact, we stopped attending church altogether.[73]

This episode could have been handled differently, but according to Reynolds the issues raised in his family could be of concern to any congregation. He raises the question, "what can happen in our churches and in our daily lives when we encounter not only people with disabilities, but also other people who are different in some way or another?"[74]

---

70. Creamer, *Disability and Christian Theology*, 115–20.
71. See Newlands and Smith, *Hospitable God*.
72. Webb-Mitchelll, *Unexpected Guests at God's Banquet*, 1.
73. Reynolds, *Vulnerable Communion*, 11.
74. Ibid., 12.

That hospitality and inclusion in congregations is not a new issue for the Christian church should not surprise anyone. It was a concern as early as the New Testament, in which Luke's Gospel talks about the issue in the "great dinner" as Yong refers to it. Here, "the stranger, the marginalized, and the excluded—as metaphorically signaled in the poor, the crippled, the blind, and the lame of the parable—are invited guests of the dinner just as the nondisabled are."[75] And so many recent papers and books in an attempt to develop a theology of disability have taken hospitality into their interface between Christian theology and the practice of the church. A look at these materials is important for the sociological understanding of disability and the church.

In her attempt to develop a "theology of access," Jennie Weiss Block argues that "if access is to be more than an idea or passing fad, our praxis must take a different direction built on acknowledgement that human vulnerability is the source of communion in the Kingdom." In fact, she and others (see below) maintain that gaining access or, for that matter, building for access, is not the same as hospitality.[76] In fact, "inclusive interdependence, and cooperation happen best among people who recognize that human vulnerability is the source of communion in the Kingdom that God desires." This position takes to task common stereotypes of disability, insisting that "as long as we continue to view a person with the disability as 'the other,' the person we need to 'help,' cast in the role of 'the least,' we close off the possibility of friendship and block the way to interdependence."[77]

But Block's analysis does not go far enough in identifying the nature and cause of what excludes, and what otherwise promotes inhospitable attitudes toward people with disabilities. Thomas Reynolds takes further steps to locate the source of these attitudes and behaviors in what he calls "the cult of normalcy."[78] First, he argues that the source of attitudes and practices cannot be obtained unless we are willing to go deeper by "naming and analyzing the social processes by which the normal and abnormal are constructed and ritually sanctioned." In order to understand a concept such as "normalcy," one must understand how it operates "as a cultural system of social control." While it operates as a "way of ordering and bringing meaning to the everyday world shared by a group" (which is good), normalcy has "an insidious undertow that accompanies it, working to draw all into a certain caste or type. Normalcy is a force that flows according to strategic

---

75. Yong, *Theology and Down Syndrome*, 222.
76. Block, *Copious Hosting*, 158.
77. Ibid., 158–59.
78. Reynolds, *Vulnerable Communion*, 48–49.

mechanisms of power that serve the conventions of the status quo, which in turn serves primarily those persons whose bodily appearance and abilities fall within a recognizably standard range."[79]

In an effort to interrogate these issues, Reynolds proceeds to provide a step-by-step examination this "cult of normalcy." He begins by arguing that there is a built-in human need for welcome, a fundamental desire for assurance lodged deep into all human psyches. Such a need seems to be based upon an "axiomatic ingredient cutting across all the ordinary circumstances of our daily lives," in that "in order to be selves, human beings require a meaningful and trustworthy world, a world with boundaries that provide security and that offer a dependable sense that all will be well." Such a place constitutes, in Reynolds's view, a home where one can live within the universe, and is therefore part of that which is disrupted by disability. Yet, home has been denied to many persons with disability.[80]

Issues of social boundaries arise when we consider ability and disability. Here Reynolds wants his readers to understand society's need to construct their social world: "Lack of ability, then, is acknowledged and measured by values that arise within the conventions and role expectations of a shared world; for ability is a factor of performing in ways that are understood by others to be meaningful and consequential."[81] This, in turn, is mediated by "a particular framework of valuation" that creates a certain "moral space, supplying specific resources for distinguishing between what does and what does not contribute to human flourishing." Later, he argues that the "welcome we seek is communally circumscribed. Frameworks create and sustain a provisional bounded sociocultural community, coordinating practices by shaping shared attitudes and values."[82]

Reynolds develops the concept of the cult of normalcy by elaborating on the "economies of exchange," defined as "a system of reciprocity that regulates interaction in a community." These interactions are embodied in that "we engage one another in concrete practices of flesh and blood." And later he states: "Economies of exchange, therefore, revolve around identification markers that display what I call *Body Capital*. The value of a body and its abilities is a matter of how it reflects common assumptions about a community's sense of the good, how it gains legitimacy, purchases recognition, or acquires worth in the community of others."[83]

79. Ibid., 51.
80. Ibid., 52–53.
81. Ibid., 55.
82. Ibid., 56–59.
83. Ibid., 60 (italics original).

Drawing on the work of disability studies scholar Lennard Davis, whose statement that "the human body is never a single so much as a series of attitudes toward it," one may define the cult of normalcy as follows:

> a set of rituals trained upon demarcating and policing the borders of a "normal" way of being. Bodies are regulated so as to remediate and thus neutralize their deviances. This is the product of an economy of exchange that fears the disruption of its management system. At base, the cult of normalcy is an evasion strategy trained upon nurturing community and manufacturing consent.[84]

Reynolds proceeds from this point on to provide details of how this "cult" (a term he uses nonsociologically) operates in the context of disability. In a sense, someone with a disability lacks social capital received from others. In turn, "normalcy creates disability as an obstacle to human flourishing, an incomplete and out-of-control body."[85] The work of the church and of theology, then, is to champion disability as a vital issue. "Privileging disability is essential to the good of society. It calls us to attend more adequately to the interpersonal nexus of vulnerable openness to others. More specifically, it calls us to responsibility as agents capable of loving and welcoming others."[86]

Love also plays a role in that it "signals the fact that I have become involved and invested, vulnerable to another."[87] Later, hope is added to the mix as tragedy so often is raised in the face of disability. "Hope," according to Reynolds, "is not merely a matter for what I hope, but with whom I hope. Hope is a creative power that is relational—for us. This distinguishes it from an ego-centered desire or wish. Love and hope are bound indissolubly."[88] However, God provides no easy answer to the presence of disability or to how people with disabilities have been treated. "God is not another term for false optimism and sense of controlled security, but rather a way of naming the element of trustworthiness in the fragility of things, a way of persistently living out the affirmation that 'it is good.'"[89]

In the end, the core of Reynolds's argument is that the church, as the people God, is a "vulnerable communion" in which all members are called

---

84. Ibid., 111.
85. Ibid., 118.
86. Ibid., 119.
87. Ibid., 141.
88. Ibid., 170.
89. Ibid., 209.

upon "to love as Christ loves," which is to recognize the need to affirm the image of God in one's self and in others. This theme is affirmed in that,

> If God's love spills outward toward creatures, sweeping immanently through the fabric of the universe, and if this love is imaged in the shape of human persons, then gratitude and hope entail giving recognition to the inherent worth of others, accepting the generosity that God has already given and letting it run over into the landscape of human relations. Finite gestures of compassionate regard for others are themselves sacred invocations that participate in the infinite, life-giving generosity of the divine.[90]

In the final analysis, according to Reynolds, the church is called to be a place where the cult of normalcy is replaced by a new order, "an order of love." This new order involves a new economy of the household of God where "we are transformed, remade interdependently with each other as vulnerable beings loved into being by God."[91] According to Reynolds, we welcome God

> as we welcome Jesus the stranger into our home. This is why disability is redemptively fundamental: by welcoming people with disabilities into our church communities, our churches become communions bearing witness to God's creative-redemptive power, a strange power that works not through strength but weakness and vulnerability to give life. And when our church communities traffic in such powers, they cannot help but spill outward to transform the world in a God-ward direction.[92]

John Swinton has extended discussion of hospitality and disability by suggesting that the church must move from "inclusion to belonging." His presentation argues that "including people with disabilities does not go far enough in overcoming the alienation, stigmatization, and exclusion of those whom we choose to name 'disabled."[93] In order to illustrate his position, he employs "thin" and "thick" models of inclusion and illustrates them through a conversation with Elaine, an elderly woman with intellectual disabilities. Based on questions such as "Where do you feel you belong?" and on Elaine's participation in various congregational activities, Swinton concludes that while her participation in worship indicates that she has obtained a certain

---

90. Ibid., 249.
91. Ibid.
92. Ibid.
93. Swinton, "From Inclusion to Belonging."

level of acceptance, her inclusion into the life of the congregation "appears to stop at the door of the chapel. She has never been invited into the homes of her religious friends, although clearly she desires this."[94] He argues that in order "to belong, you need to be missed." His reflection from the interview is that "belonging means coming to know one another in Jesus," and that which goes beyond politics to finding "community in Jesus."[95]

Toward a "High" Theology of Disability?

In taking the risk of devoting a good deal of space to outlining Thomas Reynolds's thoughts on a theology of disability, I am well aware of additional materials that could be shared in this chapter. Again, *Vulnerable Communion* is one of a handful of works aimed specifically at the theological community. It is not an "easy read" that can be handled in a few sittings. It has to be read over and over, as well as treated and included as a resource for seminary courses taught by professors of theology.

Another major work published in 2007 was Amos Yong's *Theology and Down Syndrome: Reimaging Disability in Late Modernity*.[96] This extensive volume, with 295 pages of text and another 150 pages of notes, includes references, biblical references, and an extensive index. It is a serious attempt to grapple with disability and theology in a systematic manner. Yong spends the first 150 or so pages at the beginning of his text defining the problem in secular terms and addressing challenges about disability from biblical texts. Then he proceeds to "reimage" and "renew" theology in late modernity by examining, in order, the traditional topics normally found in systematic theology, including (1) the doctrine of creation, providence, and the *Imago Dei*, (2) renewing ecclesiology, (3) rethinking soteriology, and (4) resurrecting Down syndrome and disability (heaven and the healing of the world). Yong's goal is to reimage and renew theology in late modernity in a "disabled world" by taking a "theological account of disability in general and intellectual disability in particular." (Yong's brother Mark has Down syndrome—hence the title and motivation for writing the book.)[97]

Without working through an outline of each of these pillars of systematic theology, one can obtain an idea of Yong's approach by a brief look at his chapter "Renewing Ecclesiology," which examines the doctrines of the church in light of disability. While traditional ecclesiology emphasizes

94. Ibid., 181.
95. Ibid., 183–84.
96. Yong, *Theology and Down Syndrome*, vi–viii.
97. Ibid., 151.

questions such as what is the nature of the church? Or, what is the nature of the sacraments of the church? Yong's theological work has focused on the church as "pneumatological" (Spirit-led) ecclesiology, which emphasizes "unity, holiness, [and] apostolicity."[98] The Holy Spirit is at work bringing about the transformation of the church into the image of Christ. In addition, "the governance of the church is essentially pneumatic and charismatic rather than hierarchical: the church is led by the Spirit who is poured on all flesh, even if the Spirit-filled and Spirit-led people of God are anointed to offices of service and need to discern the work of the Spirit in the midst of the church."[99] Yong also acknowledges the wider phenomenon of the Spirit, including churches in the global South, the emerging church, and "post-liberal ecclesiologies."[100]

Yong's emphasis on ecclesiology and disability begins with a discussion of L'Arche. He maintains that L'Arche "embodies and manifests the values and perspectives articulated by the more recent ecclesiologies." The L'Arche emphasis on welcoming strangers and providing a "hospitable environment" where friendships emerge and care is provided is viewed as an example of a "countercultural, egalitarian, and democratic community where strength has been manifest in weakness; where self-sacrificial love has resisted competition, and efficiency; and where the miraculous has been understood in terms of the ordinary and simple events of daily life."[101]

With L'Arche as background, and citing Paul's description of the body of Christ in 1 Cor 12:22–26, Yong maintains that a church open to people with disabilities has "a biblically informed and inclusive pneumatological ecclesiology which emphasizes both that the church is liberated from whatever disabling barriers might exclude certain of her members from full access and participation in that the 'weaker' members are accorded more honor by God and therefore are more central to the identity of the body of Christ."[102] In his view, on the practical level the church should be the place where "the relationship between the 'weak' and the 'strong' [is] such that all suffer and rejoice with the challenges and victories of each other."[103]

In a more recent book, *The Bible, Disability, and the Church*, Yong envisions "a fully inclusive church—at the congregational, parish, community, and missiological level—to be one in which people with disabilities

98. Ibid., 197.
99. Ibid.
100. Ibid., 198–99.
101. Ibid., 201.
102. Ibid., 204.
103. Ibid., 205.

are honored and in which they are fully ministers alongside non-disabled people."[104]

In contrast to Yong's systematic theology of disability, Sharon Betcher's *Spirit and the Politics of Disablement* is a response to disability couched in terms of contemporary body theology, postmodern thought, and disability studies. For Betcher, disability is extremely personal, and it is social in that she identifies disability's role as confounding the "narrated passages of tragedy to triumph, from grave to glory" for an existence that cannot be taken for granted, and one must live with the knowledge that "nothing can stabilize the risk of existence; justice can provide a clearing for livelihood. Yet the equanimity of trust offers itself as the wisdom of life."[105]

Evangelical Approaches to Disability Theology

Joni and Friends conducts the Christian Institute of Disability (CID), a theological think tank that has produced several position papers on a number of ethical issues and more general papers related to disability. It also sponsors workshops at the CID in Pasadenia, California, and in other locations around the United States. Several of these papers have been written by Kathy McReynolds from California Baptist University.[106]

Other papers from Joni and Friends include a paper, "Christianity: A Knowledge Tradition" (also by McReynolds), that seeks to build Christianity's role in responding to the "new atheists" by sharing its body of knowledge with scientists, and specifically its knowledge about disability. "The doctrines of *Creation, Sin, Redemption, Incarnation, Church, Judgment,* and *Eternity,* when taken together, provide a kind of grid through which we can understand life's most important issues. This, in turn, can yield the beginnings of a Christian understanding of disability with all the complexities it brings."[107] Truth, which is anchored in a "higher authority," is able to provide the base from which to argue the worth and dignity of people with disabilities. Other papers deal with such topics as stem cell research, prenatal genetic testing, postmodernism, and human rights. The first two take a conservative view in which clear Christian mandates that prohibit the use of stem cells, as well as prenatal testing. These arguments are rational, taking into account current arguments as well as historic philosophical and theological points of view. These two papers argue against any real capitulation

---

104. Yong, *The Bible, Disability, and the Church,* 146.
105. Betcher, *Spirit and the Politics of Disablement,* 204.
106. See Joni and Friends website (http://www.Joniandfriends.org/).
107. McReynolds, "Christianity: A Knowledge Tradition" (2010).

to the ideas behind postmodernism and against a nontheological view of human rights.[108]

In addition to Kathy McReynolds and others associated with Joni and Friends, no doubt others are involved in thinking about disability from an evangelical perspective. *Christianity Today*, a "magazine of evangelical conviction," has printed a number of articles that have featured disability issues. Most of these are geared to pushing congregations to display Christian hospitality to people with disabilities and their friends and families; these articles place attention on supporting parents who have children with disabilities. In October 2005, a brief article appeared titled "Fear Not the Disabled." It concluded with the following:

> In the debate over human embryonic stem cells, Christians are right to defend the humanity and dignity of the embryo. But our well-reasoned words are unlikely to convince people who fear disease and incapacitation if we do not also demonstrate real pro-life compassion for a whole class already here—people with disabilities. These neighbors are all around us. And we must not, like the Levite and the priest in Jesus' parable, pass by on the other side of the road.[109]

Conclusion

Over the pages of this chapter, the struggle of Christian church to deal, theologically, with disability has been documented. These efforts have moved from being small parts of ministry-oriented books about disability to book-length studies devoted solely theological themes. The older books like those authored by Govig and Wilke were pioneer efforts with only passing theological references. The new works by Yong, Reynolds, and Creamer focus exclusively on theological reflection. Even evangelicals have begun to reflect on theological/doctrinal issues raised by disability. Of utmost significance, is that, for the most part, these works have incorporated social contexts of various aspects of what it means be disabled. The idea that disability must be viewed from a nonmedical stance resonates with these authors as they seek to construct a theology that acknowledges disability's uneasy social location. In other words, they seek to explore the significance of disability amid

---

108. See McReynolds, "A Disturbing Presence"; and McReynolds, "Why Christian Doctrine Matters."

109. *Christianity Today*, "Fear Not the Disabled."

the brokenness of contemporary life to the point that they call into question the meaning of being human.

Theological reflection on disability has been enhanced by the publication of not only major monographs on the subject but articles on subtopics within the field. For example, Hollie M. Holt-Woehl has authored an article titled "Creation and Theology of Humanness," which reflects on whether creation was perfect and if the fall in the garden of Eden was the source of all human suffering.[110] Philip Thomas focuses on the image of God in light of disability by exploring how Jesus acts as the key to understanding how all persons are made in God's image even without conscious participation.[111]

Recently, an effort has been made to "change the conversation." Reynolds has published an article in which he urges readers to move beyond the "able-disabled binary that pits a normal 'inside' against an 'outside' in need of normalization, and beyond mere inclusive 'accommodation' to disability as an access issue." Instead, he proposes that disability might be viewed as a matter of human difference, received as a gift, one that disrupts easy closures and that in the end opens new transformative possibilities for being vulnerably human together in mutual relation.[112]

An additional approach suggested by Metzger is to acknowledge the evolution of disability theology over the last twenty years. Broad agreement has emerged that (1) the social model rather than the medical model is the best way to view disability, (2) any theological conversation "must begin with concrete embodied experience rather than any truth-claims by the Christian tradition," (3) "biblical and theological traditions are viewed with suspicion or assessed negatively" with respect to disability, and (4) a trend has begun away from viewing God as omnipotent toward viewing God as one who knows pain and does not seek to devalue difference.[113] In turn, Metzger suggests that "a reclamation of biblical and theological traditions that testify to an experience of the sacred as indifferent or oppressive may not only resonate but prove beneficial as well."[114]

As I have mentioned in previous chapters, most of the works reviewed in this chapter are authored by people with a personal connection to disability. They are either disabled themselves, have children or siblings with disabilities, or have extensive experiences working with people with disabilities. These newer works have demonstrated that the study area of

110. Holt-Woehl, "Creation and a Theology of Humanness."
111. Thomas, "The Relational-Revelational Image."
112. Reynolds, "Theology and Disability."
113. Metzger, "Reclaiming."
114. Ibid.

theology and disability is beneficial, in addressing not only disability issues in the church, but other areas such as theological anthropology, ecclesiology, worship, and mission. Indeed, what has been created is a community of theologians who are deeply and personally committed to constructing a theology of disability as well as to urging trained theologians to construct general works inclusive of disability and disability-related issues. Most recently, a "Summer Institute on Theology and Disability" has been developed that gathers many of the theologians whose works were reviewed in this Chapter. Global in scope, this gathering is another step to extend their work and to encourage young scholars currently at work in the field.[115]

This raises the question: how can we integrate theologies of disability (and, for that matter, all of what has been covered in this book) into the life of the church, and into the seminaries that train ministers and other church workers? The Association of Theological Schools has developed policy guidelines calling for its member theological seminaries to develop curriculum inclusive of disability, not only in special courses, but "infus[ed] . . . throughout the curriculum." The policy points to "the growing body of scholarship about theology and disability [that] provides an important resource for curriculum development."[116] As of this writing, no study has been conducted that documents how seminaries have responded to these policies. For this author's part, I have taught a special course titled "The Disability Ministry of the Congregation" at a local seminary, but have not been able to persuade the school to integrate disability issues into the seminary's curriculum so that all students have some knowledge in this area.

---

115. Gaventa, personal communication (2013).
116. Association of Theological Schools, (2012).

11

Life Worth Living: Christian Ethics and Disability

No discussion about disability and Christianity is complete without a consideration of the ethical issues involved in living with a disability. Ethical considerations are at work at every life stage, and not only for those who are impaired, but in the contexts of families, friends, caregivers, and people in general. Thus, Swinton and Brock can edit a volume on *Theology, Disability and the New Genetics*[1] and Joni Eareckson Tada and her organization Joni and Friends offers a theological perspective on disability that speaks directly to the ethical issues relevant to the disability community.[2]

Indeed, there is a real need to address society's tendency to do everything possible to avoid bringing an individual with a disability into the world and to reduce or eliminate disability should it occur at any life stage. In the United States and in other Westernized countries expectant couples are routinely screened for birth defects and counseled as to whether a child forecast to be born with disabilities (such as Down's syndrome) should be aborted. Part of such advocacy derives from the assumption that such a birth would cause "distress and suffering."[3] Since the Terri Schiavo case, there has also been an enlivened debate about whether people with minimal brain activity should be maintained on life supports indefinitely, or have these supports removed thus allowing the person to die. Euthanasia also raises the question as to whether ending life in this manner should ever be an option for people with disabilities. This, in turn, raises the further question of what constitutes a "life worth living," especially with reference to those with severe intellectual and physical disabilities.[4]

---

1. Swinton and Brock, eds., *Theology, Disability, and the New Genetics*.
2. See chapter 10, above.
3. Swinton, "Introduction," 4.
4. Reinders, *The Future of the Disabled*.

Many of these issues are rarely given full consideration by society, and discussion often takes place "under the radar" of the church. Indeed, churches can be complacent in the face of these actions and lack the knowledge, power, and skills to work with parents and medical professionals in a positive manner going beyond the simple yes or no. This is especially the case at the congregational level, where parents are admired for giving life to a disabled child but rarely is the congregation aware of the difficult tasks that parents have in caring for such a child, and the financial burdens many are faced. The same is true about the care of elderly parents, which often falls to the middle-aged female spouse even if it is the husband's parent; for some, the same can be true caring for young children as well.

On the personal level, the ethical challenge facing many people with disabilities is that when topics are raised such as prebirth genetic screening or ending the life of someone with extreme physical or mental challenges, or both, a person's very existence is called into question. While it is often assumed that such measures are appropriate to alleviate suffering, testimony from persons with birth defects or people who acquire disabilities later in life, or both, reveals that for them and their loved ones, life is worth living. As we shall learn in this chapter, the presence of suffering is not (or should not be) a criterion of whether a human life is valuable. To ignore society's assumption that a life of potential or actual suffering is not worth living is to ignore society's role in rejecting and devaluing people with disabilities. As John Swinton asserts, the real suffering that occurs in the face of disability is often caused by society's failure, not only to accept people with disabilities, but to provide the necessary measures to support people with disabilities, who not only can but want to live meaningful lives.[5]

Congregations are rarely challenged to consider what it takes to provide care for people with disabilities of all ages, or to realize that the congregation's involvement can enhance the full participation of people with disabilities in the life of the church and in the larger society. Addressing the failure of churches to recognize the importance of caregiving for people of all ages with disabilities begins with highlighting in congregations that parents of children with disabilities often mount heroic efforts to gain proper medical diagnoses and entrance to programs that address their child's educational and care needs. Families (and especially women in families) often are responsible for their child's care and also the care of their elderly parents with disabilities. The vast amount of caregiving provided informally does not require specialized training. The tasks can be as simple as running errands for an elderly person who has difficulty getting around outside the

---

5. Swinton, "Introduction," 5.

home to providing around-the-clock care for a child with severe disabilities.[6] Again, the question arises, where is the church?

The ethics of disability and caring for people with disabilities are closely intertwined. If it is the case that Christian ethics places a high value on lives of those viewed as disabled, even on those who are severely disabled, then ministry with those who are disabled (including the provision of care) should be shaped accordingly. This chapter will first discuss the issues surrounding disability ethics by tracing the eugenic tendencies that call into question the birthing and life-sustaining efforts made for people with disabilities. Then it will consider the church's efforts to respond to these ethical issues in order to see what, if any, new insights can be brought to the table based on the church's biblical, historical and theological heritage.

Eugenics and the Challenge of the New Genetics

Coined by British "scientist of heredity" Sir Francis Galton in 1883, the term *eugenics* labeled a movement aimed at "race improvement." Initially, it was devoted to eliminating "defective mentality" thought to be connected to such social ills as crime, poverty, and promiscuity. Eugenicists thought that by restricting marriages, advocating sterilization, and opening state institutions for the "feebleminded," they could diminish these societal problems. Such measures were supported by massive intelligence testing and widespread use of the terms "normal" and "abnormal" (derived from statistical notion of the normative curve) as criteria for institutionalization.[7] This was accomplished, according to disability studies scholars Sharon Snyder and David Mitchell, in four specific historical stages: (1) in the early nineteenth century people with cognitive disabilities lost their places of care within family and community and became social and state problems, (2) in the post–Civil War era, rhetoric characterized feeblemindedness as a social burden to be alleviated through custodial institutional care, (3) during the first decades of the twentieth century, rhetoric appeared characterizing feeblemindedness as a menace to society, and (4) after 1920 a psychiatry-based mental hygiene movement began to supplant eugenics; this movement emphasized helping people with disabilities adapt and adjust through services that perpetuated segregation and that could be based in the institution and/or the community.[8]

---

6. Lima, "Caregiving," 221.
7. Snyder and Mitchell, "Eugenics," 624.
8. Ibid.

To some extent, churches followed along or simply ignored these developments. Ample evidence shows that mainline Protestant pastors eagerly embraced eugenic practices as a method to keep God's creation pure. Sermons such as Phillips Endecott Osgood's "The Refiner's Fire" received top honors in a contest sponsored by the American Eugenics Society. The sermon spoke of the Christian's duty to keep God's creation pure and of eugenics as the method to enact such purging. Osgood believed that "The first urgency is to know the axioms of eugenics. We are not even well educated nor modern if we have no bowing acquaintance with its larger truths."[9] Other preachers in the American mainline echoed these sentiments, and given their place in a society where Protestants were the elites (the 1920s), eugenics held sway.[10]

The events of World War II and especially the atrocities of Nazi Germany (concentration camps and the mass murder of countless people, including those with disabilities) spelled the end of widespread eugenics advocacy. However, the story of eugenics does not end here. Discoveries in early 1950s led to increased importance for genetics and to the tracing of many disorders to abnormalities in genetic structures—abnormalities that resulted in such conditions as Down syndrome and cystic fibrosis. Later on, geneticists from around the globe developed the Human Genome Protect, whose goal is specifying "the 3 billion pairs [of chromosomes] that make up the DNA sequence of the entire human genome."[11] By June 2000, the project produced its first draft and since then has raised the hope that genetic disabilities could not only be discovered, but prevented. However, such dramatic development is in the distant future and would only affect a small proportion of people with disabilities. Thus, "the fact that we can identify the inheritance pattern or can do a genetic test tells us something about the strength of the genetic contribution to a condition, but it may not tell us much about the most significant causes of that condition in real life or its severity or prevalence."[12]

Euthanasia and the Quality of Life Question

Physician-assisted suicide (PAS) has received a great deal of media hype in recent years and especially surrounding the efforts of Dr. Kevorkian to make it a standard medical and legal enterprise. But PAS is part of a concept

9. Hall, "To Form a More Perfect Union," 76.
10. Ibid., 80.
11. Scully, "Genetics," 777.
12. Ibid., 777–78.

commonly referred to as euthanasia. According Silvers, euthanasia refers to "any action intended to hasten death for the purpose of dispensing a merciful benefit."[13] Silvers continues by outlining two "kinds of supposed beneficiaries." In the first, "euthanasia is said to benefit individuals by offering them death to relieve their suffering." In the second, it is said "to benefit whoever is burdened by or otherwise disadvantageously implicated in the lives of the aforementioned sufferers." A disability activist has characterized euthanasia as "among the theoretically benevolent, but malignant in practice, ideas that have been applied to people with disabilities."[14]

The disability studies community tends to counter euthanasia's link of disability to human suffering by pointing out that the vast majority of people with disabilities either find life worthwhile or can experience life as worthwhile with the appropriate community supports. However, there is little insight as to who would be most likely to pursue this course. Silvers argues that "as a group, people with chronic impairments or long-standing disabilities are more likely than nondisabled people to consider illness and dependence as components of ordinary life rather than as reasons to hasten death." But in some cases euthanasia or other forms of committing suicide (such as refusal to eat) tend to occur at the end of a road of a life filled with frustration and pain.[15]

In 1986 twenty-eight-year-old Elizabeth Bouvia sought to end her life because of her severe cerebral palsy and arthritis; furthermore, her marriage had fallen apart, she had experienced a miscarriage, she had little success establishing a career, and she was heavily dependent on others for feeding and personal care. The dean of the school of social work in which she was enrolled "informed her that it would be impossible for her to find a position in her field because of her severe disability." When Bouvia took leave of her studies, she lost her personal attendants and the use of a van, all of which had been provided in support of her meeting her career goals. In the face of her situation she sought to end her life (the first attempt occurring three years earlier) through the assistance of hospital staff. She even went so far as to obtain a court order prohibiting medical staff from force-feeding her. Nevertheless, the number persons opting for such a procedure is relatively small. As of 2002, she was still living.[16]

Of course, the most widely known case etched in recent memory is that of Terri Schiavo, who suffered a heart attack in her Florida home

---

13. Silvers, "Euthanasia," 2:651.
14. Ibid.
15. Ibid., 2:652.
16. Sisters of Charity, "The Case Elizabeth Bouvia."

on February 25, 1990. By the time rescue workers arrived she had ceased breathing for several minutes. Although she was revived, her brain was severely damaged to the point that there was no evidence of any awareness of herself, or any signs that she would resume normal brain activity. After a lengthy hospital stay, she was moved to a nursing facility where she remained for several years.[17] Terri Schiavo's parents were devout Catholics "who could not bring themselves to accept the termination [of the] feeding tube for their daughter." Her parents cited Vatican views that supported the continuation of her life and were able to obtain support for their position from Florida Catholics and among some Florida state legislators. However, Terri's husband felt that it was time to let her die, a position that put him at odds with his in-laws. Before long Governor Jeb Bush, a Roman Catholic, and pro-life members of the U.S. House of Representatives and Senate also became involved. Right-to-life groups gave full support to Terri's parents. The episode was publicized through round-the-clock coverage by cable news outlets.[18]

Many interested parties in the bioethics, theology, and law were completely surprised by the bitter back-and-forth struggle between the various parties. In fact, "numerous professional associations and consensus statements in medical journals had articulated the view that, under certain circumstances, life support, including food and water, could be ended for those who were terminally ill, in a permanent vegetative state, or suffering irremediably but unable to communicate."[19] However, while the Schiavo case seemed to fit these circumstances, the legal fight to keep Terri alive was carried through the Florida courts all the way to U.S. Supreme Court. In the end, rulings favored the discontinuation of her life.[20] An autopsy performed immediately after her death on March 21, 2005, discovered extensive brain damage, more than even her doctors had anticipated, as well as evidence verifying the medical judgment that she had lived over the years since 1990 in an irreversible vegetative state.[21]

A Matter of Ethics

The Bouvia and Schiavo cases, and others, raise medical, legal, and moral issues of which Christian churches need to be aware. This is especially the

17. Sisters of Charity, "Introduction," in *The Case of Terri Schiavo*, 19–21.
18. Ibid., 21.
19. Ibid., 21–22.
20. Ibid.
21. Sisters of Charity, "Case Timeline."

case because of the extensive network of secular ethicists found in hospitals across the U.S. and in other Western societies. People with disabilities have a significant stake in secular ethics. The debates discussed in this section interface with Christian ethical considerations and form a backdrop for Christian social ethical positions in several areas, including the value and meaning of life, issues of autonomy and competence, as well as issues pertaining to human rights.

For the vast majority of people with disabilities life is worth living. Therefore, when confronted with the positions held by Peter Singer, W. DeCamp Professor of Bioethics at Princeton University, disability studies scholars and activists mount a quick but well-informed response. According to Singer's point of view, parents of people born with profound disabilities or adults with severe disabilities should have the right to an abortion or to euthanasia. Singer regards infants as "sentient beings who are neither rational nor self-conscious"; that is, newborns lack the "rationality, autonomy and self-consciousness," and killing a newborn is not the same as killing a person.[22] Singer argues that preterm abortion or infant killing is advocated under two conditions. First, cases of spina bifida or hemophilia, where there is such a degree of potential suffering that life would be unbearable and the costs so high in terms of medical procedures and family care, warrant the termination of life. Second, "when the death of an infant will lead to the birth of another infant with better prospect of a happy life, the total amount of happiness will be greater if the disabled infant is killed."[23]

Singer's position is based upon a branch of utilitarianism commonly referred to as "consequentialism," which appraises "individual actions by the net utility they yield." According to Bickenbach and Wasserman, features of consequential utilitarianism can have "troubling implications" for people with disabilities. Accordingly, "the aggregation of the good found in the lives of separate individuals to make an overall assessment—which tends to treat those individuals as mere sources or receptacles of goodness—and the commitment to maximizing whatever counts as good—which in effect places a higher value on those who directly or indirectly contribute more good to the total."[24]

However, according to Brickenbach and Wassermann, some philosophers "reject pain or pleasure as a metric of well-being and tend to assess outcomes across people by their conformity to a pattern, such as equality, rather than by their aggregated magnitude." These philosophers argue "that

---

22. Singer, "Taking Life: Humans."
23. Ibid., 5.
24. Brickenbach and Wassermann, "Ethics," 620.

although there may be many kinds of life that qualify as valuable, still there are essential human 'functional capabilities' (mobility, pleasure, happiness, cognition, play, health) without which the good life is unachievable."[25] In addition, Bickenbach and Wasserman raise some very pointed observations: "Since impairments are limitations of one's capacity to perform actions, tasks or social roles, and since they often cause pain, discomfort, or distress, is it inevitable on any definition of 'good life' that the lives of people with disabilities are of less valuable? . . . Does severity of impairment matter? . . . Are limitations in cognition or the senses more a threat to living a good life than limitations in mobility and strength?"[26]

Obviously, there is more to this strain of ethical analysis than can be covered here. However, disability studies scholars have long raised concerns about viewing people with disabilities from a utilitarian point of view. Many of these scholars insist "that what makes life valuable is entirely a matter for the individual—with or without a disability—to decide (so called experts will inevitably judge lives with disabilities to be worse than individuals with those disabilities think they are)."[27] Along these same lines, Ruth Hubbard questions whether scientists should argue "that they are developing prenatal tests out of concern for the 'quality of life' of future children." Hubbard continues, "No one can make that kind of decision about someone else. No one these days openly suggests that certain kinds of people be killed; they just should not be born. Yet that involves a process of selection and a decision about what kinds of people should and should not inhabit the world."[28]

Three other issues also are raised in the context of disability ethics: the issues of autonomy, competence and the language of disability rights. Most often, issues of autonomy and competence are raised with respect to people with mental disorders, including persons with Down syndrome and persons with severe physical and mental impairments. Philosophers, including Kant, have traditionally worked with the assumption that to be human is to be rational and responsible, and that if one is incapable of operating in this manner safeguards must be established, including "a wide range of social and professional practices involving the restraint, forced treatment, and other limitations of freedom."[29]

Also mentioned in this context is the distinction between normal and abnormal. Since at least Kant such a distinction has been an operational

25. Ibid.
26. Ibid.
27. Ibid., 621.
28. Hubbard, "Abortion and Disability," 117.
29. Brickenbach and Wassermann, "Ethics," 622.

assumption, not only academically, but medically. We all make such distinctions to differentiate between those with and without disabilities.[30] Taken further are the terms used to distinguish between the two groups, such as "the normal children" and "the handicapped children" or "the normal child" versus "the hearing impaired," in the context of education. But of greater importance is that often the normal and abnormal become fixed dichotomies in operation even when the distinction is shown to be less than rigid, and changing over time.[31] James Charlton, however, would trace the origin of the normal-abnormal dichotomy to disability oppression, especially in underdeveloped societies where "disability oppression is the basis for backward attitudes" and not the other way around.[32]

According to Bickenbach and Wasserman, "the language of rights (human, civil, legal) has dominated the disability movement of the past couple of decades."[33] While this observation is relatively obvious, it bears further scrutiny. In the United States, the focus of attention has been on the Americans with Disabilities Act (ADA), its precedents, and its impact. The ADA is situated amid what can be referred to as laws guaranteeing "free association." So the ADA allows a visually impaired person to bring a guide dog into a movie theater.[34] However, as Brickenbach and Wasserman remind their readers, "this much seems to be logically required of a right: If is true that a person has a right to something, then (a) there must be someone (institution or other social arrangement) who (b) has the moral duty to provide it." This frames the discussion of disability rights in a secular vein but also provides a context from which the church can give consideration. Rights language presents a problem in this respect because most rights language is vague, and this vagueness extends from the United Nations to national governments on down to implementation of rights protection. Hence, a problem arises when asserting certain rights in concrete situations.[35]

One approach toward understanding and challenging the significance of rights for people with disabilities is to consider socioeconomic issues that impinge on their application. For starters, consider that since the ADA was signed into law in 1990 there has been almost no significant change in the proportion of people with disabilities who are employed. This is especially

30. Linton, *Claiming Disability*, 22.
31. Ibid., 23.
32. Charlton, "The Dimensions of Disability Oppression," 151.
33. Brickenbach and Wassermann, "Ethics," 623.
34. These are my own examples.
35. Brickenbach and Wassermann, "Ethics," 623.

the case with respect to those with "severe" disabilities.[36] Moreover, it is difficult to assess just how much openness has been generated in other areas covered by the law, especially in terms of access to key education programs, and accommodation among service industries connected with travel and access to everyday goods and services. In some cases, disability studies scholars have warned that access measures taken under the requirements of the law can never work for every person with disability. There are some whose needs require special adaptations beyond those viewed as "reasonable."

In addition, some disability writing seems to be missing the issues brought on by socioeconomic status. Charlton has made this an issue, even though he is working in global context. In commenting on the book Disability and Culture edited by Ingstad and Whyte, he praises their work for dealing with the social context of disability, especially with respect to issues of suffering, lameness, interest groups, the term handicapped, and the notion of deformation. However, Charlton wonders why the social-demographic issues receive so little attention—issues such as oppression, the dominant culture, justice, human rights, political movements, and self-determination.[37]

Christian Ethical Responses to Disability

At the outset, no Christian writer or group advocates for the prevention of the birth of a human being with disabilities, nor is euthanasia justified in the case of any child or adult with disabilities. To be sure, positions vary on how long a life should be sustained when all possible treatments have been exhausted. Even the Roman Catholic prelates who spoke out during the Schiavo case acknowledged the limitations of medicine in determining whether life supports were to be removed.[38] Yet this and other high-profile cases indicate that the church has not made these issues a priority. While it is relatively easy to issue statements that point to life-and-death issues relevant to people with disabilities, responding to these issues in day-in-day-out circumstances is another matter. In other words, how does the Christian congregation, including the laity as well as the clergy, respond to ethical issues raised by the presence of people with disabilities?

Evangelicals have expressed a high level of interest in ethical issues surrounding disability, including genetic testing and abortion of fetuses with a prognosis of severe physical or developmental disability, or both; whether a

---

36. Brault, *Americans with Disabilities, 2005*.
37. Referring to Ingstad and Whyte, eds., *Disability and Culture*.
38. "Catholic Controversies," in Caplan et al., eds., *The Case of Terri Schiavo*.

life of disability is worth living; and how to handle the end of life. As an example of the widespread interest in ethics and disability among evangelicals, consider two volumes mentioned here and included in the bibliography: Jennie Weiss Block's positions were discussed earlier, and in *Same Lake, Different Boat*, Stephanie Hubach seeks to provide biblical grounding for ministries among people with disabilities, ministries she spends the bulk of her book describing.[39] However, more academically oriented work is coming out from the Christian Institute on Disability, which is affiliated with the Joni and Friends International Disability Center. The institute has produced a significant number of papers that address critical disability issues and has a connection to the disability studies program at California Baptist University and especially the writing of Kathy McReynolds.[40]

In his introduction to *Theology, Disability and the New Genetics: Why Science Needs the Church*, John Swinton reminds readers that people with disabilities are to be partners in whatever discussions are held about genetics and other ethical issues that concern them. Nevertheless, "despite the public rhetoric of inclusion, equality and citizenship for people with disabilities, there remains a strange silence around the implications of genetic science and technology for the lives of people with disabilities."[41] Swinton refers to more specific ethical issues such as genetic variation, eugenics, and the new genetics. These call into question the procedures of the medical establishment, including its penchant for seeing the birth of an infant with Down syndrome as causing "distress and suffering." This happens, repeatedly, despite the evidence that "people with Down syndrome live very full and happy lives."[42] It is in this context, that Swinton raises questions such as, is the one born with a disability really a person? Are persons with disabilities able to lead lives of significance, or are they mere commodities that can be disposed of as "expendable, simply matters of choice"? And can we face up to the choices medical science has produced?[43] In the face of the challenges produced by modern medicine there is, according to Swinton, the need to affirm the "inherent value in simply being, in accepting and resting in the providence of God. This being allows us to become both the object and the subject of God's love, not because of what we can or cannot do, or because we do or do not have certain attributes, but simply because we are."[44]

39. Hubach, *Same Lake, Different Boat*.
40. See chapter 10, above.
41. Swinton, "Introduction," 1–2.
42. Ibid., 4.
43. Ibid., 8.
44. Ibid., 11.

However, this affirmation while an essential one for those who desire to reflect theologically (theology is not neutral) on the topic of disability and ethics, is not the only way of viewing the topic. From a sociological perspective, the role of the church as a social phenomenon in the larger society is crucial. Many of the theologies that have been discussed in this and in the previous chapter are weighed down by the simple fact that the larger portion of the church has not been exposed to, let alone wrestled with, the theological and ethical issues surrounding disability, however important they may be.

First, ethical thinking about disability has functioned in the medical establishment without the input of the churches (which, of course, is why there is a volume such as the one edited by Swinton and Brock). Indeed, many pregnant women in highly medicalized Western societies feel strong, sometimes coercive resistance, to their decision not to abort what has been diagnosed as a defective fetus. The "genetic counselor" plays a significant role in influencing and applying the notion that bearing a disabled child is an irrational choice.[45]

Under the assumption that the issue of whether or not babies should be born with disabilities, even severe disabilities, is of vital concern, scholars have proceeded to explore its contours. This debate has seen a significant amount of writing, including the materials in Swinton and Brock's edited volume, two volumes by Dutch theologian and ethicist Hans Reinders,[46] and a recent volume by Molly Haslam.[47] Of course others (old and new) can be consulted as needed, but at the heart of the argument is simply the question whether a human with severe intellectual disabilities or severe physical impairments, or both, is really a human being, or is it the case that such a life serves no purpose worthy of life, or if needful of care, should receive only the a minimal amount of care? The answers to these questions are relevant to society because of their significance for our understanding of who belongs and acts in life's larger arenas. Yet a focus on the severely disabled may take us too far from the vast number of people with disabilities who are not so impaired as to be prevented from participating in the larger arenas, even to the point of making significant contributions to society.

In settings where doctors and other medical personnel have the upper hand, Christian theologians and ethicists have a difficult time making inroads. Reinders argues that some space has been created by the

---

45. Brock and Brock, "Being Disabled."

46. Reinders, *The Future of the Disabled*; and Reinders, *Receiving the Gift of Friendship*.

47. Haslam, *A Constructive Theology of Intellectual Disability*.

"normalization" paradigm, which enables people with disabilities to be viewed as "potential participants in social life if only given a chance."[48] Paradoxically persons with disabilities are located in two worlds. The first is where they are viewed as being like the nondisabled but "have been wronged by their unnecessary exile from ordinary life, and . . . therefore, need our support." "The other world," according to Reinders, "is the world of prevention, which depicts living with a disability as a fate that can be worse than death and offers a rationale for justifying the practices of selective abortion and infanticide in the case of severely disabled children."[49] It is the second world that Reinders enters, describes, and diagnoses in his 2008 volume. He outlines a two-tiered division of disabled people: those who have benefited from the changes in terms of legislation and services, which can lead to greater participation in social life and to the possibility of their contributing to social life, and those who "still live in isolated situations . . . because the new vision has limitations itself that have not been sufficiently recognized so far. This is particularly true of people with intellectual disabilities."[50]

At this point, Reinders, introduces his friend Kelly. Kelly is profoundly disabled, "meaning that for all the important activities that characterize our lives—health, safety, relationships, communication, and so on—she will be entirely dependent on others." In addition, "Kelly will not reach even a minimal stage of determining what she wants for herself. Words such as 'I,' 'me,' or 'myself' will never mean anything to her, nor will any other word for that matter." These realities lead to the conclusion that people having similar impairments have been left out because "human individuality commonly has been valued in the history of Western thought." Given the value placed on individuality in Western thought, Kelly's realities also "raise questions about her being, questions that could even place her humanity in doubt."[51]

While Reinders's 2008 volume raises many questions, perhaps the most important follows: is there a theological angle that enables all humans to be embraced—even those who, like Kelly, are incapable of having any normal responsiveness to the outside world? Reinders's answer is that there is a theological angle anchored in "God's unconditional love for human beings as leverage against any view that understands human being primarily in terms of its intellectual and moral capabilities."[52] In a nutshell, Reinders argues that God's friendship is the paradigm of all relationships.

48. Reinders, *The Future of the Disabled*, 2.
49. Ibid., 4.
50. Reinders, *Receiving the Gift of Friendship*, 19.
51. Ibid., 19–24.
52. Ibid., 21.

This friendship includes all human beings because it is prior to any thought and action we humans may have. Friendship reverses "the order in which we think of human being."[53] Friendship "is received as a gift for the sake of our own person, as all true friendship is. God does not love us in order to get something from us. Likewise, we do not extend friendship in order to get something from the other"[54] Finally, in answer to the question,

> How do human beings with profound disabilities participate in God's friendship as the ultimate good of their lives? First, they participate in the freedom of being who they are and what they are without any need for further justification. Second, they participate in God's friendship in that they reap the fruits of the friendship we learn to extend to them insofar as we know how to have ourselves transformed by their presence in our lives.[55]

While Reinders's work as revealed in his two volumes is path-breaking and definitive, Molly Haslam challenges it by opening up the possibility that "we find our humanity in relationships of mutual responsiveness, in which individuals with profound intellectual disabilities participate as responders, albeit in non-symbolic, non-agential ways."[56] According to Haslam, God is not outside the "self" giving friendship to all humans, even those with profound disabilities, as Reinders suggests. Rather, for Haslam (and for Martin Buber) God is located "in the realm of 'the between.'" This implies, from Haslam's standpoint, that theologians should posit their understanding of human being "not one or the other side of the subject/object dichotomy." Such conclusions are based on Haslam's experience as physical therapist working with people with profound disabilities. (She is also a theologian.) This set of experiences indicate to her that people with profound intellectual and physical disabilities do respond to the world around them, as when one of Haslam's clients is less willing to respond to a substitute attendant than to the regular attendant, or when the client fails to look at the substitute.[57]

A different tack is taken by Joni and Friends through its Christian Institute on Disability. In her paper "Why Christian Doctrine Matters," Kathy McReynolds argues that "in recent years the evangelical church has ignored the source of its divine power: doctrine. In so doing, it has rendered itself *disabled*, incapable in many ways of carrying out its mission to reach the most vulnerable (Luke 14)." McReynolds seeks to counter the trend away

---

53. Ibid.
54. Ibid., 348.
55. Ibid., 349.
56. Haslam, *A Constructive Theology of Intellectual Disability*, 9.
57. Ibid., 10.

from doctrine (which began with Schleiermacher in the eighteenth century and continues today). The article outlines in catechetic form traditional Christian beliefs in God, Jesus Christ, the Holy Spirit, the Trinity, faith, sin, Christian virtue, and reason. Interesting is that to the question, what is sin? a two-word answer is given: abortion and homosexuality.[58] Another piece by Kathy McReynolds, "A Disturbing Presence? Disability in the Age of Enhancement," critiques the notion that giving birth to an infant with disability or living with disability oneself is a burden to family or to society. The piece discusses health care reform and seems to acknowledge disability as a "reality," but McReynolds cautions that real reform would entail a reform in our understanding "concerning what it means to be human," and enveloping within that understanding of humanity "those with a wide range of disabilities." Also discussed, is that the "biblical mandate to love your neighbor as yourself points to the importance of hospitality—a precept little understood in the individualistic West."[59]

Other papers from Joni and Friends include "Christianity: A Knowledge Tradition," which seeks to bolster Christianity's role in responding to the "new atheists" by sharing its body of knowledge with scientists, and specifically its knowledge about disability. "The doctrines of *Creation, Sin, Redemption, Incarnation, Church, Judgment,* and *Eternity,* when taken together, provide a kind of grid through which we can understand life's most important issues. This, in turn, can yield the beginnings of a Christian understanding of disability with all the complexities it brings."[60] Truth, anchored in a "higher authority," is able to provide the base from which to argue for the worth and dignity of people with disabilities. These, as well as other papers, are argued in a rational manner, taking into account current arguments as well as historical, philosophical, and theological points of view.[61]

Stanley Hauerwas is another Christian ethicist whose focus has been disability, although not from direct personal experience. Articles and lectures (which in 1986 were collected in the old single volume *Suffering Presence: Theological Reflections on Medicine, the Mentally Handicapped, and the Church*) have appeared over the years with a focus on cognitive disability, because the moral issues raised by cognitive disability "are almost the same as those entailed by our commitment to care for the sick through to agency of medicine." Hauerwas also notes that "questions of the nature and place

58. McReynolds, "Why Christian Doctrine Matters."
59. McReynolds, "A Disturbing Presence?"
60. McReynolds, "Christianity: A Knowledge Tradition."
61. Ibid.

of suffering cannot be avoided."[62] His concern is that, save among parents and relatives, society lacks the "moral will" to care for those with cognitive or intellectual disabilities. Society often says that the birth of infants with mental disabilities should be prevented since such persons inevitably suffer. Yet, Hauerwas suggests this is an imputation, in that "we thus persist in our assumption that the retarded suffer from being retarded not because we are unsympathetic with them but because we are not sure how to be sympathetic with them."[63] His analysis of suffering continues in the following critique:

> That we avoid the sufferer is not because we are deeply unsympathetic or inhumane, but because of the very character of suffering. By its very nature suffering alienates us not only from one another but from ourselves, especially suffering which we undergo, which is not easily integrated into our ongoing projects or hopes. To suffer is to have our identity threatened physically, psychologically, and morally. Thus our suffering even makes us unsure of who we are.[64]

However, from this analysis comes a surprising series of moves to help those with cognitive disabilities. Except that such help ends up stifling the need for themselves to do something rather than for others do something for them. What is really needed is the ability to share in a common humanity (my words) in which we are "freed from the false and vicious circle of having to be strong before others' weakness, and we are then able to join the retarded in the common project of sharing our needs and satisfactions."[65] Hauerwas's theological conclusion from this analysis is that the church need not condemn the weakness of the retarded, but acknowledge them to be "members of our community," in which we are interdependent.[66]

> Quite simply, the challenge of learning to know, to be with, and care for the retarded is nothing less than learning to know, be with, and love God. God's face is the face of the retarded; God's body is the body of the retarded; God's being is that of the retarded. For the God we Christians must learn to worship is not a god of self-sufficient power, a god who in self-possession needs no one; rather ours is a God who needs people, who needs a son.

---

62. Hauerwas, *Suffering Presence*, 19.
63. Ibid., 174.
64. Ibid., 175.
65. Ibid., 177.
66. Ibid., 178.

Absoluteness of being or power is not a work of the God we have come to know through the cross of Christ.[67]

Conclusion

With respect to disability ethics, is it too much to ask that the church find a way to provide supports for all those who care, for those who theologize, and for those who advocate along with people with disabilities? Is not the church a social group whose members constitute a community called by God to witness and serve? The "peace churches" have it right: "Everybody belongs; everybody serves." This is the challenge for the people who are laboring to discover how to build Christian community inclusive of people with disabilities. It is the call for pastors, Christian educators, pastoral care personnel, parents, caregivers, and people with disabilities themselves to not only talk of community but build it. And those of us who research, present, and write must pay attention to this aspect of religious life and see what it offers for understanding religious life in general.

---

67. Ibid.

12

Where Do We Go from Here?

In the introduction to this book, I outlined the goal that would shape this enterprise. I indicated that the intention of my efforts was to provide a concentrated overview the social contexts in which people with disabilities are located, both within the church and in society. I aimed this work toward pastors, seminary students and laypersons, believing that well-informed church leaders will place disability issues and people with disabilities at the center of the church's ministry.

In attempting to produce this book, I also pulled together materials that I had acquired over the past several years and shared them with my readers. In order to accomplish this task I found it necessary to seek additional items in order to "round out" the narrative I sought to produce. I found it necessary and productive to use materials acquired on the Internet. There is, of course, the risk that materials acquired in this manner will provide a less than accurate picture of the current state of the relationship between disability and the Christian church. To the contrary, I have uncovered church-related groups and the materials they produce that would not have been found by other methods.

It is my hope that this text will be employed, not only in the academy, but in the trenches, where it is often the case that people who advocate for a broader understanding of disability and disability-related issues lack sufficient knowledge to convince church leaders and those in the pews of the significance of disability for the life of the church. Indeed, as I indicated in the introduction, disability studies scholarship is for action to remedy situations where ideas and structures produce ignorance, prejudice, and outright discrimination against people with disabilities, even within the church.

I want to highlight again the "ubiquitous presence" of disability in contemporary society. I cannot stress this enough. Given medicine's ability to save and sustain life at all stages and circumstances, sooner or later, society will need to come to terms with those with disabilities. The church needs to demonstrate acceptance of and hospitality to those who are different in order to provide a model for the rest of society. Coupled with this is the need to develop an "embodied spirituality" that understands that however spiritual we might be, *in this world* spirituality is expressed through human bodies. Knowing what a particular impairment is and means has an impact on one's spiritual life. We need to know more about the lives of those with disabilities. Research needs to identify themes and the nuances that people with disabilities encounter as they respond to their impairments in the context of church life. As a start, researchers can explore religious themes in biographies of those with disabilities. Lists of such materials go back to the early 1900s. One word of caution, however, is that these writings are from the pens of those situated (mostly) in the middle and upper classes.[1] These are authors with the knowledge, skills, and cultural capital to produce such works. We need additional studies like Black and Rubenstein's study of the experience of God among aged women in poverty.[2]

Next, I want to highlight with admiration and respect those who have labored over many years to make the church more accessible and hospitable for those with disabilities, their families, and their friends. From the period just after World War II to the present, their efforts have challenged the people of God to consider that their assumed "normal" lives are not the only standard from which to judge human being; such workers have challenged the church to provide space—literally and socially—for human beings who cannot be normal. To be sure, these efforts have not always achieved their goals, but perseverance has kept disability and disability-related issues alive—for the church and these activists.

Over the years, these efforts have grown in relationship to developments in the larger social arena. In the 1950s disability-related action in the church grew in relation to the rise of special education in public schools. In the 1960s the church sought a ministry to those with cognitive disabilities in response to a secular call led by President John F. Kennedy for more services for this population. In the 1970s and 1980s the emphasis in the church was on the rights of people with disabilities in keeping with such calls by secular organizations including the United Nations. Over the years since the rise of disability studies, religious scholars have "interrogated" biblical texts, the historical experience of the church, and theological assumptions underpinning the church's response to people with disabilities. It is hard

1. Couser, *Recovering Bodies*.
2. Black and Rubenstein, *Old Souls*.

to know where this scholarship will lead, but as the second generation of these pioneering efforts emerges, there is the hope that they will impact the persons in the pews as well as what is taught at the seminary level. I also want to call attention to the need to study how the "tradition" of disability advocacy is passed down from one generation to the next. This was called to my attention by Patricia Wittberg's review of my 2006 volume. Her concern was that as the number of priests and nuns declines (speaking in reference to Roman Catholicism), the question arises as to "where that church will procure similar workers and organizers in the future." As well, she raises questions (as I do) as to how disability concerns will fare within the reorganized structures of mainline Protestantism.[3]

Third, I want to highlight the obvious fact that disability ministry and advocacy as described (especially in chapters 2 and 3) have developed largely in relation to developments within the wider social context. Each stage of the church's response to disability (especially from after World War II on) has developed *in response to* developments in such fields as special education, programs for people with developmental disabilities, deinstitutionalization, civil rights legislation, the social model of disability, and disability studies. In fact, as I indicated in chapter 3, some evangelical congregations have begun to ask whether their programs have created ghettos rather than integrating disabled participants into the congregation's mainstream.

Finally, I would like to stress the importance and limitations, of theological reflection on disability. While formal theological reflection on disability is a very recent development, theological reflection has taken place at various stages of modern disability advocacy. Most of the early reflections following World War II were included in publications aimed at promoting disability ministry. These reflections did not assist in resolving biblical and theological issues as more recent scholarship has attempted to do. And while the newer book-length works have begun to examine long-held biblical and theological assumptions significant for the future of disability ministry, the real challenge is how these materials can be disseminated so that all seminary students (and not just a few) have some exposure to disability and the issues it raises for the ministry of the church.

Yet seminarians are not the only ones who need to think theologically. How can we teach laypeople to think this way? Douglas John Hall's call for a theology to be "the testament of the body" and to be a "dialogical and communal enterprise" is worth more than passing consideration.[4] There is, then, a real need to ask if we can even raise the question about theologizing

---

3. Wittberg, Review of *Disability Advocacy*, 344–45.
4. Hall, *Thinking the Faith*, 140.

about disability among congregants who have never examined any doctrine of faith from a theological perspective. Yet, disability begs for such reflection, among pastors, laypeople, parents, friends, caregivers, and people with disabilities themselves. In calling for an "accessible theological method," Nancy Eiesland argued that "persons with disabilities must gain access to the social-symbolic life of the church, and the church must gain access to the social-symbolic lives of people with disabilities."[5] This is essential, even if some people with disabilities are incapable of understanding theology of any kind, because those who care for them must find the strength, love, and hope sufficient to sustain their efforts. This leads logically to a consideration of what needs to be done as the church faces disability and disability-related issues of the future.

Theological Education and the Church

In 2002, the Religion and Disability Program of National on Organization Disability issued a report titled "Creating Welcoming Congregations and Educating Clergy." Coupled to this was a conference in Washington DC sponsored by Wesley Theological Seminary, the National Organization on Disability, and the Washington Theological Consortium.[6] The keynote speaker, the late Nancy Eiesland of Candler School of Theology, set the direction for the event by focusing on the point "that we are all created in the image of God," and that "seminaries are called upon to affirm that God's image takes many forms, not just one of bodily perfection." Eiesland further stated that

> Claiming disability means exploring the critical divisions our society makes in creating the normal versus the pathological, the insider versus the outsider, or the blessed versus the cursed. In the seminary context, claiming disability can provide new means for accessing faith, not only for people with disabilities, but for the entire community of faith. The popular picture of the disabled life today encourages the view that people with disabilities constitute a perversion of God's creation. To counteract this perversion requires voices linguistically sophisticated, intellectually nuanced and politically astute, capable of articulating the issues implicit in the full inclusion of people with disabilities in church and society.

---

5. Eiesland, *The Disabled God*, 40.
6. Materials in this section are from Herzog, "Working Interfaith," 219–23.

Later, Bruce Birch, dean of Wesley at the time, reflected on the interface between disability and theological education:

> Whatever the nuances of our particular setting or tradition, theological schools are in the business of providing for the ministry of the whole people of God. If, on reflection, the disabled portion of God's people have been pushed to the margins, or left out altogether, then those of us who work and teach in seminaries have failed at our task . . . I would go further and say that it is also not enough to prepare those who would minister to the disabled in our communities, although sensitizing all in ministry is a worthy goal. We must be prepared to deal with the tough issues of preparing people with disabilities themselves for ministry so that ministry becomes by and with people with disabilities and not simply for them.

Dean Birch outlined "four challenges facing seminaries as they strive to fully include, serve and serve with people with disabilities." The first was to provide the support services "necessary for students with disabilities to successfully complete the curriculum with integrity and participate in the formational life of the community." The second challenge was that of physical facilities. Seminaries should have a "plan with clear priorities for identifying and removing barriers," and that "adapting physical facilities extends beyond wheelchair access to include" [1] "Rearranging classrooms and reassigning courses to accessible classrooms, when necessary"; [2] "Providing special equipment, such as a small light in a darkened classroom to allow an ASL interpreter to be seen"; [and 3] Posting "signage indicating wheelchair accessible entrances and restrooms, and the offer of assistance where barriers have not yet been removed." The third and fourth challenges outlined at the conference centered on curriculum and faculty, respectively. Dean Birch indicated that "issues of disability should be addressed in courses throughout the curriculum. In addition, seminaries need to be alert to adjustments in the curriculum appropriate to students with disabilities. Traditional preaching courses, without adjustments, will be of little use to deaf students." In addition, faculty must be trained to be sensitive to needs of students with disabilities who may be unable to use or benefit from traditional classroom techniques. For example, a student who is deaf or hearing impaired may not benefit when the teacher talks while writing on the blackboard.

Conferences such as this are a first step in attempting to expose future clergy to disability and the issues it raises for the pastoral ministry of the church. However, these conferences do little to change the culture of ministerial training. Only a few students attend, and their participation in courses on disability ministry is dependent upon whether the course is required or elective, whether potential students have space in their schedule, and whether a student is interested in disability ministry. The conference described above attracted participants from the theological schools in the Washington DC, area, but it also attracted people from around the country, people that attend these conferences on regular basis.

So how does disability gain a place in the required seminary curriculum? First, it should be part of courses in which all students are oriented to the basics of local church ministries, courses found in most seminary curriculums. Second, bibliographies for regular courses should contain some of the rich literature emerging from biblical, historical, and theological areas of study pertaining to disability. Third, seminary faculties should be required to attend conferences that expose them to disability issues and to the recent developments in disability studies in their respective fields. Fourth, seminary students and faculties need to come together on a regular basis to identify disability-related issues and to exchange ideas about the theological, historical, and biblical studies on disability and how they can be shared in the ongoing ministry of the church. Without being forced, students with disabilities should be invited to share their experiences in such a gathering.

Studying disability ministry in its contexts is not an option. Every pastor and seminary student should know basics presented in this volume. The time is past when learning about disability ministry is an option. Clergy and laity must be conversant with its ins and outs well enough to lead others in a faithful response to people with disabilities in their midst. Disabled people, themselves must be nurtured and supported as they seek to find their location within church life. It is my hope that the materials covered in this book will travel a long way toward getting everyone in the church on board.

Bibliography

Albl, Martin. "'For Whenever I Am Weak, Then I Am Strong': Disability in Paul's Epistles." In *This Abled Body: Rethinking Disabilities in Biblical Studies*, edited by Hector Avalos, et al., 145–60. Semeia Studies 55. Atlanta: Society of Biblical Literature, 2007.

Albrecht, Gary L. "Chronology." In *Encyclopedia of Disability*, edited by Gary L. Albrecht et al. 5 vols. Thousand Oaks, CA: Sage, 2006. (Note: this Chronology is found in the back of each volume of the set.)

———. *The Disability Business: Rehabilitation in America*. Sage Library of Social Research 190. Newberry Park, CA: Sage, 1992.

Albrecht, Gary L., et al., eds. *Encyclopedia of Disability*. 5 vols. Thousand Oaks, CA: Sage, 2006.

———, eds. *Encyclopedia of Disability*. Vol. 5, *A History of Disability in Primary Documents*, by Sharon L. Snyder and David T. Mitchell. 5 vols. Thousand Oaks, CA: Sage, 2006.

Albrecht, Gary L., et al. "Introduction." In *Handbook of Disability Studies*, edited by Gary L. Albrecht et al., 1–8. Thousand Oaks, CA: Sage, 2001.

Allen, Garland E. "Biological Determinism." In *Encyclopedia of Disability*, edited by Gary L. Albrecht et al., 1:172–74. 5 vols. Thousand Oaks, CA: Sage, 2006.

Altman, Barbara M. "Sociology" In *Encyclopedia of Disability*, edited by Gary L. Albrecht et al., 4:1483–87. 5 vols. Thousand Oaks, CA: Sage, 2006.

Alzheimer's Association. *2015 Alzheimer's Disease Facts and Figures*. Chicago: Alzheimer's Association, 2016.

———. "Dementia—Signs, Symptoms, Causes, Tests, Treatments, Care." http://www.als.org/what-is-dementia.asp/.

Amado, Angel Novak, et al. "Impact of Two National Congregational Programs on the Social Inclusion of Individuals with Intellectual/Developmental Disabilities." University of Minnesota: Institute on Community Integration, April, 2011. http://rtc.umn.edu/docs/CongregationalInclusion.pdf/.[These were separated into two articles: (1) "Accessible Congregations Campaign: Follow-Up Survey of Impact on Individuals with Intellectual/Developmental Disabilities (ID/DD)." *Journal of Religion, Disability & Health* 16 (2012) 364–419; and (2) "BeFrienders: Impact of a Social Ministry Program on Relationships for Individuals with Intellectual/Developmental Disabilities (ID/DD)." *Journal of Religion, Disability & Health* 17 (2013) 1–26.

American Association of People with Disabilities (AAPD). "Interfaith Disability Advocacy Coalition." http://www.aapd.com.

American Baptist Church—American Baptist Home Mission Societies. "Communities of Care: The Church and Mental Illness." Volume 2, 2014. Available in PDF format http://www.abbms.org/resources/christian_citizen/cc2014/.

———. "Resolution on the Church and Ministry with Persons with Disabilities." (Originally adopted in 1978. Amended, 1994, 1998 and 2002.)

American Council of the Blind. "Religious Resources." http://acb.org/node/1640.

Ammerman, Nancy T. "Culture and Identity in the Congregation." In *Studying Congregations: A New Handbook* edited by Nancy T. Ammerman et al., 78–104. Nashville: Abingdon, 1998.

Anabaptist Disability Network. *Connections*. (November, 2011).

Anderson, Robert C. "A Look Back." *Journal of Religion, Disability & Health* 2/2 (1996) 1–24.

Association for the Sociology of Religion, "50 Year Index American Catholic Sociological Review and Sociological Analysis." *Sociological Analysis* (1989).

Association of Theological Schools. "Policy Statement on Disability and Theological Education." The Association of Theological Schools, 2010.

Avalos, Hector. "Introducing Sensory Criticism in Biblical Studies: Audiocentricity and Visiocentricity." In *This Abled Body: Rethinking Disabilities in Biblical Studies*, edited by Hector Avalos et al., 47–59. Semeia Studies 55. Atlanta: Society of Biblical Literature, 2007.

Avalos, Hector et al. "Introduction." In *This Abled Body: Rethinking Disabilities in Biblical Studies*, 1–9. Semeia Studies 55. Atlanta: Society of Biblical Literature, 2007.

———, eds. *This Abled Body: Rethinking Disabilities in Biblical Studies*. Semeia Studies 55. Atlanta: Society of Biblical Literature, 2007.

Baden, Joel S. "The Nature of Barrenness in the Hebrew Bible." In *Disability Studies and Biblical Literature*, edited by Candida R. Moss and Jeremy Schipper, 13–27. New York: Palgrave Macmillan, 2011.

Balcazar, Fabrico, and Rene Luna. "Activism." In *Encyclopedia of Disability*, edited by Gary L. Albrecht et al., 1:24–26. 5 vols. Thousand Oaks, CA: Sage, 2006.

Baltimore-Washington Conference. "Deaf-Blind Share Impulse to Soar." 2015. http://bwcumc.org/deaf-blind-share-impulse-to-soar/.

Barker, Kristin K. *The Fibromyalgia Story: Medical Authority and Women's Worlds of Pain*. Philadelphia: Temple University Press, 2005.

Barnartt, Sharon N. "Hearing Impairment." In *Encyclopedia of Disability*, edited by Gary L. Albrecht et al., 2:847–50. 5 vols. Thousand Oaks, CA: Sage, 2006.

Barnes, Colin, and Geof Mercer. *Exploring Disability: A Sociological Introduction*. 2nd ed. Cambridge: Polity, 2010.

Barnes, Colin et al. *Exploring Disability: A Sociological Introduction*. Malden, MA: Polity, 1999.

Baum, Michelle N., and Janice L. Benton. "The Evolution and Current Focus of Ministry with Catholics with Disabilities in the United States." In *Disability Advocacy among Religious Organizations: Histories and Reflections*, edited by Albert A. Herzog Jr., 39–54. Binghamton, NY: Haworth, 2006.

Bersani, Hank, Jr. "Wolf Wolfensberger: Scholar, Change Agent, and Iconoclast." *Journal of Religion, Disability & Health* 4 (2001) 1–10.

Betcher, Sharon V. *Spirit and the Politics of Disablement*. Minneapolis: Fortress, 2007.

Bethlehem Baptist Church, Hope in God Ministries. "Ministry Outline." http://www.hopeingod.org/ministries/family/disability-ministry/.

Bethlehem Baptist Church. "A Vision for Disability Ministry." n.d. www.hopeingod.org/.
Black, Helen R., and Robert L. Rubinstein. *Old Souls: Aged Women, Poverty, and the Experience of God.* New York: de Gruyter, 2000.
Black, Kathy. *A Healing Homiletic: Preaching and Disability.* Nashville: Abingdon, 1996.
———. *Signs of Solidarity: Ministry with Persons Who Are Deaf, Deafened, and Hard of Hearing.* New York: United Methodist General Board of Global Ministries, 1994.
Block, Jennie Weiss. *Copious Hosting: A Theology of Access for People with Disabilities.* New York: Continuum, 2002.
Braddock, David L., and Susan L. Parish. "An Institutional History of Disability." In *Handbook of Disability Studies,* edited by Gary L. Albrecht et al., 11–68. Thousand Oaks, CA: Sage, 2001.
Bransfield, J. Brian. "Bible at Core of Catholic Beliefs." United States Conference of Catholic Bishops. http://www.usccb.org/bible/understanding-the-bible/study-materials/articles/bible-at-core-of-catholic-beliefs.cfm/.
Brault, Matthew W. *Americans with Disabilities: 2005.* Current Population Reports. Household Economic Studies. Washington, DC: U.S. Census Bureau, 2008.
———. *Americans with Disabilities: 2010.* Current Population Reports, 70–131. Washington, DC: U.S. Census Bureau, 2012.
Brickenbach, Jerome E., and David Wasserman. "Ethics." In *Encyclopedia of Disability,* edited by Gary L. Albrecht et al., 2:618–24. 5 vols. Thousand Oaks, CA: Sage, 2006.
Brock, Brian. "Autism, Care, and Christian Hope." *Journal of Religion, Disability & Health* 13 (2007) 7–28.
———. "Theologizing Inclusion: 1 Corinthians 12 and the Politics of the Body of Christ." *Journal of Religion, Disability & Health* 15 (2011) 351–76.
Brock, Brian, and Stephanie Brock. "Being Disabled in the New World of Genetic Testing: A Snapshot of Shifting Landscapes." In *Theology, Disability and the New Genetics: Why Science Needs the Church* edited by John Swinton and Brian Brock, 29–43. London: T. & T. Clark, 2007.
Brock, Brian, and John Swinton, eds. *Disability in the Christian Tradition: A Reader.* Grand Rapids: Eerdmans, 2012.
Bruyere, Susanne. "Vocational Rehabilitation: Law and Policy." In *Encyclopedia of Disability,* edited by Gary L. Albrecht et al., 4:1613–15. 5 vols. Thousand Oaks, CA: Sage, 2006.
Burdette, Amy M., et al. "Religion and Attitudes toward Physician-Assisted Suicide and Terminal Palliative Care." *Journal for the Scientific Study of Religion* 44/1 (2005) 79–93.
Burgdorf, Robert L., Jr. "Americans with Disabilities Act of 1990 (United States)." In *Encyclopedia of Disability,* edited by Gary L. Albrecht et al., 1:93–101. 5 vols. Thousand Oaks, CA: Sage, 2006.
Bersani, Hank, Jr. "Wolf Wolfensberger: Scholar, Change Agent, and Iconolclast." In *The Theological Voice of Wolf Wolfensberger,* edited by William C. Gaventa and David L. Coulter, 1–10. New York: Haworth, 2001.
Byrom, Brad. "A Pupil and a Patient: Hospital Schools in Progressive America." In *The New Disability History: American Perspectives,* edited by Paul K. Longmore and Laura Umansky, 133–56. The History of Disability Series. New York: New York University Press, 2001.

California Baptist University. "Master of Arts in Disability Studies." http://www.cbuonline.org/onlineprograms/.
Campbell, Jean. "The Historical and Philosophical Development of Peer-Run Support Programs." In *On Our Own Together: Peer Programs for People with Mental Illness*, edited by Sally Clay et al., 17–54. Nashville: Vanderbilt University Press, 2005.
Canonical Orthodox Bishops in the Americas. 2010 (Volume III). "Disability and Communion." http://oca.org/parish-ministry/parish-ministry/parish development/disability/.
Carter, Erik W. *Including People with Disabilities in Faith Communities: A Guide for Service Providers, Families & Congregations*. Baltimore: Brookes, 2007.
Carter, James G. "Sociology and Special Education: Differentiation and Allocation in Mass Education." In *Crucial Readings in Special Education*, edited by Scot Danforth and Steven D. Taff, 37-54. Upper Saddle River, NJ: Pearson/Merill/Prentice Hall, 2004.
Carter, Warren. "'The Blind, Lame and Paralyzed': (John 5:3); John's Gospel, Disability Studies, and Postcolonial Perspectives." In *Disability Studies and Biblical Literature*, edited by Candida R. Moss and Jeremy Schipper, 129–50. New York: Palgrave Macmillan, 2011.
Caspary, Almut. "The Patristic Era: Early Christian Attitudes toward the Disfigured Outcast." In *Disability in the Christian Tradition: A Reader*, edited by Brian Brock and John Swinton, 24–64. Grand Rapids: Eerdmans, 2012.
Center for Managing Chronic Disease, University of Michigan. 2015. "What Is Chronic Illness?" http://www.cmed.sph.umich.edu.
Centers for Disease Control and Prevention. *Autism Spectrum Disorder*. https://www.cdc.gov/ncbddd/autism/index.html.
———. *Cerebral Palsy*. https://www.cdc.gov/ncbddd/cp/index.html.
———. "Facts about Developmental Disabilities." https://www.cdc.gov/ncbddd/developmentaldisabilities/facts.html.
———. *Intellectual Disability*. http://www.cdc.gov.
———. "Key Findings: Trends in the Prevalence of Developmental Disabilities in U.S. Children, 1997–2008." https://www.cdc.gov/ncbddd/developmentaldisabilities/features/birthdefects-dd-keyfindings.html/.
Charlton, James. "The Dimensions of Disability Oppression." In *The Disability Studies Reader*, edited by Lennard J. Davis, 147–59. 3rd ed. New York: Routledge, 2010.
Chaves, Mark. *Congregations in America*. Cambridge: Harvard University Press, 2004.
Christian Church Foundation for the Handicapped d/b/a Christian Churches Disability Ministry (CCFH Ministries). 2012. "Mission Statement." http://www.ccfh.org/.
Christianity Today. "Fear Not the Disabled." Views. Editorial. October 25, 2005. http://www.christianitytoday.com/ct/2005/november/16.28.html/.
Church of Jesus Christ of Latter-day Saints. "Disability Resources." http://www.lds.org/disability/list/.
Clause, Chris. "What Is a Physical Disability: Definition and Types." In *Educational Psychology: Tutoring Solutions*. Narrated by Elizabeth Ho. http://study.com/academy/lesson/what-is-a-physical-disability-definition-types-quiz.html/.
Clay, Sally. "About Us: What We Have in Common." In *On Our Own Together: Peer Programs for People with Mental Illness*, edited by Sally Clay et al., 3–16. Nashville: Vanderbilt University Press, 2005.

Colon, Yari, et al. "Advocacy." In *Encyclopedia of Disability*, edited by Gary L. Albrecht et al., 1:42–50. 5 vols. Thousand Oaks, CA: Sage, 2001.

Couser, G. Thomas. *Recovering Bodies: Illness, Disability, and Life Writing*. Wisconsin Studies in American Autobiography. Madison: University of Wisconsin Press, 1997.

Covey, Herbert C. *Social Perceptions of People with Disabilities in History*. Springfield, IL: Thomas, 1998.

Creamer, Deborah Beth. *Disability and Christian Theology: Embodied Limits and Constructive Possibilites*. New York: Oxford University Press, 2009.

———. "John Calvin and Disability." In *Disability in the Christian Tradition: A Reader*, edited by Brian Brock and John Swinton, 216–50. Grand Rapids: Eerdmans, 2012.

———. "Theological Accessibility: The Contribution of Disability." *Disability Studies Quarterly* 26/4 (2006). http://dsq-sds.org/article/view/812/987.

Crislip, Andrew T. *From Monastery to Hospital: Christian Monasticism & the Transformation of Health Care in Late Antiquity*. Ann Arbor: Michigan University Press, 2005.

Culpepper, R. Alan. *The Gospel of Luke: Introduction, Commentary and Reflections*. In *The New Interpreter's Bible*, edited by Leander E. Keck, 9:1–490. 13 vols. Nashville: Abingdon, 1995.

Danforth, Scot. "Liberation Theology of Disability and the Option for the Poor." *Disability Studies Quarterly* 25/3 (2005) 1–12. http://dsq-sds.org/article/view/572/749/.

Daley, Brian E. "Building the New City: The Cappadocian Fathers and the Rhetoric of Philanthropy." *Journal of Early Christian Studies* 7 (1999) 431–61.

Davie, Ann Rose, and Ginny Thornburgh. T*hat All May Worship: An Interfaith Welcome to Persons with Disabilities*. Edited by Ginny Thornburgh. Washington DC: National Organization on Disability, 1992. http://www.aapd.com/wp-content/uploads/2016/03/That-All-May-Worship.pdf.

Davie, Grace. "Sociology of Religion." In *Encyclopedia of Religion and Society*, edited by William H. Swatos Jr et al., 483–89. Walnut Creek, CA: AltaMira, 1998.

Davis, Lennard J. *Enforcing Normalcy: Disability, Deafness, and the Body*. New York: Verso, 1995.

———, ed. *The Disability Studies Reader*. 3rd ed. New York: Routledge, 2010.

Dearey, Paul. "Do the Autistic Have a Prayer?" *Journal of Religion, Disability & Health* 13/1 (2009)40–50.

Dell, Robert. "Healing: The Religious Community, Spirituality, and Mental Illness." Paper presented at the National Wellness Summit for People with Mental Illness, Washington DC, September 17–18, 2007.

DeYoung, Terry A., and Mark Stephenson, eds. *Inclusion Handbook: Everybody Belongs, Everybody Serves*. Grand Rapids: Christian Reformed Disability Concerns and Reformed Church in America Disability Concerns, 2011.

Disciples of Christ. "Statement on Disability." 1985 and 1989 respectively. (No further information.)

Disciples of Christ. "Children with Special Needs." http://www.discipleshomemissions.org/pages/FCM-SpecialNeeds.

Dollahite, David C. "Fathering for Eternity: Generative Spirituality in Latter-day Saints Fathers of Children with Special Needs." *Review of Religious Research* 44 (2001) 3.

Doyle, Alicia. "Newbury Park Church Offers Disability Ministry." *Ventura County Star*, February 5, 2010. http://archive.vcstar.com/lifestyle/newbury-park-church-offers-disability-ministry-ep-369750357-350135901.html.
Dubin, Nick, and Janet E. Graetz. "Through a Different Lens: Lives of Individuals with Asperger's Syndrome." *Journal of Religion, Disability & Health* 13 (2009)29–39.
Eiesland, Nancy L. "Barriers and Bridges: Relating the Disability Rights Movement and Religious Organizations." In *Human Disability and the Service of God: Reassessing Religious Practice*, edited by Nancy L. Eiesland and Don E. Saliers, 200–230. Nashville: Abingdon, 1998.
———. *The Disabled God: Toward a Liberatory Theology of Disability*. Nashville: Abingdon, 1994.
Episcopal Disability Network. "Accessibility: Together We Can." http://www.disability99.org.
Elim Christian Services. *5 Stages: The Journey of Disability Attitudes*. Website: http://www.the5stages.com.
Elizabeth M. Boggs Center. "Faith and Autism Resource Collection." *Journal of Religion, Disability & Health* 13 (2009) 154–62.
Evangelical Covenant Church. "Disability Ministry ... Better Together." http://www.covchurch.org/disability.
Evangelical Lutheran Church in America. "Disability Ministries: Called to Be a Hospitable Church for all God's People." http://www.elca.org/Growing-In-Faith/Disability-Ministries.
———. "A Message on People with Disabilities." http://download.elca.org/ELCA%20Resource%20Repository/People_with_DisabilitiesSM.pdf.
———. "A Social Message on the Body of Christ and Mental Illness." Adopted by the Church Council of the Evangelical Lutheran Church in America on November 10, 2011. http://download.elca.org/ELCA%20Resource%20Repository/Mental_IllnessSM.pdf.
Fawcett, Kristin. "How Mental Illness is Misrepresented in the Media." *U.S. News and World Report*. April 16, 2015. http://health.usnews.com/health-news/health-wellness/articles/2015/04/16/how-mental-illness-is-misrepresented-in-the-media.
Fleischer, Doris Zames, and Frieda Zames. *The Disability Rights Movement: From Charity to Confrontation*. Philadelphia: Temple University Press, 2001.
Fox, Michael J. *Lucky Man: A Memoir*. New York: Hyperion, 2002.
Frank, Gelya. *Venus on Wheels: Two Decades of Dialogue on Disability, Biography, and Being Female in America*. Berkeley: University of California Press, 2000.
Frontera, Walter R. "Medicine." In *Encyclopedia of Disability*, edited by Gary L. Albrecht et al., 3:1067–74. 5 vols. Thousand Oaks, CA: Sage, 2006.
Fujiura, Glenn T. "Developmental Disabilities." In *Encyclopedia of Disability*, edited by Gary L. Albrecht et al., 1:394–97. 5 vols. Thousand Oaks, CA: Sage, 2006,
Garland-Thomson, Rosemarie. *Extraordinary Bodies: Figuring Physical Disability in American Culture and Literature*. New York: Columbia University Press, 1997.
Gaventa, William C., Jr. "Introduction: The Pastoral Voice of Robert Perske." *Journal of Religion, Disability & Health* 7/3 (2003) 1–11.
———. "Summer Institute on Theology and Disability, News Release." March 5, 2013. (Note: This institute has been held every year since 2010.)

Geib, Steven A. "Darwin, Charles (1809–1882)." In *Encyclopedia of Disability*, edited by Gary L. Albrecht et al., 1:343–44. 5 vols. Thousand Oaks, CA: Sage, 2006.

Genzink, Gwen Penning. "The Friendship Ministries Story." In *Disability Advocacy among Religious Organizations: Histories and Reflections*, edited by Albert A. Herzog Jr., 163–70. Binghamton, NY: Haworth, 2006.

Giardino, Angelo P., et al. "Health Care Delivery Systems and Financing Issues." In *Children with Disabilities*, edited by Mark L. Batshaw et al., 623–33. 6th ed. Baltimore: Brookes, 2007.

Goffman, Erving. *Stigma: Notes on the Management of Spoiled Identity*. A Spectrum Book. Englewood Cliffs, NJ: Prentice-Hall, 1963.

Gonzalez, Justo L. *The Changing Shape of Church History*. St. Louis: Chalice, 2002.

Gordon, James. "Is a Sense of Self Essential to Spirituality?" *Journal of Religion, Disability & Health* 13 (2009) 51–63.

Govig, Stewart D. *Strong at the Broken Places: Persons with Disabilities and the Church*. Louisville: Westminster John Knox, 1989.

Grant, Colleen C. "Reinterpreting the Healing Narratives." In *Human Disability and the Service of God: Reassessing Religious Practice*, edited by Nancy L. Eiesland and Don E. Saliers, 72–87. Nashville: Abingdon, 1998.

Hackney, Charles H., and Glenn S. Sander. "Religiosity and Mental Health: A Meta-Analysis of Recent Studies." *Journal for the Scientific Study of Religion* 42/1 (2003) 43–55.

Hahn, Harlan. "The Minority Group Model of Disability: Implications for Medical Sociology." In *Research in the Sociology of Health Care* 11 (1994) 3–24

Hall, Amy Laura. "A Ravishing and Restful Sight: Seeing with Julian of Norwich." In *Disability in the Christian Tradition: A Reader*, edited by Brian Brock and John Swinton, 152–83. Grand Rapids: Eerdmans, 2012.

———. "To Form a More Perfect Union: Mainline Protestantism and the Popularization of Eugenics." In *Theology, Disability and the New Genetics: Why Science Needs the Church*, edited by John Swinton and Brian Brock, 75–95. London: T. & T. Clark, 2007.

Hall, Douglas John. *Thinking the Faith: Christian Theology in a North American Context*. Minneapolis: Fortress, 1989.

Halstead, Lauro S. "The Lessons and Legacies of Polio." In *Post-Polio Syndrome*, edited by Lauro S. Halstead and Gunnar Grimbly, 199–214. Philadelphia: Hanley & Belfus, 1995.

Hamilton, M. *The Sociology of Religion*. London: Routledge, 1995.

Haslam, Molly C. *A Constructive Theology of Intellectual Disability: Human Being as Mutuality and Response*. New York: Fordham University Press, 2012.

Hasler, Frances. "Independent Living." In *Encyclopedia of Disability*, edited by Gary L. Albrecht et al., 2:930–35. 5 vols. Thousand Oaks, CA: Sage, 2006.

Hauerwas, Stanley. *Suffering Presence: Theological Reflections on Medicine, the Mentally Handicapped, and the Church*. Notre Dame, IN: University of Notre Dame Press, 1986.

Hendershot, Gerry. "People Seeking Pastoral Care More Likely to Have Disability." Washington DC: National Organization on Disability, 2002. http://www.nod.org/content.cfm?id=874.

———. "A Statistical Note on the Religiosity of Persons with Disabilities." *Disability Studies Quarterly* 26/4 (2006). http://dsq-sds.org/article/view/813/988.

Herzog, Albert A., Jr. *An Analysis of the Disability Rights Movement within American Mainline Protestantism at the Regional and Local Level: A Summary Report*. Report on Louisville Institute Grant 95-0050 (1998).

———, ed. *Disability Advocacy among Religious Organizations: Histories and Reflections*. Binghamton, NY: Haworth, 2006.

———. "Disability Advocacy in American Mainline Protestantism." In *Disability Advocacy among Religious Organizations: Histories and Reflections*, edited by Albert A. Herzog Jr., 75–92. Binghamton, NY: Haworth, 2006.

———. "The Disability Advocacy of the National Council of Churches." In *Disability Advocacy among Religious Organizations: Histories and Reflections*, edited by Albert A. Herzog Jr., 11–38. Binghamton, NY: Haworth, 2006.

———. "From Service to Rights: The Movement for Disability Rights in the American Methodist Tradition." *Methodist History* 38/1 (1999) 27–39.

———. "History of Disability Advocacy in the Evangelical Lutheran Church in America." Unpublished manuscript.

———. "Spires, Wheelchairs and Committees: Organizing for Disability Advocacy at the Judicatory Level." *Review of Religious Research* 45 (2008) 349–67.

———. *A History of Disability Ministry in the United Church of Christ*. 2002. Unpublished manuscript. Summary at uccm.org/disabilities/.

———. "Working Interfaith: The History of the Religion and Disability Program of the National Organization on Disability." In *Disability Advocacy among Religious Organizations: Histories and Reflections*, edited by Albert A. Herzog Jr., 207–26. Binghamton, NY: Haworth, 2006.

Hickel, Walter K. "Medicine, Bureaucracy, and Social Welfare: The Politics of Disability Compensation for American Veterans of World War I." In *The New Disability History: American Perspectives*, edited by Paul K. Longmore and Laura Umansky, 236–67. The History of Disability Series. New York: New York University Press, 2001.

Hoffman, Ingrid. "Deafblindness." In *Encyclopedia of Disability*, edited by Gary L. Albrecht et al., 1:357–60. 5 vols. Thousand Oaks, CA: Sage, 2006.

Holland, Anthony. "Alzheimer's Disease." In *Encyclopedia of Disability*, edited by Gary L. Albrecht et al., 1:91–93. 5 vols. Thousand Oaks, CA: Sage, 2006.

Holt-Woehl, Hollie M. "Creation and a Theology of Humanness." *Journal of Religion, Disability & Health* 16/2 (2012) 121–32.

Horning, Bob, et al. "A Vision for Disability Ministry at Bethlehem." (n.d.). Hope in God Ministries. Bethlehem Baptist Church. https://www.hopeingod.org/document/vision-disability-ministry-bethlehem/.

Hudson, Geoffrey L. "History of Disability: Early Modern West." In *Encyclopedia of Disability*, edited by Gary L. Albrecht et al., 2:855–58. 5 vols. Thousand Oaks, CA: Sage, 2006.

Hudspeth, Tom. "Ignore Not the Deaf." *New World Outlook Magazine*, May/June 2014. http://www.umcmission.org/Find-Resources/New-World-Outlook-Magazine/New-World-Outlook-Archives/2014/May/June/0520ignorenotthedeaf/.

Hull, John M. "The Broken Body in a Broken World: A Contribution to a Christian Doctrine of the Person from a Disabled Point of View." *Journal of Religion, Disability & Health* 7/4 (2003) 5–25.

———. *In the Beginning There Was Darkness: A Blind Person's Conversations with the Bible*. Harrisburg, PA: Trinity, 2002.

Hubach, Stephanie O. *Same Lake, Different Boat: Coming alongside People Touched by Disability.* Phillipsburg, NJ: P & R, 2006.
Hubbard, Ruth. "Abortion and Disability: Who Should and Should Not Inhabit the World?" In *The Disability Studies Reader,* edited by Lennard J. Davis, 107–19. 3rd ed. New York: Routledge, 2010.
Ingstad, Benedicte, and Susan Reynolds Whyte, eds. *Disability and Culture.* Berkeley: University of California Press, 1995.
Interfaith Disability Advocacy Coalition (IDAC). 2013. *Grounded in Faith: Resources on Mental Health and Gun Violence.* American Muslim Health Professionals (AMHP.us).
International Catholic Deaf Association. "From ICDA-Canada Section 2012 Conference at Ottawa, Ontario." *The Deaf Catholic* 59 (2012) 3. http://www.icda-us.org/wp-content/uploads/2013/01/2012_Fall_Issue-1.pdf.
Iozzio, M. J. "The Writing on the Wall . . . Alzheimer's Disease: A Daughter's Look at Mom's Faithful Care of Dad." *Journal of Religion, Disability & Health* 9/2 (2005) 49–74.
Jaeger, Paul T., and Cynthia Ann Bowman. *Understanding Disability: Inclusion, Access, Diversity, and Civil Rights.* Westport, CT: Praeger, 2005.
Johnson, Peggy A. *Deaf Ministry: Make a Joyful Silence.* Charleston: Book Surge, 2007.
———. "Embracing Deaf Ministry in the Peninsula-Delaware Conference." *New World Outlook Magazine,* May/June 2014. http://www.umcmission.org/Find-Resources/New-World-Outlook-Magazine/New-World-Outlook-Archives/2014/May/June/0708embracingdeafministry.
Joni and Friends. "The Christian Institute on Disability." http://www.joniandfriends.org/christian-institute-on-disability.
———. "Church Relations/Through The Roof Program." http://www.joniandfriends.org/church-relations.
———. "Family Retreats." http://www.joniandfriends.org/family-retreats.
———. "Joni and Friends Television Series." http://www.joniandfriends.org/television.
———. "Wheels for the World." http://www.joniandfriends.org/wheels-for-the-world.
Kaiser, Walter C., Jr. *The Book of Leviticus: Introduction Commentary, and Reflections.* In *The New Interpreter's Bible,* edited by Leander E. Keck, 1:983–1191. 13 vols. Nashville: Abingdon, 1994.
Kelley, Nicole. "The Deformed Child in Ancient Christianity." In *Children in Late Ancient Christianity,* edited by Cornelia B. Horn and Robert R. Phenix, 199–226. Studies and Texts in Antiquity and Christianity 58. Tübingen: Mohr/Siebeck, 2009.
King, Margaret L. *Western Civilization: A Social and Cultural History.* 2nd ed. Combined volume. Upper Saddle River, NJ: Prentice-Hall, 2003.
L'Arche USA Fact Sheet. https://www.larcheusa.org.
Lampe, Barbara J. "The Story of the National Apostolate for Inclusion Ministry." In *Disability Advocacy among Religious Organizations: Histories and Reflections.* edited by Albert A. Herzog Jr., 55–74. Binghamton, NY: Haworth, 2006.
Lane, Harlan. *When the Mind Hears: A History of the Deaf.* New York: Vintage, 1999.
LaRocque, Michella, and Rick Eigenbrood. "Community Access: A Survey of Congregational Accessibility for People with Disabilities." *Journal of Religion, Disability & Health* 9/1 (2009) 55–66.

Leichty, Paul D. "Mennonite Advocacy for Persons with Disabilities." In *Disability Advocacy among Religious Organizations: Histories and Reflections*, edited by Albert A. Herzog Jr., 195–206. Binghamton, NY: Haworth, 2006.

Levine, Carol. "Introduction: The Many Worlds of Family Caregivers." In *Always on Call: When Illness Turns Families into Caregivers*, edited by Carol Levine, 3–19. Updated and expanded ed. Nashville: Vanderbilt University Press, 2004.

Lewis, Hannah. *Deaf Liberation Theology. Explorations in Practical, Pastoral and Empirical Theology*. Aldershot, UK: Ashgate, 2007.

Lima, Julie C. "Caregiving." In *Encyclopedia of Disability*, edited by Gary L. Albrecht et al., 1:221–23. 5 vols. Thousand Oaks, CA: Sage, 2006.

Linton, Simi. *Claiming Disability: Knowledge and Identity*. Cultural Front. New York: New York University Press, 1998.

Longmore, Paul K., and Lauri Umanski. "Introduction: Disability History; From the Margins to the Mainstream." In *The New Disability History: American Perspectives*, edited by Paul K. Longmore and Lauri Umanski, 1–32. The History of Disability Series. New York: New York University Press, 2001.

Longmore, Paul K. "New Paradigm, New Approaches." *The Disability History Association History Newsletter* 1 (2005).

Lutheran Deaf Mission Society. "Models of Deaf Ministry." http://www.deafjesus.org.

Lutheran Disability Ministry. "Equipping the Church to Minister with People with Intellectual and Developmental Disabilities." http://ldminc.org/mission.html.

Mairs, Nancy. *Waist-High in the World: A Life among the Nondisabled*. Boston: Beacon, 1996.

Marty, Martin E. *Modern American Religion*. Vol. 3, *Under God, Indivisible, 1941–1960*. Chicago: University of Chicago Press, 1996.

Margolies, Luisa. *My Mother's Hip: Lessons from the World of Eldercare*. Philadelphia: Temple University Press, 2004.

McClain, Rick. "Being Aware of the Silent Majority." Deaf Online University. www.deaf-online-university.com.

McDonald, Katherine E. "Community Living and Group Homes. In *Encyclopedia of Disability*, edited by Gary L. Albrecht et al., 1:285–86. 5 vols. Thousand Oaks, CA: Sage, 2006.

McDonald, Katherine, and Christopher B. Keys. "L'Arche: The Success of Community, the Challenges of Empowerment in a Faith-Centered Setting." *Journal of Religion, Disability & Health* 9/4 (2005) 3–28.

McGrane, Janice E. *Saints to Lean On: Spiritual Companions for Illness and Disability*. Cincinnati: St. Anthony Messenger Press: 2006.

McLean, Athena. *The Person in Dementia: A Study of Nursing Home Care in the U.S.* Broadview Ethnographies & Case Studies. Peterborough, ON: Broadview, 2007.

McLean Bible Church. "Access: A Ministry for People with Disabilities." https://www.mcleanbible.org/connect/access/.

———. "Access Ministry Wish List." https://www.mcleanbible.org/serve/church/access-ministry-wish-list.

———. "The Friendship Club." http://www.mbctysons.org.

———. "The Friendship Club." https://www.mcleanbible.org/connect/friendship-club.

———. "Soaring Over Seven Summer Camp." https://www.mcleanbible.org/events/soaring-over-seven-summer-camp.

McNair, Jeff. "Christian Social Constructions of Church Attendees." *Journal of Religion, Disability & Health* 11/4 (2007) 51–64.

———. *The Church and Disability: The Weblog Disabled Christianity*. N.p.: Createspace, 2010.

McNair, Jeff, and Michelle Sanchez. "Christian Social Constructions of Church Leaders." *Journal of Religion, Disability and Health* 11/4 (2007) 35–50.

McReynolds, Kathy. "Christianity: A Knowledge Tradition." Pasadena, CA: Joni and Friends, 2010. http://www.joniandfriends.org/christian-institute-on-disability/policy-papers/christianity-knowledge-tradition.

———. "A Disturbing Presence? Disability in an Age of Enhancement." Pasadena, CA: Joni and Friends, 2010. http://www.joniandfriends.org/christian-institute-on-disability/policy-papers/disturbing-presence.

———. "Why Christian Doctrine Matters." Pasadena, CA: Joni and Friends, 2010. http://www.joniandfriends.org/christian-institute-on-disability/policy-papers/why-christian-doctrine-matters.

McRuer, Robert. *Crip Theory: Cultural Signs of Queerness and Disability*. Cultural Front. New York: New York University Press, 2006.

MedicineNet.com/. "Definition of Chronic Illness." http://medicinnenet.com.

Melcher, Sarah J. "Blemish and Perfection of the Body in the Priestly Literature and Deuteronomy." *Journal of Religion, Disability & Health* 16/1 (2012) 1–15.

———. "With Whom Do the Disabled Associate? Metaphorical Interplay in the Later Prophets." In *This Abled Body: Rethinking Disabilities in Biblical Studies*, edited by Hector Avalos et al., 115–30. Semeia Studies 55. Atlanta: Society of Biblical Literature, 2007.

Metzger, Bruce M., and Roland E. Murphy, eds. *The New Oxford Annotated Bible, with the Apocrypha/Deuterocanonical Books*. New Revised Standard Version. New York: Oxford University Press, 1991.

Metzger, James A. "Reclaiming 'a Dark and Malefic Sacred' for a Theology of Disability." *Journal of Religion Disability & Health* 15/3 (2011) 296–316.

Metzler, Irina. *Disability in Medieval Europe: Thinking about Physical Impairment during the High Middle Ages*. Routledge Studies in Medieval Religion 5. London: Routledge, 2006.

Michalko, Rod. *The Difference That Disability Makes*. Philadelphia: Temple University Press, 2002.

Mills-Fernald, Jackie, and Jim Pierson. *Making Changes that Lead to Real Inclusion*. Knoxville: CCFH Ministries, 2010.

Mitchell, David T. "Witchcraft." In *Encyclopedia of Disability*, edited by Gary L. Albrecht et al., 4:1639–41. 5 vols. Thousand Oaks, CA: Sage, 2006.

Mind and Soul. "10 Tips for Creating Dementia Friendly Churches." http://www.mindandsoul.info/Articles/355251.

Miles, M. "Martin Luther and Childhood Disability in 16th Century Germany: What Did He Write? What Did He Say?" *Journal of Religion, Disability & Health* 5/4 (2001) 5–36.

Moltmann, Jürgen "Liberate Yourselves by Accepting One Another." In *Human Disability and the Service of God: Reassessing Religious Practice*, edited by Nancy L. Eiesland and Don E. Sailers, 105–22. Nashville: Abingdon, 1998.

Morris, Wayne. *Theology without Words: Theology in the Deaf Community*. Explorations in Practical, Pastoral, and Empirical Theology. Aldershot, UK: Ashgate, 2008.

Morstad, David. "The Centennial of Bethesda Lutheran Homes and Services, Inc." In *Disability Advocacy among Religious Organizations: Histories and Reflections*, edited by Albert A. Herzog, Jr., 127–40. Binghamton, NY: Haworth, 2006.

Moss, Candida R. "Christly Possession and Weakened Bodies: Reconsideration of the Function of Paul's Thorn in the Flesh (2 Cor. 12:7–10)." *Journal of Religion, Disability & Health* 16/4 (2012) 319–33.

Moss, Candida R., and Jeremy Schipper, eds. *Disability Studies and Biblical Literature*. New York: Palgrave Macmillan, 2011.

National Alliance on Mental Illness (NAMI). "Facts about Stigma and Mental Illness in Diverse Communities." http://www.nami.org.

———. *FaithNet*. http://www.nami.org.

———. "Mental Health Conditions." http://www.nami.org.

———. "Mental Illness Facts and Numbers." http://www.nami.org.

———. "Serious Mental Illness (SMI) Among U.S. Adults." http://www.nami.org.

National Apostolate for Inclusion Ministry. "Tip Sheet." *NAfIM Messenger* 2010/3, 2.

———. "Winds of Change, Spirit of Inclusion." National Meeting October 4–6, 2008, Huron, Ohio.

National Catholic Partnership on Disability (NCPD). "Our Mission and Our Goal." http://www.ncpd.org/about/mission.

———. "Something to Consider for Every Parish: A Disability Advisory Committee." http://www.ncpd.org.

National Council on Disability. *Righting the ADA*. Washington DC: National Council on Disability, 2004. https://www.ncd.gov/rawmedia_repository/b6fbb02a_34f3_4bfb_a048_3385cbb184f8.pdf.

National Institute on Deafness and Other Communication Disorders. "Quick Statistics about Hearing." http://www.nidcd.gov.

National Association of the Deaf. "Resources." https://www.nad.org.

National Black Disability Coalition. 2015. *Disability Inclusion Toolkit for Black Faith and Non-Profit Organizations*. 3rd ed. http://www.blackdisability.org.

National Institute on Deafness and other Communication Disorders. "Hearing, Ear Infections and Deafness." http://www.nidcd.nih.gov.

National Institute on Neurological Disorders and Stroke (NINDS). "Dementia: Hope through Research." http://www.ninds.nih.gov/disorders/dementias/details.

National Organization on Disability. *That All May Worship*. Washington DC: National Organization on Disability, 2005.

National Organization on Disability, and Harris Interactive. *2000 N.O.D. Harris Survey of Americans with Disabilities*. New York: Harris Interactive, 2000.

———. *2004 National Organization on Disability/Harris Survey of Americans with Disabilities*. New York: Harris Interactive, 2004.

New Advent (website). "Patron Saints." In *Catholic Encyclopedia*. http://www.newadvent.org/cathen/11562a.htm?fb_comment_id=10150247809617970_10154901236342970#f19bbf1c3cfb97c/.

Newlands, George, and Allen Smith. *Hospitable God: The Transformative Dream*. Farnham, UK: Ashgate, 2010.

Newman, Barbara. *Autism and Your Church: Nurturing the Spiritual Growth of People with Autism Spectrum Disorders*. Grand Rapids: Friendship Ministries, 2006.

North American Division of Seventh-Day Adventists. "Disability Ministries." http://www.nadventist.org/article.php.

Oliver, Michael. *Understanding Disability: From Theory to Practice.* New York: St. Martin's, 1996.
Olyan, Saul M. *Disability in the Hebrew Bible: Interpreting Mental and Physical Differences.* New York: Cambridge University Press, 2008.
Omanski, Beth. "Blindness and Visual Impairment." In *Encyclopedia of Disability,* edited by Gary L. Albrecht et al., 1:185–93. 5 vols. Thousand Oaks, CA: Sage, 2006.
———. *Borderlands of Blindness.* Disability in Society. Boulder: Rienner, 2011.
Orme, Nicholas. *Medieval Children.* New Haven: Yale University Press, 2001.
Pacific Northwest Conference of the United Church of Christ. "Mental Health Chaplain Trains Clergy, Congregations on Companionship."
Page, Frank, with Lawrence Kimbrough. *Melissa: A Father's Lessons from a Daughter's Suicide.* Nashville: B & H, 2013.
Park Street Church. "History." http://cwww.parkstreet.org/history.
Pathways Awareness. *Inclusion Awareness Day Workbook.* http://www.inclusionworship.org/.
Perske, Robert. "An Attempt to Find an Adequate Theological View on Mental Retardation." *Journal of Religion, Disability & Health* 7/3 (2003) 35–52.
———. *Unequal Justice: What Can Happen When Persons with Retardation or Other Developmental Disabilities Encounter the Criminal Justice System.* Nashville: Abingdon, 1991.
Phillips, Susan D. *Disability and Mobile Citizenship in Postsocialist Ukraine.* Bloomington: Indiana University Press, 2011.
Pierson, Jim. "The Term – Disability Ministry." http://www.ccfh.org/blog/2007/09/11.
Porterfield, Amanda. *Healing in the History of Christianity.* New York: Oxford University Press, 2005.
Presbyterian Church (U.S.A.). *Comfort My People: A Policy Statement on Serious Mental Illness with Study Guide.* Louisville: Advisory Committee on Social Witness Policy, 2008.
———. *That All May Enter: Responding to People with Disability Concerns.* Louisville: Presbyterian Church (U.S.A.), 1989.
———. *Living into the Body of Christ: Towards Full Inclusion of People with Disabilities.* Louisville: Office of the General Assembly, 2006.
———. *The Presbyterian Panel: Disability Issues, May 2004* Louisville: Presbyterian Church (U.S.A.), 2004.
Pridmore, Eric. "The Christian Reformed Church as a Model for the Inclusion of People with Disabilities." In *Disability Advocacy among Religious Organizations: Histories and Reflections,* edited by Albert A. Herzog Jr., 93–108. Binghamton, NY: Haworth, 2006.
Ramsey-Lucas, Curtis, ed. "Communities of Care: The Church & Mental Illness." *Christian Citizen* 2 (2014). American Baptist Home Mission Societies. https://nmweb.abhms.org/resources/christian_citizen/docs/CC2014_v2.pdf.
———, ed. "Disability Ministry: From Access to Inclusion." *Christian Citizen* 2 (2012). American Baptist Home Mission Societies. http://s3.amazonaws.com/dfc_attachments/public/documents/3165559/TheChristianCitizen2012n2.pdf.
Raphael, Rebecca. "Whoring after Cripples: On the Intersection of Gender and Disability Imagery in Jeremiah." In *Disability Studies and Biblical Literature,* edited by Candida R. Moss and Jeremy Schipper, 103–16. New York: Palgrave Macmillan, 2011.

Rappmann, Susanne. "The Disabled Body of Christ as a Critical Metaphor—Towards a Theory." *Journal of Religion, Disability & Health* 7/4 (2003) 25–40.

Reimer, Kevin S. "Moral Transformation in L'Arche Communities for People with Developmental Disabilities." In *The Paradox of Disability: Responses to Jean Vanier and L'Arche Communities from Theology and the Sciences*, edited Hans S. Reinders, 60–74. Grand Rapids: Eerdmans, 2010.

———. Review of *Theology, Disability, and Spiritual Transformation: Learning from the Communities of L'Arche*," by Michael Hryniuk. *Journal of Religion, Disability & Health* 15/3 (2011) 332–33.

Reinders, Hans S. *The Future of the Disabled in Liberal Society: An Ethical Analysis*. Revisions. Notre Dame: University of Notre Dame Press, 2000.

———. "Human Vulnerability: A Conversation at L' Arche." In *The Paradox of Disability: Responses to Jean Vanier and L'Arche Communities from Theology and the Sciences*, edited by Hans S. Reinders, 5–18. Grand Rapids: Eerdmans, 2010.

———, ed. *The Paradox of Disability: Responses to Jean Vanier and L'Arche Communities from Theology and the Sciences*. Grand Rapids: Eerdmans, 2010.

———. *Receiving the Gift of Friendship: Profound Disability, Theological Anthropology, and Ethics*. Grand Rapids: Eerdmans, 2008.

Reynolds, Thomas E. "Theology and Disability: Changing the Conversation." *Journal of Religion, Disability & Health* 16/1 (2011) 33–48.

———. *Vulnerable Communion: A Theology of Disability and Hospitality*. Grand Rapids: Brazos, 2008.

Ridolfo, Heather, and Brian W. Ward. *Mobility Impairment and the Construction of Identity*. Disability in Society. Boulder: First Forum, 2013.

Rose, Avi. "'Who Causes the Blind to See': Disability and Quality of Religious Life." *Disability & Society* 12/3 (1997) 395–405.

Romero, Miguel J. "Aquinas on the *corporis infirmitas*: Broken Flesh and the Grammar of Grace." In *Disability in the Christian Tradition: A Reader*, edited by Brian Brock and John Swinton, 101–53. Grand Rapids: Eerdmans, 2012.

Row-Heyveld, Lindsey. "'The Lying'st Knave in Christendom': The Development of Disability in the False Miracle of Saint Alban's." *Disability Studies Quarterly* (2009). http://dsq-sds.org/article/view/994.

Rush, William. "Harvesters with Disabilities: A Journey Testimony." *Journal of Religion, Disability & Health* 7/4 (2003) 65–72.

Russell, Jeffrey B. *A History of Witchcraft: Sorcerers, Heretics, and Pagans*. London: Thames & Hudson, 1980.

Saddleback Lake Forest. "Disabilities Ministries." http://www.saddleback.com/lakeforest/children/specialneeds.

Sampley, DeAnn. *A Guide to Deaf Ministry: Let's Sign Worthy of the Lord*. Grand Rapids: Zondervan, 1990.

Sanford, Matthew S., and Kandace R. McaAlister. "Perceptions of Serious Mental Illness in the Local Church." *Journal of Religion, Disability & Health* 12/2 (2008) 144–53.

Schalick Walton O., III. "Augustine, Saint." In *Encyclopedia of Disability*, edited by Gary L. Albrecht et al., 1:144–45. 5 vols. Thousand Oaks, CA: Sage, 2006.

———. "History of Disability: Medieval West." In *Encyclopedia of Disability*, edited by Gary L. Albrecht et al., 2:868–73. 5 vols. Thousand Oaks, CA: Sage: 2006.

Schipper, Jeremy. *Disability and Isaiah's Suffering Servant*. Biblical Refigurations. New York: Oxford University Press, 2011.

———. *Disability Studies in the Hebrew Bible: Figuring Mephibosheth in the David Story*. Library of Hebrew Bible/Old Testament Studies 441. T. & T. Clark Library of Biblical Studies. London: T. & T. Clark, 2006.

———. *Parables and Conflict in the Hebrew Bible*. Cambridge: Cambridge University Press, 2009.

Schurter, Dennis. "The Religion and Spirituality Division of the American Association on Mental Retardation." In *Disability Advocacy among Religious Organizations: Histories and Reflections*, edited by Albert A. Herzog Jr., 109–26. Binghamton, NY: Haworth, 2006.

Scully, Julie Leach. "Genetics." In *Encyclopedia of Disability*, edited by Gary L. Albrecht et al., 2:776–82. 5 vols. Thousand Oaks, CA: Sage, 2006.

Shakespeare, Tom, et al. "Models." In *Encyclopedia of Disability*, edited by Gary L. Albrecht et al., 3:1101–8. 5 vols. Thousand Oaks, CA: Sage, 2006.

Shakespeare, Tom and Nicholas Watson. "The Social Model of Disability: An Outdated Ideology" In *Exploring Theories and Expanding Methodologies: Where We Are and Where We Need to Go*, edited by Sharon N. Barnartt and Barbara M. Altman, 9–28. Research in Social Science and Disability 2. Amsterdam: JAI/Elsevier, 2001.

Shelley, Marshall. Foreword to *Troubled Minds: Mental Illness and the Church's Mission*, by Amy Simpson, 9–11. Downer's Grove, IL: InterVarsity, 2013.

Shiel, William C. "Cerebral Palsy." On *MedicineNet.com*. http://www.medicinenet.com.

Shogren, Karrie A., and Mark S. Rye. "Religion and Individuals with Intellectual Disabilities: An Exploratory Study of Self-Reported Perspectives." *Journal of Religion, Disability & Health* 9/1 (2005) 29–53.

Silvers, Anita. "Euthanasia." In *Encyclopedia of Disability*, edited by Gary L. Albrecht et al., 2:631–38. 5 vols. Thousand Oaks, CA: Sage, 2006.

Simeonsson, Rune J., and Donald J. Lollar. "Individuals with Disabilities Education Act of 1990 (United States)." In *Encyclopedia of Disability*, edited by Gary L. Albrecht et al., 2:945–47. 5 vols. Thousand Oaks, CA: Sage, 2006.

Simpson, Amy. *Troubled Minds: Mental Illness and the Church's Mission*. Downer's Grove, IL: InterVarsity, 2013.

Singer, Peter. "Taking Life: Humans." In *Practical Ethics*, 175–217. 2nd ed. New York: Cambridge, 1993.

Sisters of Charity of Leavenworth Health System. "The Case of Elizabeth Bouvia." http://www.sclhsc.org/mission_vision_values/ethics/elizabeth_bouvia.asp.

———. "Case Timeline." in *The Case of Terri Schiavo: Ethics at the End of Life*, edited by Arthur L. Caplan et al., 325–45. Amherst, NY: Prometheus.

Snyder, Sharon L. "Bodies, Theories of" In *Encyclopedia of Disability*, edited by Gary L. Albrecht et al., 1:194–98. 5 vols. Thousand Oaks, CA: Sage, 2006.

———. "Disability Studies." In *Encyclopedia of Disability*, edited by Gary L. Albrecht et al., 1:478–90. 5 vols. Thousand Oaks, CA: Sage, 2006.

Snyder, Sharon L., and David T. Mitchell. *Cultural Locations of Disability*. Chicago: University of Chicago Press, 2006.

———. "Eugenics." In *Encyclopedia of Disability*, edited by Gary L. Albrecht et al., 2:624–25. 5 vols. Thousand Oaks: Sage, 2006.

Society for the Scientific Study of Religion. *Twenty-Year Index* (1981).

Southern Baptist Convention. "On Mental Health Concerns and the Heart of God." Resolution adopted by the Southern Baptist Convention Executive Committee,

June 2013. http://www.sbc.net/resolutions/1232/on-mental-health-concerns-and-the-heart-of-god.

Special Touch Ministries. http://www.specialtouch.org/author/Admin.

Stainton, Tim. "Changeling." In *Encyclopedia of Disability*, edited by Gary L. Albrecht et al., 235–36. Thousand Oaks, CA: Sage, 2006.

———. "Reason, Grace, and Charity: Augustine and the Impact of Church Doctrine on the Construction if Intellectual Disability." *Disability & Society* 9 (2009) 485–96.

Standing Conference of the Canonical Orthodox Bishops in the Americas. "Disability and Communion: Embracing People with Disabilities within the Church." http://oca.org/resource-handbook/parishdevelopment/disability/.

Stanford, Matthew. "Demon or Disorder: A Survey of Attitudes toward Mental Illness in the Christian Church." *Journal of Religion, Disability & Health* 10/5 (2007) 445–49. http://www.baylor.edu/content/services/document.php/35617.pdf/.

Steele, Richard B. "Accessibility or Hospitality? Reflections and Experiences of a Father and Theologian." *Journal of Religion, Disability & Health* 1/1 (1994) 11–26.

Steinmetz, Erika. *Americans with Disabilities: 2002*. Current Population Reports P70-107. Washington DC: U.S. Census Bureau, 2006.

Stetz, Kathleen M., et al. "Mental Health Ministry: Creating Healing Communities for Sojourners." *Journal of Religion, Disability & Health* 15/2 (2011) 153–74.

Stenross, Barbara. *Missed Connections: Hard of Hearing in a Hearing World*. Philadelphia: Temple University Press, 1999.

Stiker, Henri-Jacques. *A History of Disability*. Translated by William Sayers. Corporealities. Ann Arbor: University of Michigan Press, 1999.

Stroman, Duane F. *The Disability Rights Movement: From Deinstitutionalization to Self-Determination*. Lanham, MD: University Press of America, 2003.

Stubbins, Joseph. "The Politics of Disability." In *Attitudes toward Persons with Disabilities*, edited by Harold E. Yuker, 22–31. New York: Springer, 1988.

Stumbo, Ellen. "The Church and Disability" http://www.ellenstumbo.org.

Swinton, John. *Dementia: Living in the Memories of God*. Grand Rapids: Eerdmans, 2012.

———. "From Inclusion to Belonging: A Practical Theology of Community, Disability and Humanness." *Journal of Religion, Disability & Health*, 16/2 (2012) 172–90.

———. "Introduction: Re-imaging Genetics and Disability." In *Theology, Disability and the New Genetics: Why Science Needs the Church*, edited by John Swinton and Brian Brock, 1–25. London: T. & T. Clark, 2007.

———. *Resurrecting the Person: Friendship and the Care of People with Mental Health Problems*. Nashville: Abingdon, 2000.

Swinton, John, and Brian Brock eds. *Theology, Disability and the New Genetics: Why Science Needs the Church*. London: T. & T. Clark, 2007.

Swinton, John, and Christine Trevett. Editorial: "Religion and Autism: Initiating an Interdisciplinary Conversation." *Journal of Religion, Disability & Health* 13/1 (2009) 2–6.

Taege, Marlys. "The Christian Council on Persons with Disabilities: Goals, Network, Encourage, Impact." In *Disability Advocacy among Religious Organizations: Histories and Reflections*, edited by Albert A. Herzog Jr., 141–62. Binghamton, NY: Haworth, 2006.

Three Angels Deaf Ministries. "Why Deaf Ministry Is Needed." https://3adm.org/whydeafministry.php

Toensing, Holly Joan. "Living among the Tombs: Society, Mental Illness, and Self-Destruction in Mark 5:1–20." In *This Abled Body: Rethinking Disabilities in Biblical Studies*, edited by Hector Avalos et al., 131–44. Semeia Studies 55. Atlanta: Society of Biblical Literature, 2007.

Thomas, Philip. "The Relational-Revelational Image: A Reflection on the Image of God in the Light of Disability and on Disability in the Light of the Image of God." *Journal of Religion, Disability & Health* 16/2 (2012) 133–53.

Trinkaus, Erik. "History of Disability: Pleistocene Period." In *Encyclopedia of Disability*, edited by Gary L. Albrecht et al., 2:873–75. Thousand Oaks, CA: Sage, 2006.

Turner, Bryan S. "Disability and the Sociology of the Body." In *Handbook of Disability Studies*, edited by Gary L. Albrecht et al., 252–66. Thousand Oaks, CA: Sage, 2001.

———. *Medical Power and Social Knowledge*. 2nd ed. London: Sage, 1995.

United Church of Christ. *United Church of Christ Disabilities Ministries*. http://www.uccdm.org.

United Methodist Church of the Resurrection. *Matthew's Ministry Pamphlet*. Overland Park, KS: United Methodist Church of the Resurrection, 2010.

United Methodist Congress of the Deaf. "Joint Statement of ELDA, ECD, UMCD, UMDHM, December 6, 2014." https://www.umcd.org/newsnat/1401.html.

United Methodist Task Force on Disability Ministries. "Minutes." 2001–2012.

United States Conference of Catholic Bishops. "Pastoral Statement of U.S. Catholic Bishops on People with Disabilities" (Washington DC, 1978). National Catholic Partnership on Disability (website). https://www.ncpd.org/views-news-policy/policy/church/bishops/pastoral.

Vacek, Heather H. *Madness: American Protestant Responses to Mental Illness*. Studies in Religion, Theology, and Disability. Waco, TX: Baylor University Press, 2015.

Venier, Jean. "What Have People with Learning Disabilities Taught Me?" In *The Paradox of Disability: Responses to Jean Vanier and L'Arche Communities from Theology and the Sciences*, edited Hans S. Reinders, 19–26. Grand Rapids: Eerdmans, 2010.

Ware, Linda. "Mainstreaming." In *Encyclopedia of Disability*, edited by Gary L. Albrecht et al., 3:1052–55. Thousand Oaks, CA: Sage, 2006.

Ware, Linda, and Julie Allan. "Special Education." In *Encyclopedia of Disability*, edited by Gary L. Albrecht et al., 4:1488–92. Thousand Oaks, CA: Sage, 2006.

Warner, R. Stephen. "The Place of the Congregation in the Contemporary American Religious Configuration (1994)." In *A Church of Our Own: Disestablishment and Diversity in American Religion*, 145–82. New Brunswick, NJ: Rutgers University Press, 2005.

Weaver, Anna. "Through a Glass Darkly: How Catholics Struggle with Mental Illness." *U.S. Catholic* 75/2 (February 2010) 12–17. http://www.uscatholic.org/node/5811/.

Webb-Mitchell, Brett. *Unexpected Guests at God's Banquet: Welcoming People with Disabilities into the Church*. New York: Crossroad, 1994.

Wehman, Paul, and Patricia N. Walsh. "Transition from School to Adulthood: A Look at the United States and Europe." In *Adults with Disabilities: International Perspectives in the Community*, edited by Paul Retish and Shunit Reiter, 3–31. Mahwah, NJ: Erlbaum, 1999.

White, Stacy E. "The Influence of Religiosity on Well-Being and Acceptance in Parents of Children with Autism Spectrum Disorder." *Journal of Religion, Disability & Health* 13/2 (2009) 104–13.

Wilke, Harold H. *Creating the Caring Congregation*. Nashville: Abingdon, 1980.

———. "Signs of Liberation and Access." In *Any Body, Everybody, Christ's Body: A Congregational Guide for Becoming Accessible to All*, edited by Jo Claire Hartsig, 26–27. http://southcongregational.org/Newsletters_Calendars/anybody.pdf.

Wittberg, Patricia. Review of *Disability Advocacy among Religious Organizations: Histories and Reflections*, by Albert A. Herzog, Jr. *Review of Religious Research* 49/3 (2008) 344–45.

Willow Creek Community Church. "Disability Ministries." http://www.willowcreek.org.

Winzer, Margret A. *The History of Special Education: From Isolation to Integration*. Washington DC: Gallaudet University Press, 1993.

Wolfensberger, Wolf. "The Prophetic Voice and Presence of Mentally Retarded People in the World Today." In *The Theological Voice of Wolf Wolfensberger*, edited by William C. Gaventa and David L. Coulter, 11–48. New York: Haworth, 2001.

Wolfensberger, Wolf, et al. *The Principle of Normalization in Human Services*. Toronto: National Institute on Mental Retardation, 1972.

World Council of Churches, "The Unity of the Church and the Renewal of Humankind." Geneva: World Council of Churches, 1975.

Wynn, Kerry H. "The Normate Hermeneutic and Interpretations of Disability within the Yahwistic Narratives." In *This Abled Body: Rethinking Disabilities in Biblical Studies*. Hector Avalos et al., 91–102. Semeia Studies 55. Atlanta: Society of Biblical Literature, 2007.

Yong, Amos. *The Bible, Disability, and the Church: A New Vision of the People of God*. Grand Rapids: Eerdmans, 2011.

———. "Disability from the Margins to the Center: Hospitality and Inclusion in the Church." *Journal of Religion, Disability and Health* 15/4 (2011) 339–50.

———. *Theology and Down Syndrome: Reimaging Disability in Late Modernity*. Waco, TX: Baylor University Press, 2007.

Young, Iris. "Five Faces of Oppression." In *Oppression, Privilege and Resistance*, edited by Lisa Heldke and Peg O'Connor, 37–63. New York: McGraw-Hill, 2004.

Zachariah's Way. http://pureministryproject.com.

"The P.UR.E. Ministry Project" http://pureministryproject.com.

Zanesville Christian Missionary Alliance Church. "Disability." http://www.zanesvillecma.org/disability.

Subject Index

Access (Accessibility)
    Limits, 97–100
    Moving Beyond Accessibility, 95–96
Aquinas, Thomas, 169–70
American Baptist Church, 83–84
    The Christian Citizen, 84
Americans with Disabilities Act (ADA), 30–31, 57–59
Anabaptism, 53–54
Anabaptist Disability Network (ADNet), 54
Attitudes in the church, 97–100
Augustine, 169–70
Autism, 118–21
    Challenges to Christian ideas/assumptions, 120–21
    Definitions, 118
    Statistics, 118–19

Befrienders, 90–91
Betcher, Sharon, 204
Bethesda Lutheran Homes and Services, 76–77
Bethlehem Baptist Church, 68–69
Bible and Disability/Disability studies, 142–43
    Negative aspects, 151–52
    Demoniacs
        Healing Miracles, 155–57
        Levitical laws, 144–46
        Jacob's Limp, 143–44
        Mephibosheth, 146–48
        The Hebrew Prophets, 149–51
        Zechariah, 152

The Centurion's Faith, 153
The Gerasene Demoniac, 154–55
Healing in the house, 156–57
Blind Beggar, 157
The Man Born Blind, 111–12, 157
Healings in Acts, 158–59
Paul 160
Blindness, 109–11
    Church responses, 110–11
    Definition, 109
    Experience, 109–10
    Statistics, 109–10
Block, Jennie Weiss, 141
Bouva, Elisabeth, 212
Broken Body in a Broken World, 195

California Baptist University (CBU), 73
Calvin, John, 175, 178
Cappadocian Fathers, 167–68
Cerebral palsy, 117–18
Changelings, 176
Christian Council on Persons with Disabilities (CCPD), 51–53
Christian Church Foundation for the Handicapped (CCFH), 74–75
Christian Missionary Alliance Church of Zanesville, OH, 70
Christian Reformed Church (CRC), 54–55

SUBJECT INDEX

Chronic Disease, 93
   Impact, 94–95
   Statistics, 93–94
   Chronic Obstructive Pulmonary
      Disease (COPD), 92
Church History and Disability,
   163–64
   Ancient/Early Christianity,
      165–70
      Impairments caused by sin?
         166–67
      Treatment of disabled,
         166–69
   Middle ages
      Care vs. cure, 171–72
      Monasticism, 172–73
      Patron Saints and Shrines,
         172–73
      Paintings, 173
   Renaissance, Reformation, Early
      Modern Period
      Medicine vs. care/healing,
         174–75
      English Reformation,
         178–79
   Into Modernity
      American Colonies, 179–82
Church of Jesus Christ Latter-Day
   Saints (LDS), 85
Creamer, Deborah Beth, 195–97

Deafness, 101–9
   Categories, 101, 102–3
   Thomas Gallaudet, 103
   Deaf Culture, 101
   Deaf Ministry, 104–9
      Denominational, 105–6
      Models, 104–5
      Peggy Johnson, 106–7
   Deaf Liberation Theology,
      13–14
   Hard of Hearing, 107–9
   Oralism, 103–4
   Statistics, 102
   Treatment by church, 170
Deaf-Blindness, 110–11
Deformed Children, 165–66
Deinstitutionalization 27–29

Dementia, 136–39
   Alzheimer's 136–37
   Care, 137–39
Developmental disability
   Definition, 113
Disciples of Christ, 83
Disability
   Advocacy, 42–43
   Aging, 35–36, 37–38
   Definitions, 2, 40
   Levels of analysis, 17–19
      Individual, 32–38
      Overall structure of society,
         19–31
      Social level, 38
   Medical model, 7
   Medicalization, 20–22
   Pervasiveness, 39–40
   Program and supports, 25–26
   Rights/legislation, 26–31
   IDEA, 25–26
   Social model, 7–8
   Special education, *see below*
   Statistics, 6–7
   Visibility, 40–41
Disability and Christianity
   Interactions 3–4
Disability Ministry, 1, 66–68
   Mainline Responses, 79–84
   Research on, 87–91
Disability-related Journals, 2
Disability Studies 9–10
Downsizing, Denominational,
   56–57, 63–65

Eiesland, Nancy, 4
   The Disabled God, 188–91
Episcopal Disability Network
   (EDN), 80
Ethics, 213–24
   Brock and Swinton, 208
   Christian, 217–24
   Recent Christian Ethics, 214
   Eugenics and New Genetics,
      210–11
   Recent Christian Ethics, 214
Eugenics, 210–11
Euthanasia, 211–13

SUBJECT INDEX

Evangelical Covenant Church, 85–86
Evangelical Free Church of Newbury Park, CA, 69–70
Evangelical Lutheran Church in America (ELCA), 80–81
   Message on People Living with Disabilities, 61–63
Exposure of Infants, 166

Friendship Ministries, 77–78
Fibromyalgia, 40–41

Govig, Stewart, 185–86

Harris Survey of Americans with Disabilities 3
Haslam, Molly, 221
Hauerwas, Stanley, 222–24
Healing Community, 56
Hildegard of Bingen, 171

Independent Living, 29
Individual Educational Program (IEP), 25–26
Infertility as Disability, 148–49
Intellectual Disability
   Congregational responses, 115–17
   Experience, 32–33
   Policies, 114–15
   Statistics, 113–14
International Year of Disabled Persons (IYDP)

Joni and Friends, 14, 51, 77–78, 208
Journal of Religion, Disability & Health, 57
Julian of Norwich, 170

L'Arche and Severe Disabilities, 122–25
   Jean Vanier and critics, 123–25
Luther, Martin, 176–77

Mainstreaming 24
Malleus Maleficarum, 175
Man Born Blind, 112

Marginalization, in church/society 4–6, 8–9, 97–100
Medical model 7
Mennonite Mutual Aid (MMA), 53–54
Mental illness
   Church responses, 129–32
   Evangelical responses, 133–36
   Experience, 36–37, 127–29
   Interfaith responses, 129–32
   Statistics and types, 126–27
McLean Bible Church, 72–73
   Accessibility Summit, 72–73
McReynolds, Kathy, 204–5, 221–22
Moltmann, Jurgun, 193
Multiple Sclerosis, 35–36

National Black Disabilities Coalition (NBDC), 57
National Organization on Disability, 55–57
   Accessible Congregations Campaign, 60–61, 89–90

Orthodox Tradition, 57

Peace Church Tradition, 84
Perske, Robert, 186–87
Patmos Church, 69
Park Church, Boston, 70–71
Physician Assisted Suicide (PAS), 211–13
Physical Disability
   Defined, 92–93
   Impact, 94–95
Presbyterian Church U.S.A.
   Living into the Body of Christ, 63, 82
   Presbyterian Panel, 82–83
Protestantism, general
   Mainline, 43–49
   NCC, 42–45, 47–49
   Cooperative Publication Association Publications, 43–45
   Reformed Tradition, 54–55, 84–85
Protestantism, Conservative, 51–53

Rehabilitation Act of 1973, 29, 46, 65
Reinders, Hans, 219–21
Religion and Spirituality Division, American Association on Intellectual and Developmental Disabilities, 56–57
Reynolds, Thomas E., 197–201
Roman Catholic Church 49–51, 86–87
    National Apostolate for Inclusion Ministries, 50
    National Catholic Partnership on Disabilities, 50–51

Saddleback Church, 71–72
Seventh-Day Adventist Church (SDA), 85
Schiavo, Terri, 208, 213
Singer, Peter, 214
Sociology of Religion, 11–12
Special Education, 22–25
    Legislation, 24
Special Touch Ministries, 75–76
Swinton, John, 192–93

That All May Worship, 55–57
Theology, New Resources, 183–84
    Body Theology, 195–97
    Evangelical Approaches, 204–5
    Inclusion and Hospitality, 197–202
    Liberation Theology, 192–95
    Pre Disability Rights Era, 184–88
    High theology, 202–4
        Amos Yong, 202–4
        Thomas Reynolds, 198–201
Theological education, 228–30

United Church of Christ
    National Committee on People with Disabilities, 80
United Methodist Committee on Disability Ministries, 59, 81–82
    Association of Physically Challenged Ministers (APCM), 59
United Methodist Church of the Resurrection
    Matthew's Ministry, 79–80

Wilke, Harold, 56, 140, 184–85
Willow Creek Church, 71–72
Witchcraft, 175–76
Wolfensberger, Wolf, 187–88
World Council of Churches, 1975

Zachariah's Way, 76

Scripture Index

Genesis
32:23–32   143–44

Leviticus
21:17–23   144–46

2 Samuel
4:4, 9:1–8   146–48

Isaiah
29:17–21   149
35:5–7   150
45:9–12   150

Matthew
8:5–17   153
9:1–8   156–57
9:32–33   154
11:2–6   154–55, 158
12:9–14   156–57
12:22–32   154
20:29–34   156

Mark
2:1–12   156–57
3:1–6   156–57
5:1–20   154–55
10:22   157
10:46–52   157

Luke
5:17–26   156–57
6:6–11   155
7:18–23   154–55, 158
11:14–15   154
14:13–24   156
18:35–43   157
24:36–43   190

John
5:1–15   157–58
5:4   158
9   157

Acts
3:1–10   158–59
3:6   159
3:8   159
8:56–58   159
9:1–19   160
13:6–12   160
14:8–18   159
14:9   159
22:4–16   160

Romans
6:9   160

2 Corinthians
13:4   160

www.ingramcontent.com/pod-product-compliance
Lightning Source LLC
Chambersburg PA
CBHW021700230426
43668CB00008B/679